Dealing Gently with the Ignorant and Wayward

Joe Evans

&

Parson's Porch Books

www.parsonsporchbooks.com

Dealing Gently with the Ignorant and Wayward
ISBN: Softcover
Copyright © 2019 by Joe Evans

*Dealing Gently with the
Ignorant and Wayward*

Dedicated to Lily Evans. Every time I sang you, "You Are My Sunshine," I meant it.

Contents

Preface

The sermons in this book were preached during my second year of ministry at First Presbyterian Church of Marietta, Georgia. This great church, who nurtured me as a child and through adolescence, even supporting me through college and seminary, called me to be their Senior Pastor in the summer of 2017. This call came in the aftermath of division. After our denomination met and approved new standards of marriage equality in 2015, the nearly 200-year-old congregation split. Around 300 members broke ties with First Presbyterian Church to start a new church in a more conservative denomination of Presbyterians, ECO. The three years following this split and preceding my arrival were marked by a genuine determination to survive, great moments of healing, and courageous leadership.

The sermons in this book stretch across 2018, one year in the life of this great congregation. This was a year when God moved the congregation beyond survival and healing to growth and celebration. These sermons were easy for me to write and preach because all around me, the Holy Spirit was alive and well, and the Gospel was not confined to the pages of Scripture, for the congregation of First Presbyterian Church was living it.

Part 1: Leadership

Scripture depicts heroes with a great deal of transparency. Of all the great heroes of the Bible, King David rises to the top, and still, the account of his life in 2nd Samuel honors his accomplishments while telling the truth about his humanity. In the following sermons focused on three great leaders in the Bible: David, Moses, and Elijah, I reflect on the truth of who we all are and how God is at work in our lives despite our imperfections.

Who Will Build the Temple?
Ephesians 2: 11-22 and 2ⁿᵈ Samuel 7: 1-14a

Preached on July 22, 2018

Recently, I took our girls to see *The Incredibles 2*. It's a new animated movie to the theaters, and we all liked it a lot. Seeing a movie is a good thing to do on a summer afternoon. You have to pay $20.00 for popcorn, but it's a fun thing to do.

Before the main attraction, there was an "appetizer movie." It was a short cartoon to get us warmed up, and it had a genuine impact on me that I want to tell you about. This short cartoon featured a lonely woman who took her time to make her husband and herself the most delicious steamed dumplings for their lunch. She made them for him with painstaking care. She created the filling from fresh ingredients, folded the dough around that filling with beauty and precision, then steamed these precious dumplings and presented them before her husband as though they were a love letter. However, he then scarfed them down in seconds while never taking his eyes off the TV. Having eaten, he was off to work, leaving the woman to eat her dumplings in lonely silence. We watched as she sat, staring at her lunch, when, strangely, her last dumpling came to life.

A dumpling is the perfect food to make into a baby. This dumpling baby had fat, doughy cheeks that the lonely woman pinched. Eventually, the little dumpling sprouted arms and legs, enabling it to move around. That meant that the lonely woman was no longer alone. She took her dumpling baby out to grocery shop. He went with her to tai chi in the park. Having this dumpling to love, care for, and feed made the lonely woman happy. However, then the dumpling baby grew.

One day, he saw some boys playing soccer in the park and didn't want to do tai chi anymore. He wanted to play soccer. This independent desire is where the problem began because the lonely woman didn't want her little dumpling playing soccer. She wanted to keep him close by her side, so she jerked him back.

You can see where this is going. The lonely woman loved her dumpling and didn't want him to go anywhere or get himself hurt, but the dumpling wanted to grow up. Eventually, as time marched on, he went out and came back home with a tall, blond girlfriend. The dumpling told his human parents, "We're getting married." When the lonely women protested by stomping her foot and crossing her arms, the dumpling and his blond fiancée try to storm out. However, before he could make it out the door, the lonely woman scooped up her dumpling boy and ate him.

That was a dramatic twist.

It didn't end there, though. Maybe you can imagine that in this cartoon, the dumpling that the lonely woman doted over was a stand-in for her real son. The cartoon went on to show us that as her human son grew up, he pushed her away, too, and the more he pushed, the tighter she tried to hold him close, until eventually he ran off.[1]

That happens sometimes. It's like the song "38 Special;" we cling too tightly and lose control. We tighten our grip rather than accept the reality that people will fight to be who they are and against who we want them to be. Maybe you haven't carried around a dumpling or taken it to tai chi, but have you ever wanted to hold close someone who was pushing you away? Maybe this cartoon was a little strange; still, it reminded me of dropping Lily off at Kindergarten.

The first two weeks or so were great. Then, at some point, something changed. She didn't want to go anymore. She'd cry and cry rather than rush into the school as she had before, making the impulse to just let her stay home really strong.

One morning, I dropped her off. She didn't want to go. She was so little, and after leaving her in her classroom, where I'm sure she was perfectly happy, I made it back to the car and sat in the driver's seat and cried. It was awful. Maybe, like me, you can relate to the impulse to scoop up a little dumpling and never let her go because letting kids grow up is so painful.

Loving someone and having to let them go; there's just nothing easy about it. Allowing people to be who they are rather than who we want them to be or being who we are despite the pressure to be someone else, is not easy. However, these challenges are a part of our life together, both in families and in a community.

Such challenges were in David's life, too.

Consider David's father. He was supposed to call all of his sons to see the Prophet Samuel, that he might pick one of them to be the king of Israel. However, his father left little David out in the field because sometimes it's hard to allow your children to be who God calls them to be.

---

[1] https://m.youtube.com/watch?v=fZN02raRHC0

Then, there was this conflicted relationship David had with King Saul. Saul loved David until he got too big for his britches and stepped out of Saul's shadow to become king himself.

So often there's a conflict between the projection we cast on our loved ones and who they actually are. When the boy grows into a man or when the dumpling exerts a little independence, something happens in the hearts and minds of those who want the dumpling to stay within arm's length.

You've heard about David's wife Michal who despised David in her heart. You might have wondered why she despised him. She despised him because David turned out to be the kind of king who danced rather than the kind of king that she expected him to be, so, as it was with David, it is with us: life is full of human relationships with push away and pull back. A dance of childhood loving closeness one minute, exerting adolescent independence the next, and today we see that King David's relationship with his God was not so unlike his human relationships.

"Now when the king was settled in his house, and the Lord had given him rest from all his enemies around him, the king said to the prophet Nathan, 'See now, I am living in a house of cedar, but the ark of God stays in a tent.'"

All David wants to do here is build the Lord a house. He wants to keep God close by. This is a kind thought, a loving gesture; yet, have you ever been given a present that the giver wanted to give more than you wanted to receive?

I know a man in Tennessee named David Locke. Mr. Locke used to say, "Always accept what someone gives you because sooner or later they'll give you something that you actually want." That's one way to think about it, but that's not how God thought about it.

David wants to build God a house, but did David ask God if God would like one? No.

There are two kinds of unwanted gifts. There are the unwanted gifts that people give you because you need them and you don't know it, like nose hair clippers. Husbands, if your wives gave you nose hair clippers it's because you need them, and I know you didn't ask for them, but you should accept the gift for your own good. Then, there's the other kind of unwanted gift, the kind of gift that's been wrapped in a motive. This kind of gift says more about the person giving it and his hopes for who you'll be than his understanding of who you actually are.

How many little girls woke up to find that Santa had brought them a tutu instead of the pocketknife that they asked for? How many mothers opened up an *Instapot* on Mother's Day and wanted to use it for target practice? These gifts often say more about who the giver wants you to be than who you actually are, and that happens because it's hard for some people to let those whom they love be themselves.

For years, I had to go to dance recitals for my sister, Elizabeth. She really did ask Santa for a tutu because she loved to dance. I remember that, every once in a while, a group would come on stage that had a boy in it. On the stage would be that whole group of girls and one boy. I remember my mother saying, "the bravest person in this auditorium is that boy's father."

She said that because allowing someone whom you love to be who God created him to be takes strength. Allowing God to be who God actually is rather than who we want God to be takes strength as well. That takes a particular kind of strength that we call faith.

Now comes the real story, the life lesson:

> But that same night the word of the Lord came to Nathan: Go and tell my servant David: Thus says the Lord: Are you the one to build me a house to live in? Whenever I have moved about among the people of Israel, did I ever speak a word with any of the tribal leaders of Israel, "Why have you not built me a house of cedar?"

God never said, "It sure would be nice to have a solid roof over my head."

God never said to David: "Look at you, resting easy, and I'm in this old tent."

It wasn't like that. God was happy that David was settled in his house, but God didn't want a house of His own. That was what David wanted God to want. David, like all of us, has this problem of projection. He was limiting God according to his image of God. He was boxing God in according to his perception of who God is and what God wants. Again, this is a normal enough thing to do, but it's dangerous because mothers have to let their little dumplings grow up and be who they were created to be.

Likewise, a husband has to listen to his wife so well that he knows her. He must listen so well that he's heard what she fears, knows what she worries about, and can be reasonably sure of what she likes and doesn't. Then, he can buy her what she actually wants and not what he wants her to want.

The same is true for our relationship with God.

We Christians have to listen to God. We have to conform to His will because God will not conform to ours, though so often we will try to get God to or will speak as though God always takes our side. We must remember that, while God is always with us, God does not support all that we do. God is not just along for the ride.

Last week, I saw a picture of a Labrador Retriever. These dogs are known to be compassionate and loyal, and below the picture was the heading, "man's true best friend." Below that heading was a test to prove that statement: "Men, if you want to know who your true best friend is, lock your wife and your dog in the trunk of your car for an hour. Then let them out and see who's happy to see you."

That's funny, but you shouldn't put your wife in a trunk. You shouldn't put your dog in a trunk either, and you definitely shouldn't try to put God in the trunk and take God along for the ride, regardless of where you are going.

Bumper stickers used to say, "Jesus is my co-pilot." Remember those? Then, a counter bumper sticker came out: "If Jesus is your co-pilot then you're in the wrong seat."

Sometimes, we just want God to go along with us and bless our ride regardless, but what if we're going in the wrong direction? What if God is calling us to turn around?

What if God doesn't want us to build him a house?

Preachers have that problem. I was preaching at a camp meeting a few years ago. We were outside. Cars were parked all around. I thought I had this great sermon about how God often speaks through interruptions. Someone's car alarm started going off and interrupted my sermon. I gave a frustrated look in the direction of the perpetrator. An embarrassed man turned the alarm off so I could continue with what I wanted to say. Then it went off again, and again we waited while he turned off the alarm. I continued, but when the alarm went off for a third time, I finally realized how well I was proving my point that God interrupts but we just keep on going.

We want to build God a house, but what if God doesn't need one?

We want our children to change, but what about the change that needs to occur in us?

We sing "God Bless America," but God cannot bless our every endeavor, for so much of what we do is contrary to God's Word.

Too often, we only want God to support what we're already doing. We look to Scripture, not for challenge, but for affirmation, only consider this: is God's Word not a refiner's fire?

If only we weren't so resistant to being refined.

It reminds me of one story of how Columbia Theological Seminary got started. The great Presbyterian churches of the Antebellum South used to send all their fine pastoral candidates up to Princeton Seminary in New Jersey for training. The problem was, they'd all come back abolitionists. Rather than listen to what these preachers had to say and hear the truth that God calls us to see our brothers and sisters as people and not as property, we just built a seminary in the South where we wouldn't have to hear it.

Does God need us to build him a house?

Does not God need us to instead listen to his Word and be changed by it?

And will God not freely give greater blessings than we could ever dream of should we be so bold as to change according to His divine will?

> The Lord declares to you that the Lord will make you a house. When your days are fulfilled, and you lie down with your ancestors, I will raise up your offspring after you, who shall come forth from your body, and I will establish his kingdom. He shall build a house for my name, and I will establish the throne of his kingdom forever."

Let us always remember that unless the Lord builds the house, those who labor, labor in vain.

Amen.

The Invitation
2nd Samuel 11: 1-5 and Song of Solomon 2: 8-13
Preached on July 29, 2018

When we lived in Tennessee, we had a big backyard. The lots in our neighborhood were large. Moving here to Marietta, we knew we would have to compromise. We wanted to be close to the Square, the Church, and our girl's school, so we had to buy a house with a smaller backyard. The smaller lot we settled on is perfectly suitable and has less grass to mow, but we're now closer to our neighbors, which has made us aware of how loud we are.

We are. It's true. We're loud, and the loudest of us all, the bane of our neighborhood, is the coonhound we adopted from the pound back in Tennessee.

We were at a neighborhood dinner last fall. All of the attendees there were introducing themselves by saying things like, "We're the Smiths, and we're the ones who have been having the pool installed. Sorry about that." Then everyone laughed politely, excusing and understanding the slight inconvenience. Eventually, Sara said, "We're the Evans family, and we're the ones with the hound dog who barks all the time." No one laughed.

Therefore, when we went out of town last week, we were worried about what was going to happen with these neighbors who agreed to watch our dogs. We emphasized how free they should feel to shut June bug the coonhound inside if there were a cat around that she couldn't stop barking at. Our kind neighbor assured us that everything would be fine, only then, she contacted us on our way back into town with some bad news. A possum had made itself a home under our deck.

June bug knew that it was there, but she couldn't get to it because this deck is right on the ground. She wouldn't stop barking at it. Our neighbor shut our dog inside where her barks were at least muffled, and when we got home, our first order of business was to sell the house and leave the neighborhood before they ran us out.

No, that's not really what happened. First order of business was to buy a trap and catch the possum.

I had to shop around to buy the kind I wanted. I finally found the humane kind at Lowe's. The only problem with the humane kind is that you have to release what you've trapped. Fortunately, I knew the code to my neighbor's garage and planned on leaving the captured possum in there.

I'm just kidding. I was planning on releasing it in the woods a couple miles from the house; however, before setting the trap, Sara asked me how I was feeling about trapping this wild animal. I told her that I was feeling a little sorry for the possum because after a nice meal of possum bait, it'd be spending a cold night inside a metal trap.

Sara said, "Just think about how happy this possum will be living in the woods instead of having a coonhound bark in its ear incessantly." That was a good point, but after catching and releasing it, I watched as the dirty old marsupial waddled off into its new home, and I couldn't help wondering about this accepted practice of trapping a possum and taking it somewhere else against its will. I was thinking about how you can do all kinds of things to a possum without asking its permission. A human is allowed to ignore the will of a pest, but to abuse power is to treat a person like a possum.

It is an abuse of power for a man to treat another human, not like a person, but like an animal. That's wrong.

It is wrong for a king to treat citizens, not like self-determining individuals with minds, bodies, and rights, but as subjects who need to be told what to do.

It is wrong for the people's representative, God's chosen king, to manipulate the truth to suit him, and dispose of those whose testimony might discredit him.

It is an abuse of power for a tyrant to look down from his roof to see a woman bathing, and to see her as something that he wants and that he might take.

It's a tragic truth that these are all things that King David did. We read in our first Scripture lesson:

> It happened late one afternoon, when David rose from his couch and was walking about on the roof of the king's house, that he saw from the roof a woman bathing; the woman was very beautiful. David sent someone to inquire about the woman. [Then] David sent messengers to get her.

That's not how it's supposed to happen, but that's how David did it as he becomes the kind of king that the Prophet Samuel warned Israel about.

Do you remember what the Prophet Samuel said?

Rev. Lisa Majores reminded me that the Prophet Samuel warned the people when they asked for a king. The Prophet told them that, "He will take your sons. He will take your daughters. He will take the best of your fields. And in

22

that day, you will cry out because of your king whom you have chosen for yourselves."

No one would have thought that gentle David would become such a king. No one expected him to become the kind who looks down from his roof to see what he might take, but this is the way of human corruption. This is what too often happens in the hearts of men when given power.

There's no need to go down the list of powerful men who did what David did. You know who they are already, so today I won't name names or go on about condemning those who are guilty of abusing their power. The truth will come out with or without this preacher.

What I feel called to speak about today is what it's supposed to look like.

School starts again this week, and every parent thinks that school is about learning, but every student knows it's really about socializing. With socializing comes friendship; then later, dating.

In either case, it's important to know how it's supposed to look. It's important to know how it was intended to be, for throughout life, there will be those who look at you and see something that they want. However, there will be others who will really see you, and with love in their hearts, instead of seeing you as something that they might have, they will see you as someone who might want what they have to give.

Listen again to the words of our second Scripture lesson:

"My beloved is like a gazelle or a young stag. Look, there he stands behind our wall, gazing in at the windows, looking through the lattice. My beloved speaks and says to me: 'Arise, my love, my fair one, and come away.'"

My favorite detail in those verses is where the young man is standing. You might wonder, "Why doesn't he just knock on the door?" If you've never been a 15-year-old boy, you might not know this, but he's hiding behind the wall because he's terrified.

I remember what my mother said to me as I was gathering the courage to call a fellow high school student to ask her out on a date. She said, "If I had any idea how timid 15-year-old boys really were, I would have been a much more confident 15-year-old girl."

That's how it's supposed to be. The young man has something to offer, and what he has to offer is his heart. This is a gift he wants to give, but he's terrified because the one whom he wants to give his heart to has the power to accept it and treasure it or crush his 15-year-old heart with her rejection.

That's nothing to worry over. That's how it's meant to be, so consider for just a moment the difference between this young man who hides behind the wall, looking through the lattice to catch a glimpse of his beloved, and King David. King David looks down from his roof to see a beautiful woman whose name he doesn't even know.

Consider the difference between this young man who speaks and says, "Arise my love, my fair one, and come away," and King David, who doesn't even say anything to Bathsheba. He just sends for her.

Consider the difference in who has agency.

Consider the difference in who has control and power.

Where is the woman with the chance to say "yes" or "no," and where is the woman trapped, like a possum in a cage?

It is so important to issue an invitation, for while you can't control whether the invitation will be accepted, and, while your heart may get broken in the process, if the one you are inviting doesn't have the power to say "yes" or "no," there can be no real friendship. If there is no agency, certainly there can be nothing more than that. If there is no invitation, there can only be something that is so much less than love.

Without an invitation, there is only abused power. There is one who has the power to choose what he wants, and another who is an object to be taken. On the other hand, with an invitation, there is an open door to love.

That's important to remember in life. It's important to remember that from the beginning of friendship and into dating. It's even important to remember that in understanding our relationship with God.

The great C.S. Lewis said that we are like children, happily making mud pies in a back-alley, when we have been invited to the seashore. With this invitation, what we have is the choice between the life that we know and the abundant life that we don't know but are invited to.

God knows how much better the beach is to making mud pies in the back-alley. God knows this as much as Sara knows that a possum would rather live in the woods than be trapped under our deck, only God, who issues us this invitation, would never trap us and take us to the beach for our own good because that's not love. Instead, our God simply issues the invitation.

The invitation is to come away: "for now the winter is past, the rain is over and gone. The flowers appear on the earth; the time for singing has come, and the voice of the turtledove is heard in our land. Arise, my love, my fair one, and come away."

You see, the young man in the Song of Solomon is not just a young man. The ancients kept this love poetry in our Bible so that we would know this great metaphor: that God's love for us is like the love of a young man for a young woman. That the Lord gives to us an invitation, and we have the choice to go or not because that's love.

Love is not a power-drunk king who looks down from heaven on a people that he wants for his own pleasure. Instead, love is a young man in the Song of Solomon or a Gentle Savior in the Gospels. Love is like our Gentle Savior who holds out His heart to His people saying, "take and eat, this is my body, broken for you."

We had the power to reject Him, and we did.

What is the cross if not the sign of God's abundant love, freely offered, and humanity's sin, which chose to slam the door in His face? Yet, even after rejection, He rose and offers us His love again today.

We are not possums.

We are not objects.

It is our choice to say "yes" or to say "no;" that's how love is supposed to look, and that's how it has to be.

Will it break God's heart if we turn our backs? Maybe, but our God, who is the very definition of what love truly is, would never look upon us and take what He wants. He'd only call on us to consider again what it is that He has to give.

With an invitation, God invites us to have not just life, but abundant life. He invites us to enjoy, not freedom as the world knows it, but freedom from regret and freedom to rest in His mercy.

It is vitally important that we as a church remember the beauty of this invitation as we go out into the world and as we welcome visitors into our doors.

If this is your first time here, I confess that there's always a part of me that wants to give you a pledge card right away. However, the emphasis of the Gospel is not on what you have, but on what God has to give.

This is a church founded on the Good News of the Lord Jesus Christ, and here lives are transformed by faith, hope, and love. The Gospel is alive here, and that's what we emphasize: God's invitation to the whole world to enjoy abundant life.

Amen.

Food for the Journey
Ephesians 4: 1-16 and Exodus 16: 2-4 and 9-15

Preached on August 5, 2018

Sara and I have been watching a TV show called *Suits*. It's sort of like a PG-version of *Mad Men*, except *Suits* is set in contemporary New York City, and the main characters all work at a law firm instead of an advertising agency. The male main characters wear these really sharp tailored suits, which is why the show is called *Suits*, I guess. It's really fast-paced and exciting. The whole show is focused on these two guys, Harvey Specter and Mike Ross. They storm into meetings and courtrooms, corner bad guys through verbal acrobatics, then take beautiful women out to dinner.

It's exactly like being an attorney in real life, right?

Maybe some attorneys in the room can correct this misconception. I've heard that the real life of an attorney goes at a slower pace. We all know that Hollywood tends to skip the boring parts of any story it tells. This trait of the Hollywood version probably explains why I decided in 3rd grade, right after seeing *Indiana Jones*, that when I grew up, I'd be an archeologist. Because of this aspiration, my Mom signed me up for an archelogy camp, but all we did was sift through dirt and brush off rocks with a paint brush. It wasn't anything like the movie.

It's a hard reality to accept that most of the time real life moves more slowly than it does on TV or in movies, especially when it comes to people accepting change.

They say that in every good story, something has to change. Whether a person, an institution, or a change of heart, something has to change. In the entertainment industries, that change happens in the course of a few hundred pages of a book, in the thirty minutes of a TV show, or in the two hours of a movie, while real-life change often takes much longer.

I remember wondering why the Israelites wandered through the desert for forty years. It doesn't seem like it should take that long to go from slavery in Egypt to freedom in the Promised Land. Scholars have even said that it should have only taken eleven days to walk from Egypt to Israel, but that's the thing about real change. Real change often doesn't happen that fast. Around this church, just as in the human heart, change can take a while.

Consider how we have two buses here at the church. We refer to them as the old bus and the new bus, only the new bus is now more than twenty years old. I guess we're still getting used to it.

You see, change doesn't always happen quickly. You can't always make it from Egypt to Israel in eleven days. If we're still referring to it as the new bus twenty years later, then making a big change, like going from slavery to freedom, must take longer. If you can do that in forty years, you're making pretty good time.

Change is often slow, probably because a lot of people don't like it.

You heard them: "The Israelites complained against Moses and Aaron in the wilderness. [They] said to them, 'If only we had died by the hand of the Lord in the land of Egypt, when we sat by the fleshpots and ate our fill of bread.'"

Now imagine being one of those Israelites and complaining to Moses, asking, "Why did you save us from slavery? It wasn't that bad." This is the craziest thing to say, but this is exactly how people are. This is exactly how it really happens.

Probably the scariest moment of my life was in labor and delivery. All at once, my pregnant wife was pulled out of her room by a crowd of worried faces and taken to the operating room. I was left standing there wondering if I was about to lose Sara and our new baby. I remember having no idea where to go or what to do. I remember just being more scared than I'd ever been before or since.

Thanks be to God, everything turned out fine. Sara had an emergency C-section that resulted in a healthy baby and a healthy mother. While I was so thankful for this outcome, about a year later, while I'm still recovering from the trauma, Sara wants to talk about having another baby.

I wanted to ask, "Why, Sara, would you even think of returning to the flesh pots of Egypt? Don't you remember what it was really like?" Of course, she didn't remember exactly what it was like because if mothers remembered accurately the trauma of childbirth, then no one here would have any siblings. If human beings remembered accurately all the traumatic circumstances that they'd been delivered from, they'd never return, but according to the Bureau of Justice Statistics, five out of six state prisoners are arrested again within nine years of their release.

5 out of 6!

It's hard to imagine anyone saying, "It wasn't so bad in prison: three meals a day, a nice jump-suit." No one really says that, but can they imagine a better future? Is anyone leading them to it, or do they get halfway and decide to turn back around to what they know?

Don't be fooled. The journey to freedom is a long one, and part of the reason it gets longer is because of the way our memory works.

On the other hand, the movies go from the Emancipation Proclamation straight to total and complete equality. In real life, it's taking so much longer, and one reason it's taking so long is because so many are trying to go back to where they were before. Just look at the world today with all its racial problems and listen to what some people are calling for. Listen to how they remember where we've been, forgetting the evils we've been delivered from.

We're just like the Israelites because we, too, get halfway there and want to turn around. Then, we look for someone to blame. You heard it:

> The Israelites said to [Moses and Aaron], "If only we had died by the hand of the Lord in the land of Egypt, when we sat by the fleshpots and ate our fill of bread; for **you** have brought us out into this wilderness to kill this whole assembly with hunger."[emphasis added]

That's normal enough, too.

Do you know what a church does when it hits hard times? It wants to get a new pastor.

Do you know what parents do when concerned over their children's education? They blame the teachers.

And what do countries do in times of crisis? People chant, "drain the swamp."

However, the most dangerous kind of leader to call on when a church, a school system, or a nation has hit hard times is the kind who says, "I can save you. Just leave it to me."

Great leaders don't fall into this trap. The people blamed Moses, but he didn't shoulder all the blame, nor did he make promises he couldn't deliver. That's because real leaders, in times of crisis, call on people to stand up on their own two feet by saying things like, "It's not what your country can do for you; it's what you can do for your country."

You remember that?

Real leadership, on the most challenging journeys of life, looks like what we saw in our first Scripture lesson from the book of Ephesians, where Paul begs each Christian to "lead a life worthy of the calling to which you have been called."

"Each of us" he wrote, "was given grace," and the role of the ones who spend all their time talking (the apostles, prophets, evangelists, and pastors) is "to equip [you] the saints for the work of ministry, for building up the body of Christ."

While I look with awe and reverence at the portraits of the great pastors who have served our church, who is it that teaches our children to sing, "Jesus loves me this I know?"

We commissioned our children's Sunday school teachers this morning and celebrate their ministry because they are leading lives worthy of the calling to which they have been called. They are making our church stronger, not waiting for others to do it for them.

To broaden this thought beyond teachers, I ask you to think about what happens when it gets hot in here. Do you know who fixes the air conditioner? It's not me.

Then this morning, when I walked into the church, the first person I saw was our security associate, Antonio Evans, who was wearing a hairnet. "Antonio, what are you doing wearing a hairnet?" I asked. He said, "I'm making coffee and cooking a quiche. I'm being the church."

Isn't that the truth?

We are on a journey to the Promised Land, and each of us has a job to do that helps to get us there. Even if, along the way, from time to time, we try to turn around to go back to where we've been, look for someone to blame or for someone to save us, the Lord is all the while providing us food for the journey so that we have the strength to press on.

Moses said to Aaron, "Say to the whole congregation of the Israelites, 'draw near to the Lord.'" In the evening, quails came up and covered the camp. In the morning, there was a layer of dew around the camp. When the layer of dew lifted, there on the surface of the wilderness was a fine flaky substance, as fine as frost on the ground. Moses said to them, "It is the bread that the Lord has given you to eat."

Life is full of these difficult journeys of change, and some of them drag us onward kicking and screaming. Our only choice is whether or not we'll resist them, and our only hope is finding a way to see God at work in them.

Now, look around today. It's in moments like this one and on days like today when we hear again that great call to keep going and to run our race. It's on days like today that we see in this bread and cup prepared for us the reminder that even when we don't want to go one step further, He is with us still, calling us onward and towards the goal.

Amen.

Under the Broom Tree
Ephesians 4: 25 – 5: 2 and 1st Kings 19: 1-18
Preached on August 12, 2018

My junior or senior year of high school, I was on the Marietta High School baseball team. That's not to say that I played baseball. I was on the team, but I didn't play a whole lot.

My dad went to most all of the games anyway, and one game I got to play a lot. I was three for three. I got a hit every at bat and drove in three or four runs. There was a short write-up in the paper because I hit a single that drove in two runs, which gave us the lead. I was so proud of that newspaper clipping that appeared in the *Marietta Daily Journal* that I only recently stopped carrying it around in my wallet.

After the game, my dad wanted to celebrate by taking me out to a steak dinner, and since it was an evening game, the only place still open and serving steak by the time the game ended was Waffle House, so we went. He bought me a T-bone, and I'll never forget it.

It was a victory feast, and I'll never forget it because not every meal is like that.

We were once invited to what was meant to be a campaign victory party. A friend was running for public office, and we arrived at the venue as the results were just starting to come in; however, the numbers were going in the wrong direction. This friend, who was expected to win in a landslide, ended up losing the election, and when he finally showed up, we could tell he didn't want to be there. No one felt like eating any of the food. No toasts were given. We drank some, but it wasn't Champagne because the character of the party wasn't victory but defeat.

When I compare these two memories, my victory dinner at Waffle House and the campaign party that occurred after my friend's defeat, I realize that it's not just the presence of food that inspires our appetite. Our appetite also depends on whether or not we feel like we deserve to eat what's been prepared.

A victory feast is one thing. The kind of meal we've just read about in our second Scripture lesson is another.

This meal occurs right in the middle of major events you may know about.

Queen Jezebel had brought priests from her homeland into the nation of Israel. They were called the Priests of Baal, and, after watching his brothers and sisters adopt this pagan religion, the Prophet Elijah stood up and challenged the Priests of Baal to a great contest. There'd be two bulls on two altars. The Priests of Baal called on their god to rain down fire on the altar, and Elijah did the same. The god who answered by fire would be named the true god of Israel.

It's hard when you get punished for doing the right thing, but that's pretty much what happened to Elijah. While he was faithful, and the fire of the Lord fell on his sacrifice, burning it up and turning back the hearts of those in Israel who saw, Queen Jezebel wasn't giving up that easily.

Rather than repent like the others, Queen Jezebel wanted Elijah dead, so, fleeing from her wrath, the Prophet ran. That's the background for our second Scripture lesson. Finally exhausted, he sat down under a solitary broom tree and asked that he might die, saying, "It is enough, now, O Lord, take away my life, for I am no better than my ancestors."

On the one hand, knowing what's just happened, it doesn't make any sense for him to say something like that. For generations and generations, we've been telling the story of the Prophet Elijah who called down the Lord's fire from heaven to defeat the prophets of Baal. The problem is, from what we've read this morning, you can tell that from Elijah's point of view, nothing really changed.

When Elijah says, "It is enough, now, O Lord, take away my life, for I am no better than my ancestors," he means that, while he was on the winning side of one contest, he's lost the war. While he was faithful, he still considers himself a failure, for Queen Jezebel is still in power. She still commands the soldiers who are hunting him down, and if she is still in power with such authority, then while he fought the good fight, while he ran his race, there's nothing to keep her from doubling the number of Baal's prophets and erasing this one victory from the pages of Israel's history.

Do you know what that feels like?

Do you know what it feels like to have given your very best, and to have come out feeling like it was all for nothing?

Do you know what it feels like to have done the right thing, stood with integrity, only to be silenced?

Do you know what it feels like to have exercised more and eaten less, but when you got up on the scale, you were two pounds more than you were before?

We tell our kids to try out for the team, but to do so they have to risk something. They have to gather up the courage to put themselves out there, and still they may go to the bulletin board to see that their names are not on the list.

Should that happen, and they're brave enough to tell you, you had better be ready to take them out to ice cream, only remember that it's hard to enjoy the party if you lost the election.

It's even hard to know what to do as people gather around to say, "You gave it your best. We're still proud." because if you've given it your all and still came up wanting, what you really want to do is lie down under a broom tree and die.

I remember a friend in college. He was a great basketball player, so his team passed him the ball as the time ran out on the clock. They were down by one. If he made the shot, they'd win the game, so he took the shot but missed it.

After the game, while he was walking off the court, his girlfriend walked up with a glass of water, and he knocked it out of her hand. Why? Because love is a hard thing to accept if you don't feel like you are worthy of it.

"It is enough, now, O Lord, take away my life, for I am no better than my ancestors."

That's what he said. That's how he felt, and I've been under that broom tree, too.

You know I'm the one who usually writes the Prayer of Confession in your bulletin. Other members of the church staff fix the grammar and polish it up, but I can write these things week after week without too much trouble because getting in touch with my sin is so easy. My sin is ever before me. All I have to do is write it down.

Do you know what's harder for me to do?

Accept the words from the Assurance of Forgiveness.

I have a good friend named James who told me that the Assurance of Forgiveness is the hardest part of the worship service for him to believe. Think of that in relation to all the other claims we make in here.

In here, we say that God created the heavens and the earth. For James, that's no problem.

We say that Jesus was conceived by the Holy Ghost, born of the Virgin Mary. For my friend, that doesn't take a leap of faith to believe.

We say that, on the third day, He rose again from the dead and ascended into heaven, and my friend James, he's got it. On the other hand, to believe that despite all the wars he's fought and been defeated, the races he's run and lost, or even as God knows his inmost parts, the secrets he can't tell, and the regrets he can't help but remember, this friend of mine wonders, "how could God love me still?"

Thinking those kinds of thoughts, Elijah lay down under the broom tree and fell asleep. Suddenly, an angel touched him and said to him, "Get up and eat," though you know Elijah wanted to knock that jar of water out of the angel's hand.

Instead, he ate and drank because God doesn't care about winning or losing so much as He cares about feeding His children.

There's a preacher up in New York City named Tim Keller. The great Libba Schell sent me a quote of his last Thursday:

> To be loved but not known is comforting, but superficial. To be known and not loved is our greatest fear. But to be fully known and truly loved is, well, a lot like being loved by God. It is what we need more than anything. It liberates us from pretense, humbles us out of our self-righteousness, and fortifies us for any difficulty life can throw at us.

At the end of her email, Libba also reminded me how in trivia the other night I thought the longest book in the Bible was Numbers and not Psalms, but that proves the point, right? What is love but to know that, win or lose, I'm still loved?

There's a hymn that says it this way: "no more a stranger, or a guest, but like a child at home."

Likewise, when God came to earth in human form, Scripture tells us that God so loved the world that He gave His only Son, not that the world would be condemned by Him but that all might have life in His name. He didn't go around wagging His finger and adding to our shame. No! He called a bunch of sinners to His table, and He washed their feet and fed them.

Did they deserve it?

Did they feel like they belonged?

Was it a steak dinner at the Waffle House victory feast? No. It was the kind of meal where they heard what I did from my dad. It was like Jesus saying to them, "I'm your father, and you're my son, and I am thankful to sit down at any table with you anytime, whether you're on cloud nine or walking through the valley of the shadow of death."

That's the story of God as told in Scripture. That's the Good News of the Gospel of Jesus Christ. But that's not always easy to accept, nor is it what we always hear.

Back in Tennessee, there was a church with a billboard out front. Every year, about this time, when it was so hot you couldn't go outside without sweating through your shirt, they'd put out on that billboard: "Sinner, You Think It's Hot Now?"

The problem with that kind of message is that, while it's meant to scare you into that church, it just convinces a whole bunch of people that they don't belong inside the church's doors and that they never will, so the admonition from Ephesians is this: "Be imitators of God."

Go out into the world and show those who think that their worth hangs in the balance that they're beautiful.

Go and tell the frustrated that they're enough.

Go and tell that mother who's just barely holding it together that everything is going to be OK, and maybe she won't want to hear it, but tell her anyway.

This morning my sermon wouldn't print. You know that feeling?

I got up from my desk and walked over to look at the printer. I stared at it for a while. That didn't do anything. I pushed a couple buttons. Still nothing, so I had to take my laptop into the Sanctuary and put it right on the pulpit. I felt so stupid.

You know what helped? Looking in my wallet at the two little notes that replaced my old newspaper clipping, hearing the Assurance of Forgiveness spoken by Rev. Lisa Majores, being greeted with the Peace of Christ by Erroll, Beth, and Cal, and when Katherine Harrison walked out of the Sanctuary at the end of the service, she winked at me.

Be imitators of the God of grace, by giving the grace that He has given you. And thank you for giving that grace to me.

Amen.

Part 2: Wisdom

Wisdom literature makes up a significant part of our Bible. The following sermons, based on two books of Biblical wisdom, Proverbs and James, attempt to lift up the kind of counter-cultural insight that these books provide. These words of truth matter now more than ever. Our prayer to God today must be that of the *Book of Common Worship*: "Among all the changing words of this generation, speak to us your Word, which does not change."

Turn in Here
Ephesians 5: 15-20 and Proverbs 9: 1-6
Preached on August 19, 2018

Zoey Brogan just read a beautiful passage from the book of Proverbs, and it was right to have a female voice read this passage because it's *Woman* Wisdom calling us to come to her for insight. I say us because that's whom she's talking to. She's not talking to anyone else. She's not talking to your neighbor or your sister's husband. She's talking to you and me.

Knowing that to be the case, you can tell that there's a difference between the way we read Proverbs and the way we might be tempted to read a book of Law like Deuteronomy or a letter from Paul. It's possible to read either and assume that the instruction isn't really for us but someone else, like drunkards or adulterers, maybe. Sometimes that may be the case, but we're wasting our time reading Proverbs without ourselves in mind because none of us is so wise that he doesn't need to seek out Wisdom's help.

Let me give you an example of what I mean.

With another shark movie in the theaters, I made an interesting discovery just this week. According to a recent study, on average, there are six shark-related deaths each year. [2] That's tragic, of course, but there are over 2,900 hippopotamus-related deaths each year.

Think of that for just a minute. Think of that disparity, and, yet, there was *Jaws*, *Jaws 2*, and *Jaws 3*. Plus, now there's *Sharknado*, and the new *Megalodon* is the top-grossing movie in theaters, but can you think of one horror movie involving a hippopotamus?

When I think of a hippopotamus, I think of the Ann Murray record my mom used to play for me: *There's a Hippo in My Tub*. What's wrong with Ann Murray giving kids this horrible image? Why was she singing this horrible song? She'd never sing about a great white shark in her tub, would she? And yet, consider the numbers. Consider for just a moment how much more afraid a rational person should be of a hippopotamus than a shark.

Here's the problem, though: we aren't rational. Plus, we resist change, even when we know we're being irrational.

---

[2] https://www.mnn.com/earth-matters/animals/stories/11-animals-more-likely-to-kill-you-than-sharks

I'm thankful for work done by one church member, David Waldrep, who's lobbied to get some legislation through the State House so that driving while texting is now against the law. That will go a long way, but we should know better than to text and drive all on our own. However, we aren't rational, and we resist change.

We will all fight to keep things as they are, even if doing things the way we always have is killing us.

Eating at Brandi's Famous Hot Dogs isn't doing anything for my physique, but I can't stop going there, can I? Even if I know better, I don't necessarily do better, so Woman Wisdom calls us, all of us, to "turn in here."

Zoey Brogan read it beautifully:

"Wisdom has built her house; she has hewn her seven pillars.

She has slaughtered her animals, she has mixed her wine, she has also set her table."

She does this because she invites us to come and eat with her and to "lay aside immaturity, and live, and walk in the way of insight."

That sounds great, but it requires changing our ways and admitting that she's talking to us.

Some of our habits are so ingrained that we don't even see them, and if you don't believe you have any ingrained habits, then tell me why you're sitting in the same pew that you always sit in this morning.

Wisdom is calling you and me, and according to the book of Proverbs, with wisdom, we will grow in knowledge and understanding.

With wisdom, we will be saved from the way of evil.

However, just as the first step in education is admitting what we don't know, and just as the first step towards forgiveness is confessing that we're not perfect, so wisdom begins when we lean not on our own knowledge or insight.

You know that one. Cheryl Reeves' grandmother quoted it all the time, and maybe yours did, too, but from the King James Version:

"Trust in the Lord with all thine heart; and lean not unto thine own understanding."

I had to learn that one the hard way. In ninth grade at Marietta High School, I failed Spanish 101. That's not something that I'm proud of, but it's true.

That's just what happens when you don't pay attention in class or do any of the homework.

In tenth grade, I took it again, and I remember my teacher, Señora Smitherman, telling me that the difference between the F that I made the first time and the A that I made in her class was that, in her class, I was always the first to ask a question.

Wisdom calls, "turn in here!" but, too often, we keep going, either unwilling to accept her help, or convinced that she's not talking to us and that we're doing just fine on our own. Either way, in place of wisdom, we make the fool's choice to lean on our own limited understanding. However, in Ephesians we read:

"Be careful then how you live, not as unwise people but as wise, making the most of the time, because the days are evil. So, do not be foolish, but understand what the will of the Lord is."

How important these words are because it is so easy to allow our days to pass by without thinking about what we're doing.

A friend of mine named James Fleming once scolded his retired father for taking two hours to polish his shoes. He asked, "Dad, why is that taking you so long? I polish mine in fifteen minutes."

His wise, old father responded, "Twenty-four hours in a day son; got to fill it with something."

But what?

It creeps in so innocently.

Ballet lessons are on Monday. There's nothing wrong with that.

Tae Kwan Do is on Tuesdays. That's good, too.

Then, church is on Wednesday.

Daddy works late on Thursdays.

Mom was invited to go out with a group on Friday.

Saturday there are soccer games.

Sunday used to be a day that no one dared touch, but not anymore.

I like to have things to do, and I love being able to run to Home Depot on a Sunday afternoon, but if we just go with the flow of the 21st Century, accepting the norms of our consumer culture, we're going to catch ourselves coming and going.

That's why Wisdom calls us, "Turn in here!"

"Come and eat of my bread and drink of the wine I have mixed. Lay aside immaturity and the desire to fit in with the craziness that everyone is calling normal and walk in the way of insight."

I need to listen to her because I find myself saying, "I just have too much going on."

Guess who can stop it?

Guess who can change it?

All any of us has to do is veer off the well-worn road of doing things the way you always have to turn in to the way of wisdom.

You see, we have to listen to her because we're not rational beings. We'll self-destruct if left to our own devices.

We're busy being scared of sharks, but you know the animal that kills more people per year than any other? The mosquito that flies in and out of our backyards every moment of every day.

We know to be cautious of the big, scary things, but what if it's our normal lives that are killing us? What if it's our daily routines that need to change?

"Turn in here!" she says because if we don't turn off this road that we're on, what's going to happen?

We are the most medicated country in the world.

Our bodies and our souls hurt.

For some of us, it's as though we know something's wrong, yet it's just so easy to keep going, so we do.

The other option comes in Wisdom's voice crying out: "Turn in here."

Look to her for answers.

Today, we gave third graders their very own Bibles because as a Christian church, we believe that within the pages of Scripture are words of guidance and hope in a world full of words that should not be trusted.

For a real-life example of words that cannot be trusted, you may have received an email yesterday from me, requesting that you help me out with a favor. All I needed, according to this email scam, was a few gift cards for a couple hundred dollars. I was asking you to buy them and send them to me. It was all very convincing, especially because the grammar and spelling in these emails made me sound like English was my second language, making the email consistent with my typical grammar and spelling.

I apologize for this email. I didn't send it, and we've taken steps to make it stop, but this email does help to illustrate my point. We live in a crazy world where you can't even trust the words of an email that looks like it was sent from your pastor.

Don't take my word for it.

Don't take Hollywood's word for it. They'll brainwash you.

Don't take Washington's word for it.

Don't take Wall Street's word for it because among all the changing voices of this present evil age, only one voice can lead you to new life.

Wisdom is calling.

Rather than accept the patterns that our culture calls normal and the lies told that pass for truth, let us be about reading and studying the words of Scripture, listening to Wisdom always.

Amen.

In a Mirror
Deuteronomy 4: 1-2 and 6-9, and James 1: 17-27
Preached on September 2, 2018

James is a difficult book. We're in it, though. Now, we're in it, and I want to stay in it for a few weeks because, while difficult, it's good for us to take this book of the Bible seriously.

That's because James is a life-giving book of the Bible. However, my Mom asked me a couple months ago about a good Sunday school curriculum on the book of James for her class in North Carolina to use, and I told her to pick another book. I said, "Mom, you don't want to get into James. It's rough." We do need to hear it, though. It's in the Bible for a reason. However, legend Martin Luther, the great church reformer who started the Protestant Reformation 500 years ago, took his students to the river and instructed them to turn to the book of James in their Bibles, rip it out, and throw it into the water.

Now, why would he instruct his students to do that?

Luther told them to rip out the book of James because this book can give you the idea that your salvation depends on your behavior. If you read James without thinking about God's grace, this book can give you the idea that ours is a religion of morals and being good, and it's not. Instead, ours is a religion of undeserved grace, for we believe that we are saved, not because of what we do, but because of what Christ has done on the cross. We're saved by his blood, not by our good behavior. That's the essence of Christianity; however, that doesn't mean our behavior is irrelevant.

We have to turn to James because, even if we are washed in the blood of the Lamb, that doesn't mean we can go around acting crazy.

Even if we are like prodigal sons and daughters, returned home and welcomed with open arms despite our years of carousing, that doesn't mean we should go back to "loose living."

Even though we were baptized in water, made heirs of the Kingdom of Heaven, we still go out into the world, and the way we live may be the closest thing to a Bible that some people ever see. Therefore, James says to us, "Be doers of the word, not merely hearers who deceive themselves. For if any are hearers of the word and not doers, they are like those who look at themselves in a mirror; for they look at themselves and, on going away, immediately forget what they were like."

44

You know what that means?

That means that all the time I'm telling you to remember who you are, and I'm doing that for a good reason. "Remember always who you are," I say at the end of every worship service, "for you are God's own. As God's own, clothe yourselves with compassion, kindness, humility, and patience. Forgive each other, just as the Lord has forgiven you."

Why do I care so much about these words that I repeat them to you week after week? It's because if we come into this room and hear that we're God's own, what good is it if we walk out of here and immediately forget?

How does it sound if we talk and talk about forgiveness while we're at church, but upon going home, we keep an account of grievances against our neighbor?

How does it look if we are told to "clothe ourselves with kindness and humility," but then go and speak to our waitress at the Red Lobster as though we were the Queen of England and she were the dirt under our shoes?

That's what they'd always remind us before we left on big trips in our old church bus back when I was in high school. You know the bus I'm talking about. It's parked in the West Lot, and it may not run well enough to leave the West Lot for a while, but, back then, Mike Clotfelter and Tim Hammond would drive us in it all the way to Mexico. It says First Presbyterian Church right on the side, and back when it ran, that was a dangerous advertising opportunity. It was a bus with your church's name on the side, filled with a bunch of teenagers.

That's why Dr. Speed, who was the Senior Pastor then, would come and address us all, saying, "Remember that where you go, you go representing our church and our Christian faith." I remember him saying that to all of us like it was yesterday, but I also remember once that we parked at a McDonald's. This was back when McDonald's still had ashtrays and salt and pepper shakers on the table. Someone discovered that if you spun a quarter on the table just right, then while it was spinning, you could slam down one of those shakers on top of it. Because the bottom was plastic, the quarter would break through, and all the salt or pepper would come out of the bottom and onto the table.

This was one of those things that was a challenge to master.

Teenagers like a challenge, and we didn't have cell phones back then to keep us occupied, so we were bored. After eating, we all were in the mood for a challenge, so we spun our quarters on the tables and busted every salt and pepper shaker in the restaurant. Then we climbed into the bus. Right there on the side of it were the words "First Presbyterian Church of Marietta, Georgia." Then we had to climb right back out to apologize to the manager of the McDonald's.

Why would we do such a thing?

Because to some degree or another, we are all like those "who look at themselves in a mirror; for we look at ourselves and, on going away, immediately forget what we were like."

That's why I tell you to remember always who you are. These words are so important that I say them at the end of every worship service; however, these words and the way of life that goes with them are so profound, that sometimes I can't get the words out of my mouth.

Does that ever happen to you? Do your words ever get stuck?

I learned something interesting about that last Wednesday. I was listening to a radio show about Elvis Presley and how he would often forget the words to one of his most popular songs, "Are You Lonesome Tonight?"

You know this one:

>Are you lonesome tonight?
>
>Do you miss me tonight?
>
>Are you sorry we drifted apart?
>
>Does your memory stray
>
>To a brighter sunny day
>
>When I kissed you and called you sweetheart?

You know these lines. They're pretty easy to remember, and that was the part of the song that he could always get right, but then came the spoken verses where he wasn't singing, but just talking. Elvis was supposed to say:

>You know someone said that the world's a stage
>
>And each must play a part
>
>Fate had me playing in love
>
>With you as my sweetheart
>
>Act one was when we met, I loved you at first glance
>
>You read your line so cleverly and never missed a cue
>
>Then came act two, you seemed to change, and you acted strange

And why I'll never know.

Honey, you lied when you said you loved me.

Now the stage is bare and I'm standing there

With emptiness all around

And if you won't come back to me

Then they can bring the curtain down.

It was during this part where on at least twelve occasions, Elvis went blank. He'd be live, on stage, in front of a crowd of people, and he'd forget the words to this song that he'd sung thousands of times before. Here's the interesting part: the very first time his mind went blank was right after Priscilla left him.

You see, these words were like a mirror, and when he said them, reality hit him like a ton of bricks. It will make you sad to hear the recordings. Hearing will make you pity the King, but when he got done singing those words that revealed the truth, he went right back to the same behavior that pushed Priscilla away in the first place.

"For if any are hearers of the word and not doers, they are like those who look in a mirror, but on going away forget what they saw."

In the same way, when we worship God in this place, by confessing our sins and hearing words of forgiveness, it's like we are holding up a mirror to ourselves. God holds up a mirror that tells us who we really are namely, God's own, who are always sinning yet are forgiven, fallen yet lifted up, broken yet healed, and imperfect yet redeemed.

There are moments in worship, like when we sing the words to "Amazing Grace," where the truth of who we are in the eyes of God hits some people like a ton of bricks. Next time we sing it, you ought to put your hymnal down and look around to see all those who have tears in their eyes. Some can't make it through the first stanza without being overcome with emotion, and why is that?

It's because we know that we were once blind, but now we see, and that we were lost, but now we're found.

When we sing all that, we see the truth of who we are. But what does it mean if we leave this place and go back to living the way we did before?

Elvis stumbled right after saying words like, "Honey, you lied when you said you loved me.

Now the stage is bare and I'm standing there." It was a sad situation that these words uncovered, and what did he do about it? Nothing.

You see, obedience to the Law; it's not about avoiding eternal punishment. No. Instead, it's about putting love into action.

My father-in-law does that. He doesn't drive fifteen miles under the speed limit because he's scared of getting a ticket. He drives fifteen miles under the speed limit because when his granddaughters are in the back seat, he knows he's carrying precious cargo.

Parents do that, too. We tell our daughters over and over again, probably ten times a day, "You are so beautiful." They are, but I keep telling them that because I want to see them live like they know it by raising their hands with confidence and walking into school like they're somebody. That's when it counts. They have to put their father's love into action. They have to know it, not just when Daddy's in front of them saying it, but when he's not.

That's what we all have to do. We all must put the Father's love for us into action because we all leave this church, and when we sit down at our table at the Red Lobster, everyone's going to know where we've been.

By the clothes that we wear, everyone will know that we've been to church, but they'll know that we are Christians, not by our clothes, but by our love.

Amen.

No Partiality
Proverbs 22: 1-2, 8-9, 22-23; and James 2: 1-17
Preached on September 9, 2018

Today is a special day at First Presbyterian Church.

If you're here for the first time, I'm so glad you're here for this worship service, and I hope you'll come back again next week, but I feel like I have to tell you that it isn't always like this.

It's always good to be here. Every Sunday, it's good to be here at First Presbyterian Church, but it isn't always like this.

This is a special Sunday because today we celebrate the Scottish roots of the Presbyterian Church. These roots take us back to several moments in history. One in particular is August 17, 1560, when John Knox and five of his colleagues presented the first reformed confession of faith written in the English Language to the Parliament of Scotland. This was a pivotal moment, and we'll use a portion of that very confession as our Affirmation of Faith later in the service.

I want to point that out because today is about more than kilts and bagpipes; it's also about lessons learned from our ancestors. Today is about the faith passed down to us, but sometimes the faith part gets forgotten. That happens.

Last weekend was a celebration of the Jewish roots of Temple Kol Emeth, a Synagogue over in East Cobb. It wasn't the faith passed down from one generation to the next that got the news coverage in the *Marietta Daily Journal* for this event. No, what made the front page was the bagel-eating contest.[3]

A man named Brandon "Da Garbage Disposal" Clark, originally from St. Louis, won the bagel eating contest by eating seven bagels in five minutes. This feat is amazing, but how much more amazing is the heritage and faith inherited by these Jewish people?

Consider the legacy passed down from their foremothers and forefathers of perseverance through all kinds of oppression, Nazi and otherwise.

---

[3] https://www.mdjonline.com/news/competition-fierce-at-noshfest-s-annual-bagel-eating-challenge/article_12b97f1a-b046-11e8-9b40-6fcd1c8bc01c.html

Also, did you know that there are more Jewish Nobel Prize winners than any other ethnicity?[4]

Then, to inspire our awe and wonder, there are the Scriptures that the Jewish people compiled that today make up most of the most important book ever written.

It's not that eating seven bagels in five minutes isn't impressive. It is, only there ought to be more to a celebration of Jewish heritage than that. Likewise, there's more to this celebration of the Scottish roots of the Presbyterian Church than kilts.

I like kilts, but I'm not even Scottish as far as I know. My family came here to Marietta from Virginia Highlands in 1986, and that's about all the genealogical work I've done. I'm not here because of genetics. I'm here because of their faith that I've inherited.

While some can trace their roots to these great families represented by the tartans on display, this worship service today is so truly about what we all can learn from the people who passed down their faith to us.

Today we celebrate John Knox. I mentioned him before. He was a major figure in the Presbyterian Church. He was such a force that Mary, Queen of Scotts is often quoted as saying, "I fear the prayers of John Knox more than all the assembled armies of Europe." In standing on his convictions, he and many others were persecuted by both England and France and were sent to labor camps. They were punished for what they believed, but they persevered so that our Presbyterian tradition gained a strong foothold in Scotland. That Presbyterian faith of John Knox crossed the Atlantic Ocean, so that there were more Presbyterian signers of the Declaration of Independence than any other religious group. By the early 1700's, Presbyterians had started Princeton University, and by the start of the Civil War, they had founded over a fourth of all the colleges in the United States.[5]

Skip ahead to World War II, and the most well-known preacher in the country was a Scottish born Presbyterian named Peter Marshall. At that time, he served New York Avenue Presbyterian Church in Washington, D.C., and was the chaplain to Congress. Before that, he was a student at Columbia Theological Seminary in Decatur and often visited this very church to preach and sing.

---

[4] https://www.quora.com/Why-are-there-so-many-Jewish-Nobel-laureates-in-comparison-to-other-groups
[5] https://www.presbyteriancolleges.org/being__presbyterian_related_

As Peter Marshall was from Scotland, it was he who brought this tradition of Kirkin' of the Tartan to America, where the tartans, or flags, of each family were brought into the church that they might be displayed and blessed by God.

That's where this worship service comes from. Peter Marshall brought it over, but this tradition that we follow in the worship service today first emerged in Scotland in the 18th Century, at a time where the signs of Scottish culture had been outlawed. In those days, Scottish families could only celebrate their culture and identity in secret.

Imagine that.

To live in a land where you have to hide who you are.

This worship service is founded on the Scottish tradition of celebrating their heritage in the presence of God after years of only celebrating in secret, so, here, when all tartans are raised, it's the sign that all families, all peoples, all tribes, all nations and creeds, we all were created by God who spoke back at the dawn of time and called humanity to existence on the sixth day, then said, "It was very good."

This worship service calls us to remember again that God doesn't make junk. All of us stand today and receive our blessing, remembering that doing so is a privilege. We must remember that it is a privilege to raise a tartan and be blessed by God without any shame or fear of rejection for who we are and who were created to be, and it is a privilege that we now must share.

We said before: "We raise the tartans before Almighty God in gratitude for heritage and pray God's blessing on His servant people in all lands."

That's a powerful phrase: "God's servant people in all lands," but that's what we said earlier in the service, so we pray for God's blessing not just on the MacDonalds, MacFarlanes, MacGregors, and MacMillans, but also on the Smiths, Hernandezes, Abbasis, and the Sings.

We pray for God's blessing on all tribes, remembering the Scotts who once were tempted to be ashamed of who they were created to be. We Presbyterians, Scottish or not, today, we stand together saying, "The Lord shows no partiality!"

It's just as Paul said it in his letter to the Galatians:

"There is no Jew or Greek,

Slave or free,

Male and female; for all of you are one in Christ Jesus."

Having believed this truth ourselves and publicly receiving God's blessings after generations of hiding who we are, now we have to put belief into action, for as James knows: "Faith without works is dead."

Any Episcopal in here will know the way the Prayer Book echoes the same sentiment:

"That we show forth thy praise, not only with our lips, but also with our lives!"

Therefore, as we remember today those oppressed Scottish Presbyterians of long ago, how the English outlawed the bagpipes that they played, the kilts that they wore, and the Gaelic that they spoke, yet how, in this worship service, their native tongue was blessed, we also must ask ourselves, "Who would we be to go out into the world criticizing the accents of our neighbors?"

You know what it's like to feel ashamed of your accent.

I was once in New York City, and I told a guy I'm from Georgia. He said, "I know."

James asked all those who would look down a person because of how they appear: "Do you with your acts of favoritism really believe in our glorious Lord Jesus Christ?"

For if a person with gold rings, or an English accent, with fine clothes or in a mink coat, with money in his pocket or power at her disposal comes into this Great Hall, and we say, "Sit here in the place of honor," but then say, "All rednecks and immigrants to the back," have we not become hypocrites?

It's a reminder like that one that our world needs more than kilts or a bagel-eating contest, for discrimination touches every ethnicity. Racism has reared its ugly head throughout the ages.

Just as they outlawed our bagpipes, they destroyed the drums of African slaves.

Just as they forbade our kilts, so they cut the Cherokee's hair.

Just as they pressured the Scotts to Anglicize their language, not so long ago, Texas Governor Miriam Ferguson said, "If English was good enough for Jesus, it's good enough for Texas school children." I don't have to tell you how misguided such a statement is, but it's just as misguided to allow such prejudice to continue without calling it wrong.

Knowing how discrimination hurt our ancestors and defies the teachings of the Gospel, we must stand against it now. As the Scots were oppressed, so we must fight racism today.

That's why we can't sit idly by as children in headscarves are treated like terrorists.

We can't watch without asking questions as children who cross the border are treated as criminals.

We can't just keep quiet while men and women are abused because of whom they love.

And we can't blindly dismiss the players and cheerleaders who kneel during the Anthem, even if it makes us mad, without first trying to understand what they're kneeling for.

If we enjoy God's blessing today, celebrating our heritage in safety and freedom now, we must also work that all should have the privilege of being proud of who they are and where they come from, knowing who created, redeemed, and blesses them.

Our God shows no partiality, and neither can we because all are one in Christ Jesus our Lord.

Amen.

Taming the Tongue
Isaiah 50: 4-9 and James 3: 1-12
Preached on September 16, 2018

This passage of Scripture that I've just read from the book of James reminds me of two quotes about the power of words. One is from the great Jewish theologian Rabbi Abraham Heschel, who said that "words create worlds." The stories that we hear and the words we let in create the world that we inhabit, so the child who is told that she is beautiful and brilliant is very different from the other who is told that she'll never amount to anything. This difference has less to do with genetics or opportunities than the story that each is told, which informs how she sees herself.

In the same way, those who find themselves sucked in to the 24-hour news cycle can't help but live in a world of fear and anxiety. The words we hear create the world we live in, so you may want to call the people who never watch the news "ignorant," but you know what I call them? Happy.

Likewise, a scientist subscribing fully to the Big Bang Theory, believing that we humans are nothing more than the result of a random collision of forces millions of years ago, may also live as though her very life were but a random collision of forces without meaning or purpose.

That happens because the words we let in create the world that we inhabit

In addition to the science that we learn, we Christians also have the benefit of the Creation account in Genesis. The words of this account don't nullify rational thought but compliment it with God's story, so we believe that God spoke, not randomly, but on purpose. With God's words, all that we know was created, which then enables us to live in a world, not of random collisions, but of faith, hope, and love.

It's not so complicated. Rabbi Heschel's point is simple enough: words matter. Another Christian theologian named Damayanti Niles speaks of the importance of words as well, for she said that with our words, we create stories that become the baskets in which we carry our relationships.

The words that we speak and hear create the stories that either hold us together or tear us apart. The story of Grandma who always cooked our favorite yeast rolls will forever cast her as someone we can trust, but the story of the grandfather who was invited to speak at the Boy Scout meeting but showed up drunk will forever cast him as one who cannot be depended on no matter how many times he apologized. That's because regardless of what he said, what James would add to our understanding of the power of words is that when our words fail to materialize into our actions, the fabric that holds our relationships together frays and even breaks.

You know this already because you've seen what I'm talking about in action nearly every day of your life.

Whether it be a parent, a teacher, or a president, when the person we trust lean too heavily on the phrase, "Do as I say, not as I do," we hear the words of a hypocrite.

Likewise, a pastor who ignores you can't show up one day out of the blue and bring you comfort. It won't work. If you hear words of forgiveness preached by someone who you've seen yell at a waitress for bringing out the wrong drink order, you question the real state of his heart. As James asks, "Does a spring pour forth from the same opening both fresh and brackish water?" No. That can't happen. Either from your depths, you produce living water, or you don't. It doesn't matter what you say if your actions reveal that the true state of your heart is that of a brackish cesspool.

You know who has a good heart? Rev. Joe Brice.

His gallbladder wasn't so good, so he had it removed, but that guy's heart is a spring of living water. I know that because last Wednesday morning, I got to hear Rev. Joe Brice preach a funeral, but it was a hard one to do. It was a hard one because neither one of us has been here very long, so Joe had to start this funeral sermon by acknowledging the fact that he'd only known Vera a short while. Then, he went on to say that in the time he'd known her, he knew she'd not been in her full stature, so his experience of her wasn't enough to really express the fullness of her life.

Joe just acknowledged all that. He said,

> I didn't have the pleasure of knowing Vera very well, just a brief time when she was hospitalized, but I have had the pleasure of learning so much about her from her family and friends. You know, some people ask me, "Isn't what you do as a pastor so difficult? You know, the hospital visits, the funeral services?" Yes, there are difficult aspects to this role. Mostly dealing with the Christians is the hard part, but there is such a deep joy that continually washes over me when I have the honor to walk sacred steps with people during the holiest times of their life journeys.

After saying that, he looked at the family: "It is a joy and an honor to be trusted with the stories of Vera's life." Then, he told the stories. He told the stories that he collected from her children, grandchildren, and friends, and he was able to tell them because he sat with them and listened.

He also told the Gospel story, and that, together with the family stories, captured a woman. In that way, together at the funeral, we were all able to give thanks to God for her as we entrusted her to God's care.

It was a good funeral even though Joe didn't know her as well as he would have liked. He got to know her by listening to the stories that the family told, but have you ever been to the other kind where the preacher refers to the deceased by the wrong name?

We use our words to weave the cloth that might hold us together. These words can be so life-giving that, even at the grave, we are inspired to rejoice, singing our "halleluiahs." By a preacher's words, we may be reminded of the Great Story that changes everything we know, the story of Christ's redeeming death that brings new life, but by a preacher's actions, some are led to question everything they know.

Words are so powerful, and when they are rendered empty by the speaker's actions, they can cause a crisis of faith.

Therefore, "Not many of you should become teachers, my brothers and sisters," is what James says, "for you know that we who teach will be judged with greater strictness."

Think about that, schoolteachers. The power that you actually wield is almost as great as the power that parents think you wield.

So it is with preachers. I remember well going into Dr. Jim Speed's office just after high school graduation where I told him I planned to go on to Presbyterian College to major in religion, in preparation for studying to become a Presbyterian minister.

You know what he said? He said, "Be careful, Joe, because you're talking about getting involved in every person's most important relationship: between them and their God."

He's exactly right about that because when the person who preaches forgiveness betrays you, it hurts in such a profound way. It does something to the world that the preacher's words have testified to.

It's not just that the clergy is discredited; it's that the faith he or she inspired in the people who listened is discredited.

That's happening now to our brothers and sisters in the Roman Catholic Church, but, truly, this is something that happens everywhere. That's why I want to tell you something else Dr. Speed told me. It was right after I graduated seminary, and I drove up here to ask him the secret to being a pastor. I wanted to know the secret to being the pastor of a church that grew as much as this one did. You know what he said?

He said, "Don't give me too much credit, Joe. Marietta was growing then. Pretty much all I had to do was keep the doors open and avoid doing anything stupid."

That sounds easy, but you'd be surprised how hard I've worked to avoid doing anything stupid.

As James said, "All of us make many mistakes," so ultimately who is it that can be trusted completely? Who is the Teacher who always deserves to be heard?

Edith Foster read this passage from Isaiah:

The Lord God has given me the tongue of a teacher,

That I may know how to sustain the weary with a word.

The Lord God has opened my ear,

And I was not rebellious,

I did not turn backward,

I gave my back to those who struck me,

And my cheeks to those who pulled out the beard;

I did not hide my face from insult and spitting.

By His endurance and His steadfast love, we see that the Suffering Servant that the Prophet Isaiah describes not only has the tongue of a teacher but lives the life of one who deserves to be heard. This Suffering Servant of Isaiah describes the Lord Jesus Christ, who speaks to us words of rebuke that we don't want to hear and words of love that we fear we don't deserve. He speaks them both from a heart of faithful and undying devotion. He speaks from a heart that is the Spring of Living Water, so, we preachers, if we only point to ourselves, any who listens will eventually be disappointed for none of us is perfect, but those of us who testify to Him are worthy of being heard.

There's a preacher out in Denver named Nadia Boltz-Weber. Each time a new group of people join the church that she serves, she says to them, "Sooner or later, I'm going to disappoint you. That's because I'm a human being, and I can't help it, but still, after I've disappointed you, you may be tempted to leave this church to go someplace else. If you do that, you'll just find another human pastor who's going to disappoint you there, too. I encourage you to stick it out because, in that moment when you realize your pastor isn't perfect, you grow instead to trust in the Lord who is."

Among all the words of this present evil age, I charge you to be discerning.

I get so tired of hearing about "fake news" because it's not as though some news is fake and other news is true. It's that all the news we hear is imperfect until we come face to face with the Good News.

It's what He says that can save us, so, if you listen to the news for two hours a day, read from the Gospel for four until you get straightened out.

If your boss tells you you're a loser, come to this baptismal font and hear the truth: that you're a child of God, and if you hear words that make you hopeless, don't you ever forget that Christ has died, Christ is risen, and Christ will come again.

Amen.

Draw Near to God and
God Will Draw Near to You
Psalm 1 and James 3: 13 – 4: 10
Preached on September 23, 2018

One of my favorite restaurants in the whole world is the OK Café on the corner of West Paces Ferry and 41, right there just off I-75. I've eaten there so many times that I don't need to look at the menu, and the menu hasn't really changed since the first time I sat down in one of their red booths to eat. It's one of those timeless places that hasn't changed a whole lot, but I have, so part of the reason I love going to the OK Café is because it makes me think about all that's changed in my life over the years I've been eating there.

The memories I have of being eight years old and going there with my dad are just as important to me as the food. When I walk in, I think of how much my mom likes their Red Zinger iced tea, or when, right before they got married, Sara and I took my old friend Matt Buchanan and Jessica, who was then his fiancée, there for dinner. Now Matt and Jessica have a nearly-teenaged daughter. That's the kind of big change that happens over the course of several years and going to the OK Café makes me think about all that.

Even more so, the Chevron gas station across the street from the OK Café makes me think about how things change because right after graduating college, when Sara and I were first married, I worked for a lawn maintenance company. Pretty much every day, we'd park near that Chevron so we could eat lunch with all the other lawn maintenance crews at the picnic table in the back under a big magnolia tree. That picnic table is still there, and all these Atlanta landscape crews still stop to eat lunch right at that spot, so when I went to the OK Café last week, I stopped to buy gas at that Chevron, and there they all were. Nothing much has changed, but I've changed.

Back in those days when I ate at that picnic table, I was tan from working outside, and I spoke Spanish all day to communicate with my crew. Once, when I walked into that Chevron to buy a coke, the guy at the register said to me, "Buenos dias."

Well, last week all the guy at the register said was, "Good morning." I was a little disappointed, but that's to be expected because, while it's the same

Chevron with the same picnic table under the same magnolia tree, I've changed. I no longer fit into the world that I was once proud to belong to.

Now, that idea brings us to the matter at hand from the book of James. If you know what it's like to change in such a way that you no longer fit into the world you once belonged to, either because you moved to the city and your friends back in the country think you talk like a Yankee or because you got divorced and now your couple friends are weird about inviting you to dinner parties, use that feeling of no longer fitting into the world you once belonged to as a lens to really understand what James is trying to say to us today. It's important to hold onto that feeling of no longer fitting in to where you once belonged because we Christians are now citizens of the Kingdom of God. Why, then, are we still trying to fit into this world that's not our home any longer?

We feel the drive to fit in, but should we?

In reality, we aren't meant to fit in here, anymore.

Because of the life-changing Gospel of Jesus Christ, something inside us has changed. "But," as James says, "if you have bitter envy and selfish ambition in your hearts," then you are guided, not by heavenly wisdom, but by what is "earthly, unspiritual, devilish…"

There are two ways. There are two kinds of wisdom. One is of this world, and the other is of the world to come. James demands that we ask ourselves, "Which way are we choosing?" for, "You want something and do not have it; so you commit murder. And you covet something and cannot obtain it; so you engage in disputes and conflicts."

James is sure that too much of the time, our behavior makes us hypocrites. It just doesn't make any sense for us to keep on living according to the customs of the earth when we are citizens of the Kingdom of Heaven, but, as James says, there are "cravings… at war within" us.

We accept the standards of our society where everyone spends too much money, then we allow the reckless pursuit of wealth to trump our moral compass.

We lay down with the dogs of reckless power, following their actions and listening to their every word, then wind up waking up with their fleas.

We think we're just watching the commercials for restless leg syndrome, but before we know it, we're talking to our doctor about it, and she's writing a prescription for some disease that we never knew existed before we saw the commercial during the evening news. If anyone really has that restless leg syndrome, I'm sorry for being a jerk about it. It sounds awful, but the point

I want to make is that sometimes we are influenced in ways that we don't even realize because the fallen world that we don't belong to anymore still influences the way we think and the way we act.

There it all is in first half of chapter 4, verse 4:

"Adulterers! Do you not know that friendship with the world is enmity with God?"

The truth is that we have to change our ways. The change in our hearts that comes with our Christian belief must also create a change in our actions. We must become as pilgrims on the earth that we might be prepared to settle in heaven, so James says to us:

"Resist the devil, and he will flee from you. Draw near to God, and he will draw near to you."

Maybe you'd agree that this does sound like exactly what we ought to do, but maybe you're getting a little tired of all this preacher's "should's" and "ought's."

That can be exhausting.

You know, the thing about James that I don't like is that at first James makes me feel the same way as a trip to the dentist. It's like he's looking in my soul and saying, "Joe, you really ought to clean up in here." Of course, I should, but why? How?

What's so important in this long lecture that James gives us for these five chapters is that there's joy to be found in following his advice. You know that's true because trying to fit into the world as we know it will ultimately make you miserable.

I heard a story once about how hard it can be to please your father.

The story is about the first female President of the United States. She called her dad and invited him to go to the inauguration. He told her that he didn't have a ride to get there or a suit that fit any more, so he probably shouldn't go. Well, the President-to-be wasn't going to take that. She wanted her daddy there. She wanted him to be there so he could be proud of what she'd accomplished, so she sent over a tailor to his house. She paid for his suit, then sent a helicopter on Inauguration Day to pick him up. He rode to D.C. in that fancy helicopter, the Secret Service met him at the landing pad and escorted him right up to the front row where he could see his daughter put her hand on the Bible to be sworn in as President of the United States just as plain as day.

You know what her daddy said?

61

He said to the guy sitting next to him, "You see that lady up there. She's my daughter, but her brother played for Georgia."

You see, you can work hard to be somebody in the eyes of your earthly father, but there's no guarantee that you'll ever shine in his estimation.

We can work hard to fit in at the high school, but as soon as you save up the money to buy whatever clothes you're supposed to have, the trend changes, and you're out again.

In the same way, in this world we live in, even the ones who make it to the top and have all the stuff that is supposed to make someone happy are miserable. You can read about it in *Us Weekly*. The misery of the rich and famous is well-documented and there for you to read about in the check-out line of your neighborhood grocery store.

The call from James is not a five-chapter, finger-wagging lecture, but a mirror that we can hold up to this world that we're trying to fit into.

We worry about not being somebody in the eyes of the world; however, no matter how hard we work, we might still wind up feeling empty. On the other hand, to be somebody in the eyes of God:

That's like "soaring on the wings of eagles."

That's like "running and not growing weary."

That's like drinking the kind of water that satisfies, and you know what it takes to be somebody in the eyes of God according to our passage from James? All it takes is humility.

For a long time now, every meeting of our youth group has ended with the whole group forming one big circle, so that together they sing the words of James chapter 4, verse 10: "Humble thyself in the sight of the Lord, and he shall lift you up." The version that we read from this morning translated the words just slightly differently, but the meaning is the same. Regardless of how you say it, all we have to do to draw near to God is face the fact that the way we've been doing it isn't working.

It's just like how the first step towards going down the right path is walking into the gas station and asking for directions.

We have to humble ourselves before the Lord because those who aren't willing to admit that they need a savior can't benefit from the one that we have in Jesus Christ.

We have to humble ourselves before the Lord because until we're willing to admit that we're broken, we can't be mended.

Until we're ready to admit that we're sick, we can't be healed.

Until we're ready to say we're blind, we'll never see.

Until we're ready to say as the Prophet Isaiah said, "Lord, I'm a man with unclean lips living among a people with unclean lips," the Lord can't make us clean.

Yet, once we surrender and once we accept it, then we wonder why for so long we've been laboring in vain.

To say it as the psalmist did in our first Scripture lesson:

> Happy are those who do not follow the advice of the wicked,
>
> Or take the path that sinners tread,
>
> But their delight is in the law of the Lord,
>
> And on his law they meditate day and night.

If we want to be like the trees planted by streams of water that this psalm talks about, we, too, have to be ready to admit that where we've been living and what we've grown used to is so much like a desert that the people of this world look everywhere for a drink that they'll never find.

We'll never be able to buy our way to satisfaction no matter how much money we have.

We'll never be able to legislate our way to happiness no matter how much power we have, and we'll never be able to medicate ourselves to joy no matter how many pills we take.

You see, while the world makes promises, it cannot deliver.

There is only one source of living water.

There is only one life-giving stream, and it runs through the city not made by human hands. That's the place that we call home.

If you want to go there with me, take stock of your actions. Take stock of your heart. Have you adopted the ways of the world? Are the habits that we mortals accept as normal behavior ingrained so much that you're on your way to going down with it? Or is your heart so changed that you're preparing to live in a New Heaven and a New Earth, where the lion lays down with the lamb and the Lord is there to wipe away the tears from our eyes that we might live in joy forevermore?

When I die, I don't want anyone to say, "He sure was an upstanding citizen of the city of Marietta." I want them to say, "That Joe Evans was always a little weird, but that's because he didn't belong here. He was always preparing himself to live in the New Jerusalem, the Kingdom of God."

Draw near to God, and God will draw near to you.

Amen.

Speak with Boldness
Esther 7: 1-6 and James 5: 13-20
Preached on September 30, 2018

During seminary, as I trained to become a pastor, my first internship was at the old Georgia Baptist Hospital where I was to learn from their chaplains about visiting people in the hospital. By the time I was in seminary, it had been renamed the Atlanta Medical Center. Once a week, I was charged with visiting patients on the ICU floor, so I went from room to room, introducing myself to strangers and asking them about their personal struggles.

It was a role I felt completely unqualified to fill. I couldn't believe they just let me do that. I'd walk right in and meet people in the middle of whatever medical crisis they were facing. I'm sure it was the worst day of many of their lives; then, here I come. Sometimes, they seemed to tolerate my efforts; other times, they were glad to see me go. For me, all of it was terrifying because I had in my mind an idea that these poor people might want to talk with me about the great theological issues of life. That one might ask me:

"Why do bad things happen to good people?" or, "Why, young chaplain intern, is there suffering in the world?"

Of course, it got worse after my friend Fred Wise told me about his experience. He was called into a hospital room where a man had just died. He asked the man's wife if he might pray with her and her sister, which Fred did. He asked God to comfort them in their time of grief, and gave thanks for this man's life, but at the end of the prayer, the man's wife looked like she was expecting something more out of Fred, so she asked, "Well, aren't you going to try to raise him from the dead?"

This story basically confirmed all my worst fears about visiting people in the hospital as a chaplain intern. However, in reality, the most I was ever asked to do, beyond say a simple prayer, was to give someone a backrub. Thinking of Fred's story on the one hand and the reality of what I was ever actually asked to do, I realize that my fears built up so much that I was nearly afraid to do anything at all.

Do you remember as a child being nervous about talking to your friend after he'd lost his grandmother? Were you nervous, wondering,

"What will I say?

What if he cries?"

Were you also so nervous that maybe you waited until the time had passed to say anything at all?

I remember the pastor who preached my Great Uncle Jim's funeral. He told the story of being a nine- or ten-year-old boy. His father had just died, and his house was full of people. It was so full that he couldn't really make out much of it. His memory of the day was of a bunch of men and women wanting to say some words that would make this young boy feel better. The only vivid memory this preacher had of that sad day was climbing the steps, and, as he did, someone took his hand and squeezed it. That was all, but that was all my Great Uncle Jim needed to do. Despite all the years that had passed between the day of his father's funeral when he was a child and the day of my Great Uncle Jim's death, that preacher, now retired, remembered that simple gesture that told him he wasn't alone on one of the worst days of his life.

It is a scary thing to do what James is calling us to do. From this book of the Bible that we've been dealing with all month, I just read another passage with plain and clear instruction that pushes many of us beyond our comfort zones:

"Are there any among you suffering? Are any among you sick? They should call for the elders of the church and have them pray over them, anointing them with oil in the name of the Lord."

Doing such a thing as that sounds scary, but it's only scary because our imagination can convince us that in the presence of our suffering or sick friend, we're going to be asked to do some huge thing. Maybe we will, but more likely, they'll never even remember what we said; they'll only remember whether or not we were there.

I remember going to visit Roy. He was on oxygen and rarely left the house, except to go and eat at Red Lobster. His wife, Dodie, asked me to come over to bring him communion, but when I got there, I walked in the house and realized I had forgotten the home communion set. Years later when I left that church to go to Tennessee, you know what Dodie gave me as a going away present? A home communion set. When Roy died, I called Dodie, even though by then I was serving a different church in a different state. I called just to tell her I was sorry, and she cried, not because I knew the perfect thing to say, but because I took the time to call.

Think about that.

Have you ever waited and waited to call a friend who is going through a time of chaos for fear of saying the wrong thing? That happens. People do say the wrong thing. We had a friend in Tennessee who didn't know what to say to a mother who'd just lost her son, but she knew her son had played football for Alabama. To fill in the silence in the receiving line at the funeral all she could think to say to this grieving mother was, "Roll Tide."

And that's not the worst thing anyone's ever said at a funeral.

Worse to say are those empty platitudes, like, "God must have needed another angel in the choir." We say those kinds of things because we don't know what else to say; however, we have to remember how much power to heal there is in just showing up in an authentic and honest way. There is plenty of strength in standing before the power of death fortified with the truth of the Gospel and the truth of ourselves.

We don't have to know what to say.

We also don't have to know what to do, but we do have to show up.

I remember when Joanne was dying. Hospice arranged for a nice hospital bed to be put in her dining room so she wouldn't have to go up and down the stairs to her bedroom. Her husband slept on the coach in the next room, and, even though it was Christmastime, they hadn't bothered with a tree. They hadn't really bothered with much of anything other than soaking up every second that she had left. Her friends in the choir all wanted to do something, but Joanne and her husband didn't want visitors; yet, one of them called and asked her husband just to open the windows in the dining room. Right outside those windows, the choir sang Christmas carols.

That's an incredible thing, isn't it?

It really is. That's what her church did for her. A church is an incredible thing.

Churches are just full of people, but life-changing things happen here most every day when people have the courage to step out in faith as James implores.

If you read your newsletter (and if you haven't, you should), there's an article in there about a couple who's moving to France to be closer to their daughter. The only problem is that their dog is too old to make the flight. Their daughter, a former church member, sent us a message, wondering if there was any way we could help place this dog in a home.

The dog's name is Charlie and Martie Moore adopted him. The daughter who contacted us initially wrote me a note, saying, "Thank you so much for helping us find a home for Charlie. He is so happy with Martie. It was meant to be. It has also meant a lot to my parents who have had a tough time with ALS, and this gesture has given them some peace along the journey."

Consider that! The difference that can be made with such a simple act of kindness!

There's something else; there's someone who's been sliding a candy bar into my mailbox every Sunday. This morning, it was a whole bag of York Peppermint Patties. I don't know who it is that's doing it, but it means so much to be thought of that I don't even know what to say.

I suppose it's a simple thing, but it doesn't feel simple. It feels like somebody loves me, and that's never small.

Even in the face of evil, a simple act of authentic kindness is enough to defy the power of sin and death. Listen to this: we were in Boston this week. Flights on Southwest were just $50, so we decided to make the trip since the girls were out of school, and we like to show them parts of the world that expand their horizons. Boston is a city in a way that Marietta's not. It's big. It's so big that, while Dr. Ken Farrah taught us to pray every time we hear the sirens of an ambulance back when he was our Sunday School teacher, in Boston you hear sirens so often you're pretty much praying all the time, wondering what good a little prayer's going to do.

We walked the Freedom Trail, which was wonderful, and right next to the Freedom Trail is a noteworthy Holocaust Memorial. There's one simple glass tower dedicated to each of the concentration camps, numbers on the outsides etched in the glass of all the people murdered at each one. The numbers reach to the sky, but on the inside of the tower, where you walk through, there are quotes from survivors. This one was especially profound:

"Ilse, a childhood friend of mine, once found a raspberry in the camp and carried it in her pocket all day to present to me that night on a leaf." [6]

Imagine a world in which your entire possession is one raspberry and you give it to your friend.

The world might make us feel small, as though our actions have no meaning or as though there's nothing really to be done. "Who am I to make a difference?" we've learned to ask. Surely that's how it was with Esther.

Who was she, but the Jewish girl who had somehow lucked out and made it into the palace? No one there knew she was a Jew, and they didn't need to know. If she hid her true identity, she'd be spared from all the hardship her people faced living as an oppressed minority under the Persian Empire.

This is how it is sometimes. Some people can pass, and they learn to get by. That was Esther. She was beautiful, and so she was given a pass. The only price you have to pay when you get such a pass is always living with the fear of getting caught and accepting the reality that you can never really be

---

[6] Gervasi Weisseman Klein, Holocaust Memorial, Boston Mass.

yourself.

Such a life teaches you to keep silent and to pretend that you're not who you are and to look pretty doing it. Many women who are living in a man's world know what this is like. Esther's life was given value by the Emperor, but not because of her mind or her talent. She was valued because of the way she looked, so she knew to wake up every morning, put on her makeup, laugh at the Emperor's jokes, and keep her authentic self covered up.

None of this feels very good, but people do it all the time. However, the only father she had ever known needed her. Her people needed her, so she spoke out against the evil Haman to prevent a genocide. She took a risk and voiced her convictions. She risked her life and was honest about her identity, and look what happened. She saved her people.

Of course, it must have been hard if not nearly impossible.

It's nearly impossible to no longer hide but to really show up with your truth. It's not easy, but doing so changes things, so while there will always be powerful men who benefit from the silence of women, the message from Scripture is clear: show up and "speak with boldness." Speak from the truth of your heart because within us all is the power to topple tyrants and change the world.

We may not have the power to raise the dead, but within us is the power to testify to the God who can.

Within us is the power to comfort a friend in grief, just by reaching out and squeezing his hand.

We can bring the promise of Christmas to a home in the valley of the shadow of death.

Within us is the power to bring peace along a difficult journey.

The world may always be the kind of place where it feels prudent to keep silent, but Scripture is clear: speak up! Scripture calls us to speak up, not with empty platitudes, but with the truth of your heart. While it's so easy just to keep quiet and to hope that trouble will pass like a storm cloud in the sky, better yet is to remember this: "My brothers and sisters, if anyone among you wanders from the truth and is brought back by another, you should know that whoever brings back a sinner from wandering will save the sinner's soul from death and will cover a multitude of sins."

With that, James ends his letter, and, with that, he challenges us to begin living our lives with faith, hope, and love.

Amen.

Part 3: Hope

The following sermons are based on the book of Job. Like James and Proverbs, Job is considered wisdom literature, but it also transcends the genre by illustrating a faithfulness that defies hopelessness. During this series of sermons, the lessons of Job were illustrated by the perseverance of the church that I serve. Having split just three years before, in October of 2018, the readers of the local paper voted First Presbyterian Church the Best Place to Worship in Cobb County.

From the Ash Heap
Hebrews 1: 1-4, 2: 5-12; and Job 1: 1, 2: 1-10
Preached on October 7, 2018

The whole month of September, Sunday after Sunday, I preached from the book of James. I felt like after all the time we spent with James challenging us to be better Christians, we needed something a little uplifting. I felt like maybe we needed some encouragement, but now, here we are in Job. Job is another challenging book; however, I'm thankful to be reading it. I'm thankful to be reading it because if we find ourselves in the ash heap with Job this morning, we find ourselves in a place that we've all been before, a place that we all need Job's help to understand.

You know about the ash heap.

The ash heap is a place where everything has unraveled, and we're tempted to give up, to quit.

If we find ourselves there, then things haven't gone how they were supposed to go. What's worse is that, not only are we broken down and discouraged, but if not our spouse, then someone else is always there nearby the ash heap urging us "to curse God and die," as Job's wife did.

You know what I'm talking about because everyone does.

Consider our friend Dansby Swanson.

Since the Braves are in the postseason, last Wednesday, at all the Marietta City Elementary Schools, students were encouraged to wear their Atlanta Braves hats and t-shirts. Our daughter Lily wore her Dansby Swanson jersey. All the kids in the school who, like her, chose to wear number 7, were called out to the front steps of West Side for a picture. Lily said there must have been fifty of them in all, all wearing their Dansby Swanson shirts. Dansby's mother, who works at West Side Elementary School, came out. When she saw them all, she cried because her son, who's worked so hard to make it to National League Playoffs, has injured his left hand and doesn't get to play.

He might be sitting in the dugout later today for the game, but it's really the ash heap. He doesn't want to be in the dugout. He wants to be out in the field. It's surely a big disappointment that he's going through.

I dare say, however, that he's going to be alright because people like Dansby Swanson who find themselves in the ash heap, despite the temptation to allow the injustice to consume them, persevere.

73

That's why, as they interview candidates to be our next associate pastor, I asked the search committee to ask every candidate, as the chair, Hal McClain, once asked me, to tell the committee about the worst year of his or her life.

You can tell everything you need to know about a person by hearing how they respond when they find themselves in the ash heap.

When you're in the ash heap, what will you do?

I can also say that Dansby Swanson is going to be OK because he's made it out of the ash heap before. After his first season, he was a candidate to win the Rookie of the Year Award. Then, the Braves moved their stadium here to Marietta, his hometown, and made him the poster boy of their whole advertising campaign. After all that attention, Swanson ended the season statistically as the worst defensive shortstop in baseball.

Can you imagine what that was like?

Sure, you can because you've been there, too.

Everything was supposed to go one way, only then, the winds shifted, the tide went out, and all at once, your boat ran aground, and the clear skies became foreboding.

To many, such a change is interpreted as a tremendous injustice or an unfairness that they never get over because they weren't prepared for life to deliver lemons, and they don't know how to make lemonade.

I'm reading a book about a mother who, in an attempt to encourage her son to pray, finds out that among his first prayers to God, he voiced his greatest prayer request: to receive a bag full of apple-flavored lollipops coated in caramel, so she snuck the lollipops under his pillow that night. On the one hand, that seems like a good idea. We want our kids to pray, so why not encourage them by finagling a way for a prayer here and there to be answered?

The problem is that sometimes we pray for lollipops, and we end up in the ash heap because God isn't like Santa Claus. We can't "receive the good at the hand of God, and not receive the bad."

The bad has a lesson for us to learn as well.

A life that's all roses only prepares us to live in the rose garden and not the real world. It's important that we all know what to do when it rains on our parade because at some point, we might be driving a trailer full of cows down I-75 South that topples over just before rush hour.

74

What we do in such a situation matters because the measure of a man is not determined when he's relaxing on the beach. A woman's life won't be defined by what she does at a picnic in the park on a Sunday afternoon, but when her world falls apart. What will she do then?

That's when we come to know what faith is really all about. We don't know what prayer is until we've stood at the door knocking week after week to no answer.

Then, Lot's wife comes to our side saying, "Do you still persist in your integrity? Curse God, and die." That's when we learn something.

Job hits rock bottom, and he still won't sin with his lips. That's what the book is all about: Job facing the true unfairness of human life with faith, but plenty have faced such hardship, only to learn that they'll do anything to get by.

That's what George Will wrote about this week.

I've been reading George Will for a long time.

My grandfather used to cut out his columns and send them to me. It started when I was eleven or twelve years old. A thick manila envelope would come in the mail, addressed to me from my grandfather. I'd open it up so excited, thinking he was sending me baseball cards or something else that I'd actually want, but instead, it'd be packed full of George Will articles.

Last Thursday, he reminded us readers about Robert Penn Warren's book "All the King's Men." In this legendary book, the main character, Stark, says: "Man is conceived in sin and born in corruption and he passeth from the stink of the [diaper] to the stench of the shroud." Then, when an aide tells Stark that a particular act of securing dirt on a fellow politician is beneath the dignity of a governor, Stark replies that "there ain't anything worth doing a man can do and keep his dignity."

George Will followed with this: "We should hope, against much current evidence, that this is not true."

We look, then, to Job because there is more than one way to deal with desperate times, though this narrow path may not be modeled for us readily.

We look, then, to Job, asking: "Shall we receive the good at the hand of God, and not receive the bad?" or give up, abandoning our morals?

You don't need to answer that question. By your actions over the past three years, you already have.

I'm a witness to your Job-like faithfulness in times of unjust tragedy.

Today is the first Sunday of October. Three years ago this week, Dr. Dave Mayo preached his last sermon from this pulpit as the Senior Pastor of this church. Three years ago this very week, he left his position here to lead about 300 members of our church in a schism, dividing our congregation in two.

Three years ago this very week, the choice you faced was like every other group of people who ever found themselves in the ash heap: would we curse God and die, giving up and closing our doors?

That was a real possibility. Instead, you accepted the truth that the road to the Promised Land is not a simple walk through the desert, but a journey that might lead you to an oasis one day and an ash heap the next.

The only way you won't make it there is if you quit walking.

You lived it out, that if we receive good from God, we must also dare to believe that God also works through the bad. As I look around this church now, as I see your faces today, I give thanks to God for everything that He has done, for today, while so much has fallen away, what remains is life.

What's still here is joy. What we have is hope, so we move into the future not with malice, but with forgiveness.

For today, despite the past, we have an eye to the future and faith in our hearts, believing that while God may sometimes give us more than we think we can handle, the Lord is with us in the ash heap just as the Lord is with us on the mountain top.

With such faithful vision as that, we see as Christ saw. For had Christ been without faith, His last words would have been: "My God, my God, why have you forsaken me?"

Yet, those aren't His last words.

Do you remember what He said to the one hanging on the cross right next to Him?

"Today, you will be with me in paradise."

Christ, the innocent One who suffered, as Hebrews tells us, is the "pioneer" of "salvation" made "perfect through sufferings." Even in our suffering, let us follow Him to Paradise.

Amen.

To Vanish in Darkness
Hebrews 4: 12-16 and Job 23: 1-9 and 16-17
Preached on October 14, 2018

I once spent a summer in a maximum-security women's prison. I wasn't incarcerated there. I was learning about being a chaplain by shadowing the one who served that prison, though I probably learned more that summer from the women who were incarcerated there than the chaplain I was shadowing. There was one woman in particular. From her, I learned a most profound lesson about resilience when I went to hear her sing on the second floor of the building where those inmates who, like her, suffered from mental illness lived.

I was sent up there because all the women there liked to sing hymns, and somehow or another I was invited to hear them. They gathered in one room. They were all in their brown prison jumpsuits. One of the women must have been seven feet tall. I heard later that she was locked up because she had attacked a man with a rake. She sat down next to me. I introduced myself. We exchanged pleasantries, and then it was time to sing.

One by one, they got up to sing. I don't remember who was first, but there was this one in particular that I remember. She wore thick glasses. She was probably twenty, and she stood before us all and sang a song that defied the hopelessness and sadness of that whole prison. She sang, "His eye is on the sparrow, and I know he watches me." It's a simple song, but it was a picture of defiance. The hope that she embodied when she sang those words challenged everything about those gray prison walls.

I tell you this story because that woman showed me something that I'm still learning about. I'm still learning about what it means to be faithful regardless of where life takes me, and I want to learn how to be as faithful as that young woman. For me, life is full of ups and downs, and sometimes the way I feel about my place in the world goes up and down right along with it.

Take this last Monday for example. Last Monday started off great. I'm back in school working for my doctorate, and when I got to class on Monday, our professor returned our first two papers, and I got an A on them both.

The other thing that happened last Monday was I sat down on our daughter Cece's bed to read her a bedtime story. Immediately, I heard a loud crack as her footboard broke, and I ended up on the floor.

Cece laughed at me. Sara and Lily came down the stairs to laugh at me, too, and so a day of academic accomplishments ended in humiliation, but that's how life is.

Because that's life, we can't put too much emphasis on accomplishments because accomplishments can be followed with failures.

We can't put too much emphasis on wealth or property because what we have might be here one day and gone the next.

That's what happened with Job.

The book of Job tells the story of a man who loses everything. This telling illustrates an important truth of life: that we can't put too much emphasis on fame or fortune, youth or beauty, wealth or property because we might be getting straight A's one minute, only to break the bed the next. Still, we can't let a broken bed break us.

The alternative is embodied by this woman who sang in the prison.

Every day, she woke up and saw the sunshine through bars on her window. She put on the brown jumpsuit of an incarcerated criminal. If you need help feeling like a loser, those two things alone will do it nearly every time. Put on top of that the stigma attached to mental illness, and most people are scraping themselves up off the floor, but not her. No. Despite everything that had gone wrong and every accomplishment that came to nothing, she knew something that sometimes I forget:

"His eye is on the sparrow, and I know he watches me."

That's a powerful declaration of faith in a place like a prison.

And it's a declaration like that that will get you through a prison sentence or any of the other ups and downs of life because, while Christ watches over us always, we can't always count on anybody else.

Another thing about prisons is how easy it is for some people on the outside to forget about the people inside.

It's the same with hospitals and nursing homes. These are places where too many people are suffering all alone. They are without people by their sides or really understanding. It's just the opposite of when you have a new baby.

For some major events, we are surrounded, and for others, we're not.

It's a strange thing that when you have a new baby in the house, everybody wants to come visit. Even when parents are weird about who touches the baby, still everyone wants to come over. It's not always that way when people are suffering.

You know, when Lily was a baby, we bought these shoe cover things. We had these blue disposable things that we asked everyone to slip on over their shoes so they wouldn't track into the house any contaminates from the outside world. Getting into our house when we had a new baby was like getting into Fort Knox. We expected everyone to suit up as though they were entering a sterile laboratory. We made everyone sanitize their hands and put those things over their shoes. We'd put you out if you sneezed. Visitors who had a runny nose could just leave their gifts and casseroles at the door. We made it difficult, but people wanted to come see the baby anyway. It's not always like that when someone's suffering.

It's hard to go visit people in the prison, hospital, or funeral parlor, but some people do it. Job's friends went to visit him, too, in the midst of his suffering. Scripture tells us that:

> When they saw him from a distance, they did not recognize him, and they raised their voices and wept aloud; they tore their robes and threw dust in the air above their heads. [Then] they sat with him on the ground seven days and seven nights, and no one spoke a word to him, for they saw that his suffering was very great.

I remember a professor in seminary telling us that this is one of the great examples of real friendship. They go and just sit with their friend in his time of need. That's what we all long for when we're suffering ourselves. "But then," my professor said, "then, they opened their mouths."

Job dares to speak to his friends from the depth of his despair, but you know what his friends did? By their replies, they made him feel even more alone.

Job curses the day he was born, and Eliphaz tells him he suffers because he has sinned.

Job says, "My suffering is without end," and Bildad tells him he should repent.

Job declares, "I loathe my life," and Zophar tells him he deserves his punishment.

It goes along like this from chapter 3 all the way to chapter 31. For 28 chapters, Job's suffering is compounded because in his suffering, he finds that he's all alone. That's why he says what he did in our second Scripture lesson for today: "If only I could vanish in darkness, and thick darkness would cover my face." He says that because there is a place lower than the ash heap. Below the ash heap is that place where you suffer in silence. In looking for understanding from your friends, they instead try to explain your suffering away. That's not just a place of sadness; that's a place of disappearing into nothingness.

Plus, he's looking for God in the midst of all of this, and his friends tell him to straighten up. They tell him, "Get it together!"

Do you know what it is that's just happened to him? He became the one everyone was praying for, but no one wanted to be seen with. Then, in chapter 32, they leave him all alone.

Do you know what that's like?

Sure, you do.

In class this week, I heard from a friend who's an associate pastor for this great, big youth group. He watched as thirty middle school girls walked out of their cabin one Saturday morning at their youth retreat. Twenty-nine of them had on the same black yoga pants and a long-sleeved t-shirt. One poor girl didn't get the memo.

You know what that's like?

We parents say that it's what's on the inside that counts, and we mean it, but how we contradict ourselves when we pay $400 on homecoming dresses that emphasize more than our daughters' personalities. Why do we do that? We do that because no one wants his kid to be left out of the group. No one wants his kid to be the one that everyone turns her back on because she doesn't have the right clothes or the right hair or the right car.

We live in this world where we are always working to fit in.

We are always working to be accepted, but acceptance is just like so much else in this life: it can be here one day and gone the next.

Consider Job. He's not in the ash heap this morning. No. He's actually some place worse. He said,

"God has made my heart faint; the Almighty has terrified me; If only I could vanish in darkness, and thick darkness cover my face!"

He finds himself there because, in addition to losing all that he had, he also lost his friends.

Now here's a place where many people go, but not all of them return.

This is the place where we're stripped of everything: everything that made us feel secure. Everything and everyone who gave us identity and worth are gone. There, all alone, we begin to vanish into the thick darkness.

That's what happens when the bed breaks and we break with it.

We step on the scale, and that number determines how we'll feel about ourselves for the rest of that day.

We try to understand our place in this world, and we use numbers: how many people liked my photo. How many friends do I have? What's my score?

It gets worse.

I remember once when my grandparents wanted to take Sara and me out to dinner. We met at their house, and right before we left, my grandfather said, "Let me run upstairs and check my stocks so I can see how nice of a restaurant I can take us out to." As he said, that my grandmother was rolling her eyes because she knew that some things go up and then they come down, and should we be so foolish as to place too much importance on such numbers, our worth will always be held captive by forces outside our control.

Still, that's what we do.

Economic depressions inspire emotional depressions.

Hard days make for hard looks in the mirror where we question ourselves.

Suicide rates rise because this thick darkness covers too many faces, and not enough of us know how to sing: "His eye is on the sparrow, and I know he watches me."

It's not just that He watches, though; it's that He's right beside us.

From Hebrews, we read, "For we do not have a high priest who is unable to sympathize with our weakness, but we have one who in every respect has been tested as we are." We "approach" His throne of grace with boldness because He's walked a mile in our shoes and understands what others fail to comprehend.

His presence must be the solid rock that we build on our lives upon because He gives us freely what this world tells us we must work hard to gain.

The world tells you that to be somebody, you have to make a great name for yourself, but He's already made you somebody.

The world tells us that to be accepted, we have to dress right and do what's expected of us whether we want to or not, but He's already accepted us.

That's what this woman in the prison knew so well; she knew that even when she lost her freedom and was confined to a cell, even after she was stripped of her clothes and given a brown jump suit, even after her friends and family turned their backs and left her alone, she knew something that too few of us remember: that His eye is on the sparrow, and I know He watches me.

That's what baptism means; you see. All that we work for, He gives so freely. Remember that and be at peace.

Amen.

Dealing Gently with the Ignorant
and Wayward
Hebrews 5: 1-10 and Job 38: 1-11 and 38: 34 – 39: 4

Preached on October 21, 2018

I titled this sermon, "Dealing Gently with the Ignorant and Wayward." That's a line from the first Scripture lesson from Hebrews, where the author claims that Christ, our Great High Priest, deals gently with the ignorant and wayward, which is good news to me because I am often both of those things.

This is the third sermon on the book of Job. For the third Sunday in a row, we turn to this book that's hard to understand: a book that I've been wrestling with and trying to preach a good word from. I could have called an expert on Job for help, but I didn't.

That may be the very definition of ignorance: having the opportunity to gain knowledge but choosing, instead, to dwell in ignorance.

I could have asked our resident Job expert for help, but I didn't.

Dr. Brennan Breed is our new Theologian in Residence. He's an Old Testament Professor at the Columbia Theological Seminary, and he's teaching a great Sunday school class in the Sanctuary. You knew that already, but what you maybe didn't know is that so much of his work as a scholar is dealing with how we should understand Job. He is, by all definitions, a "Job scholar," but I was slow to ask him for help. Why? I realized that I wanted to write these sermons all by myself.

Sure, I read some books, but I could have called one of the guys who wrote the books.

I realized that last Sunday. Here I've been wrestling with Job, trying to understand it, and I could have just asked for help, but I was slow to do so because I am often ignorant and wayward.

I've been this way for most of my life.

My mother's in town. She can tell you about other times I've chosen ignorance.

Since she's in town this weekend, I'd like to tell you two stories about my mother that might embarrass her. The first takes place at a fancy restaurant, maybe the first fancy restaurant I'd ever been to. I was six or seven and my order came with a piece of parsley on it as a garnish.

I'd never seen something so fancy before. I asked my mom what it was for, and she said it was just to make my plate look pretty. I asked her if it was edible, and she said, "Try it and find out."

Not all of her parenting techniques are what you'd call typical.

Then once, when I threw a temper tantrum, frustrated with something that she'd asked me to do, something really unfair like asking me to clean my room, she said something equally surprising.

I was probably seven, and I told her I'd be running away. She said, "Well, let me help you pack."

That was not what I was expecting her to say, but then, it got stranger.

"What are you going to eat out in the world all by yourself?" she asked.

I didn't have a plan for eating, so we made some crackers and peanut butter. She wrapped them in a handkerchief and tied the bundle to the end of a stick, just like the hobos used to do. Then, I barged out of there to start a life on my own, living by my own rules without my mother interfering all the time.

I walked up the sidewalk about a hundred yards, but all that walking made me hungry. I sat down and took out my crackers. Once I finished eating them, because I had depleted my store of food, I swallowed my pride and went back home, realizing I didn't want to do things all by myself. My mother welcomed me back in because she also deals gently with the ignorant and wayward.

On a grander scale, I believe God does the same for Job in our second Scripture lesson.

It seems to me as though God is saying to our friend Job: "You don't like this world I've created? Well, let me help you pack."

God shows up and says to Job (Job, this man who's had all these complaints): "Gird up your loins like a man, I will question you… where were you when I laid the foundation of the earth? Surely you know!"

God says, "What would you eat if I didn't make it rain?"

"Can you lift up your voice to the clouds, so that a flood of waters may cover you?"

"You don't even know where the mountain goats give birth, but you're ready to take issue with how I'm running this place?"

It's an incredible and beautiful speech, and surely it shook Job to his core, which is OK because sometimes we all get too big for our britches.

We say, "I don't want to ask for help; I'd rather do it myself."

Mom asks us to clean up our room, and we want to hit the road, but once we're out on our own, we realize how big the great, wide world really is, so it can be comforting to be put back in our place.

That can be embarrassing but comforting. I think that's what happened to Job.

I remember something similar happening in an assembly at Hickory Hills Elementary School when I was a student there. The speaker was an inventor, and she wanted to know if any of us kids had ever invented anything. She called up all the little inventors, and one by one they went down the line, reporting on their inventions. One kid had invented a basket that went on the back of his bicycle and held his lunchbox; another made pants with Velcro around the knee, so he could take the bottom part of his pants legs off, and they could quickly turn into shorts (I hope that kid made some money by now because now you can buy those things). What I remember best, though, was this little kindergartner who got up there and told us all that one time she and her grandma got a pitcher of water and a packet of mix, and they invented some Kool-Aid.

We all laughed at that, of course, but how arrogant all of us can be.

While we didn't create this world, so often we walk around like we own the place.

God invited Adam to name the animals, so what do we do? We shoot them and mount them on our walls like we're the Kings of the jungle.

The Lord spoke and created continents, but just because we draw borders upon them, that doesn't mean that they're ours.

Stewardship Season is here again.

Now, I know you don't like Stewardship Season all that much. Believe it or not, I don't like asking you for money very much, either, but with Stewardship Season comes this very important reminder that's so much like God's reminder to Job. Stewardship Season is the time where we look at our pledge cards and decide how much of our money we'll so generously give to the church, but God is asking, "You think any of that money's yours?"

C.S. Lewis says it's like our father gave us ten dollars and sent us to the store to buy him a Father's Day present, only we spend nine dollars on ourselves and one on the gift. We might as well be claiming we invented Kool-Aid.

God asks us: "Where were you when I laid the foundation of the earth?

"Or who shut in the sea with doors when it burst out through the womb?"

"And I know that you have that nice office and a fancy paycheck, but just who do you think you are and where would you be had I not given you the means to make that money in the first place?"

In our second Scripture lesson for this morning, the Lord answers Job. It's the kind of answer that turns our lives upside down but right-side up because all of a sudden, we realize that we've eaten all our crackers on the sidewalk a hundred yards from our house.

We can see how ignorant and wayward we really are.

We are always trying to control.

We are always fearing the truth.

Have you seen the things that people do today to hold onto power?

It's time to go back home, isn't it? To submit to the higher authority.

It's time to let Him hold the whole world in His hands because we can't hold it ourselves.

It's a good thing "He is able to deal gently with the ignorant and wayward." because that can be us, but don't be afraid because when God puts us back in our place, we are free from all the anxiety that comes from trying to play God ourselves.

There's this great quote from G.K. Chesterton: "How much happier you would be, how much more of you there would be, if the hammer of a higher God could smash your small cosmos".

That's what God did to Job, and I'm thankful, for when God does the same for me, I see that the world He has created is so much greater than the little fiefdom I've tried to control.

It's a gift to realize how little we know, for in confessing our ignorance, the world of knowledge opens up. Once we stop trying to control what the truth is, the truth will set us free.

It's also a gift to return to God, for when we remember that there is a God in heaven, we realize we don't have to be Him.

A grandfather told me about it last week.

I was asking Andy Tatnall what it's like to see his daughters hold his grandchildren. He said, "I wish I could have seen that moment when they were younger. Had I had this picture of them being such wonderful parents in my mind while they were young, I would have been a more relaxed father because, when they were young, and I was their father, I spent so much time worrying about how they would turn out. Now that I've seen them be these incredible parents, I realize I worried over them when I could have been enjoying them."

May the Lord deal gently with us, the ignorant and wayward, and ease us all back from our desire to control what we cannot, that we might enjoy this world He has created.

Amen.

An Inheritance
Job 1: 1-5 and Job 42: 1-6 and 10-17
Preached on October 28, 2018

John Michael just read the verses that make up the very beginning of the book of Job, and I just read the very end. I wanted to read the beginning and the end together as our first and second Scripture readings because a couple weeks ago, I heard an Old Testament Professor, Dr. Bill Brown, explain that the book of Job ends almost exactly where it began. After all the suffering in the middle, in the end, his fortunes are restored. The Lord gave Job twice as much as he had before, but the way Job acts in the end is pretty different from how he acted in the beginning.

Did you notice that?

I never had before, but Dr. Brown points out this significant difference: in the end of the book, we read that "Job gave his daughters an inheritance along with their brothers." This kind and countercultural gesture stands in contrast to the first chapter of Job. There, Job is described as a man so "blameless and upright," so consumed with "fearing God and turning away from evil" that when his seven sons would "hold feasts in one another's houses" inviting their three sisters "to eat and drink with them," he was obsessive about atoning for any mistakes they might have made. After the feasts, Scripture tells us: "Job would send and sanctify them, and he would rise early in the morning and offer burnt offerings according to the number of them all; for Job said, 'It may be that my children have sinned, and cursed God in their hearts.' That was what Job always did."

That's a nice idea, but there's a problem with that.

There's a problem with sacrificing one animal for each of your kids because there are some things that you just can't do for them.

You can't be a Christian for your kids, for example.

There're all kinds of things parents are tempted to do for their children, but the line between helping and enabling is thin but crucial. Imagine that your sixth-grade son leaves for school but left his homework on the kitchen table. You know that he needs to turn it in that day, that he's worked hard on it and will be penalized when he can't turn it in. Surely, you're tempted to bring it to him at the school, but you don't want to get in the habit of doing things like that. If he's thirty-five, living in the basement, and you're still bringing

88

him his brief case at the office when he forgets it on the kitchen table, that's embarrassing for everybody involved.

Last Wednesday night, our District Attorney, Vic Reynolds, was here at the church. He was in a panel moderated by the always-Honorable but recently retired Chief Justice Harris Hines. On this panel that was discussing the opium epidemic facing our community, D.A. Reynolds said, "There's nothing that will give a human more dignity than a job."

Everyone on the panel was talking about drugs and why people use them. Mr. Reynolds said that if people don't have anything to do with their lives, if there's nothing there to fill their days, and if they're not just lonely but also disempowered, a good way to build them up is to get them a decent job so they'll see what they're capable of. On the other hand, Job got in the bad habit of doing too much for his children.

That's not good, but it happens.

There's a quote on our plaque honoring all the boys who earned the rank of Eagle Scout through our Troop 252. My brother's name is on there. If you look at all the names there, you will recognize a bunch of them. Along with the names, there is a quote at the top from Teddy Roosevelt: "Far and away the best prize that life offers are the chance to work hard at work worth doing." I know some of those Eagle Scouts rendered that quote ironic because the work done to earn the rank was done by their daddies.

We parents can't do too much for our kids. Especially, we can't be Christians for them.

An old preacher used to say, "God has children, but no grandchildren." Just because his mama was a prayer warrior and his daddy was an elder, and they both sat on the front row every Sunday, that doesn't mean that their son's relationship with God is taken care of because God has children, but no grandchildren. All of us must be washed in the blood of the Lamb for ourselves. The hymn goes: We all must walk that lonesome valley, and nobody else can walk it for us. You've got to walk it by yourself.

However, parents try to walk it for their children.

I try to for our kids. Yet, even if their daddy's a preacher, they're the ones who are responsible for their relationships with God. We can help, and God is always reaching out to them, but nobody else can do it for them.

On the other hand, Job offered those sacrifices just in case his kids might have sinned.

You know, we can encourage our children, but we can't do everything for them, or they'll get all messed up.

A son who got a small loan from his father when he was a young man that he turned into a fortune is one thing. The father who made his son a millionaire by the time he turned three is something entirely different.

There are some things that people have to do on their own, and if too much is given to them, they'll take all the credit without doing any of the work.

"Some people are born on third base and think it's because they hit a triple," is what a preacher I know likes to say. That's true.

I do it all the time.

I walked into a Bible study last Tuesday. I was supposed to start the class right at 12, and there I was. I walked into that room right at 12 to start the class. As I did, all the ladies in there clapped. I thought they were clapping for me, and when I got home, I told Sara, "You can't believe how much those ladies love the way I teach Revelation. They clapped when I entered the room." Turns out they only clapped because I finally showed up on time.

You see, people take credit for too much. And when we do everything for our kids, they don't grow up grateful. Rather, they grow up entitled, so the way Job ends is different from how it begins. In the end, Job doesn't offer sacrifices for them; he gives all of them, even his daughters, something to inherit.

The trick that the book of Job teaches is that great parenting is giving them enough help so that they can do it themselves. It teaches that a wise parent gives enough money so his children can go out and make something of themselves, enough opportunities for education so that they can get educated, and enough guidance that they can meet God on their own because we can't do it for them.

Do you know what often happens? We drag them here all their lives. Then, they finally get confirmed in seventh grade, and we treat it like they're graduating from church.

A youth minister told me that one time. He also said that we ought to be careful about honoring high school graduates in a worship service because some of them will think that now they're done with religion just like they're done with high school. That's what will happen unless we can find a way to make this house of worship their house, too.

We've asked John Michael to read Scripture this morning. That's an important job, and we didn't ask him because he looks sharp up here behind

90

the pulpit. No. We asked him because he has something to teach us and because he has something to give this church, too.

Everyone deserves the chance to give.

I gave blood in between services today.

Sara asked me if I thought that was such a good idea. I said, "No, it's not." If I pass out, John Michael's taking over for me. I was thinking about not giving blood, but it's easy not to give blood if there are plenty of people who will do it if I don't. This time was different. If we didn't make thirty-two pints, the Red Cross was going to quit having blood drives at our church, so I rolled up my sleeves and did it.

I'm glad I did because I'm O negative, and they give babies my blood. It makes me proud to give, but I have a million excuses why I can't. Then, when I know I'm needed, it feels so good to make my contribution.

That's what Job gave to his children in the end. He gave them the joy of doing work worth doing.

That's what Stewardship is all about. I know there are a million reasons not to give to the church this year, but don't let the reason that you don't give be that plenty of people around here will do it if you don't because this church is yours, too.

I say that to you if you're ninety-eight or if you're only eight months old: you have something to give this church. You have something to contribute, and you can't let anyone else do it for you.

When I was seventeen, the youth group of this church elected me to be their President.

Now, before that time, I hadn't really been that big a part of things. My parents taught Sunday school, and because my grandmother pinched my mother during the sermons when she was a child, we didn't make it to worship when I was a kid a whole lot. She didn't want to have to pinch us.

Somebody said that the best thing about being a preacher is you don't have to sit next to your kids in church. Staying out of here during worship when I was a kid was nice, but you know what was better? When the youth group elected me to be their President.

That was a big deal. I don't even really know what my official role of youth group President was, but I can tell you what I thought it was. I thought I needed to be at everything, so when I was senior in high school and my parents were all set to take us all to London for my cousin's wedding, but it was the same week that the youth group was going to Montreat for the Youth

91

Conference, I said, "Sorry, Mom and Dad, but I can't go. I have presidential responsibilities."

I might not have said it exactly like that, but what I'm trying to say is that instead of this church doing everything for me, all at once, I was put to work. That work I did and the simple honor of being asked to contribute made all the difference in the world to me.

We wonder why young people have this problem with commitment, yet, why shouldn't they if, in the end, we'll just do it for them?

That's what changed with Job.

Bill Paden has an even better story than mine. He had tickets to Super Bowl I. He was already in Los Angeles on business, but do you know what he did? He flew back here and missed the game because on that Sunday he was to be ordained as a Deacon of First Presbyterian Church.

Two of his grandsons have just been asked to be deacons for the first time as well, and Bill's passing something on to them. This whole church is passing something on to them. It's an inheritance like the one that Job gave his children in the end of the book. It's not the kind that's so big they'll never have to work again. This inheritance puts them to work; this inheritance enables them to contribute to make this church their own.

That's the big difference between what Job does at the beginning of the book compared to what he does at the end. After all he suffered, at the end of the book, he's given up making sacrifices on behalf of all his children and decided, instead, to give his daughters an inheritance along with his sons.

Now that's a revolutionary thing to do but think about what it would have meant to them. Instead of trying to protect them from the world, now Job's given them a chance to make their own way in it.

Instead of doing everything for them, now Job's given even his daughters the means to do for themselves.

Instead of making sacrifices on their behalf, now they can make their own sacrifices, live their own lives, and worship their God.

It's a major difference. You can't help but think that this difference is the result of all that's happened to him, for when we are faced with the chaos of the world, the devastation, the hardship and injustice, the choice we often face is whether we'll hide the world as it is from our children or give them the tools to deal with it.

This week, as a church, we face just how hard the reality of our world is.

David Blake, a child of our church, was finally found near Little Kennesaw Mountain. We all must wonder how to talk with our kids about it because the reality of depression can't be hidden, or it will take even more.

Job tried to do it all for his kids. He tried to protect them, but far better is to pass on an inheritance so that all our children and our grandchildren might make this faith their own and say of their own volition despite all the storms of life, still: "I know that my redeemer lives."

Amen.

Part 4: Anticipation

Paul wrote in Romans that the whole Creation groans, as in the pangs of childbirth, waiting for what is to come. A mother's love for her children, and the anticipation that a pregnant mother feels, are both apt metaphors for God's love for us. This next group of sermons begins with mother Hannah's love for her son Samuel and ends with a sermon based on mother Mary's love for her son Jesus.

Hannah's Song
1 Samuel 1: 4-20 and 1 Samuel 2: 1-10
Preached on November 18, 2018

Both of these passages that I've just read are about Samuel. Samuel is the prophet who made David and others kings over Israel, and Samuel is one of my favorite people in the Bible. The Bible tells us a lot about him. We just read about the circumstances surrounding his birth, so now we know so much of his backstory that we even know what his mother was thinking before he was born.

If Samuel knew what we do now, that kind of insight would surely have given him an advantage over many children because knowing that you're loved and wanted by your parents can shape your self-understanding for your entire lifetime. The child of a mother disappointed about her pregnancy and who was told that she ruined her mother's life of independence turns out differently from the other who always knew that she was the apple of her daddy's eye. Knowing what your parents felt about you changes how you see yourself and knowing that you were loved changes everything.

Sara and I are hoping we've communicated something of our love to our daughters. We hope that we've passed on to them something like what Hannah shares with us in Scripture.

When she was pregnant, Sara and I got conned into a photography session at her cousin's house.

We love this cousin of hers and her husband, and we still do even after what they did to us.

What happened is they got free family photos if they could convince enough of their friends to come over to their house to pay to have their pictures taken. We were among the suckers, so we went over there. I already hated this kind of thing. We got dressed up. I had to force a smile for the photographer, which is hard for me to do because I know how weird I look when forced to smile for a picture. Worse is that then, the photographer wanted us to stage all these poses. The worst was that the photographer asked me to touch my wife's pregnant belly with my nose.

That's right.

I couldn't believe the photographer asked me to do it, and Sara couldn't believe that I actually would, but I did and doing so made Sara laugh so hard that joy erupted on her face. Right then, the photographer took our picture.

Today, that picture hangs right over our bed.

It's there for our girls to see.

We want them to see it. When we had it framed, Sara said, "Now they'll know how happy we were thinking about their births. Every time they see this picture, they'll see that we couldn't wait to meet them. Now they'll know that before they were even born, we loved them."

Consider Samuel. If Samuel also knew what we just read, these Scripture lessons would have done the same thing for him.

If he could remember what his mother, Hannah, was thinking before he was born, then when he was tempted to believe the voice of self-doubt inside his head, all he had to do was think back on this account of his mother, who cherished him as a gift from God.

If he couldn't sleep for all his frustration with this crazy world of ours, maybe all he had to do was hum to himself the song that she sang him, which made up our second Scripture lesson. Reminded of those words, surely his reality was reframed by his mother's love.

If he started to believe what the bullies said, if he ever wondered whether the dark cloud would ever lift or the sadness would ever end, then these stories from before he was born were surely like a warm blanket on a cold dark night, holding him tight until the sun rose again.

I hope Samuel knew all that backstory that our two Scripture lessons offer because Samuel was up against so much. He was a virtual orphan living in the Temple. The priest's sons mistreated him, and he only got to see his family once a year.

If you read the Harry Potter books, you have an idea of what it must have been like to be Samuel. If you didn't read those books, it's OK. They're just about an orphan who has no real idea how loved he is. All the time, he was beaten down because he was born in a house where his aunt and uncle mistreated him. He was basically their live-in maid, but then, one day, he discovered that he was loved by his mother. Knowing that changed everything for him because love always changes everything.

However, the world would have us forget it or would rather us not ever hear about it.

That's why it's easy for me to imagine Hannah's fear as she left her son at the Temple.

You leave a boy at the Temple, and how is he supposed to feel but hurt and abandoned?

It's worse than forgetting your child at the funeral home.

Even though he was hardly abandoned, it would have been hard to convince him otherwise, for not knowing the whole story, that's exactly what it looks like. The world would gladly have Samuel or any of us believe the worst explanation that our imaginations can cook up.

I heard the Rev. Joan Gray say that we must always be upfront and transparent because what people make up is always worse than the truth. Imagine, then, how important it was for Hannah to do anything she could to make sure that her son knew the whole story of her love for him.

The whole story is just as we read it in our first Scripture lesson. Hannah longed for a child, but pregnancy, which can seem like it comes so easy to everyone else, remained out of her grasp. Unable to conceive, she did what many of us do in times of extreme desperation: she made a deal with God.

"Oh Lord of hosts," she pleaded, "if only you will look on the misery of your servant, and remember me, and not forget your servant, but will give to your servant a male child, then I will set him before you as a nazirite until the day of his death."

Surprisingly (or un-surprisingly), the Lord accepted this bargain. That meant Hannah had to honor her end of the deal: a hard, if not impossible, demand.

Think of her happy times with that child: the first time she felt the baby Samuel kick still in the womb, the time some artist tried to make her husband put his nose on her pregnant belly, the first time she held him in her arms, the first time this mother, Hannah, heard baby Samuel coo or saw him smile. All the while, in the back of her mind, shrouding all these good things, surely was the promise that she had made. She knew that once he was weaned, she would take him to the Temple and would return home without him, leaving him to wonder as he grew up a servant in the household of God: "Who am I, and what does this mean?"

She wouldn't be there to answer and to help him understand if he asked, "What did I do to deserve being left at the Temple without a family?"

She wouldn't be there to tell him about her deal with God.

Should Samuel grow up wondering, "How could a mother be so cruel as to turn and walk away from her own flesh and blood," she wouldn't be there to correct his misunderstanding.

The mind of a young boy is fertile ground for misunderstanding, too. The mind of anyone is fertile ground for misunderstanding. That's why Hannah, knowing that she would not be there to wipe away all his tears, sings a song that she hopes will speak for her to tell her son that he was loved.

She wanted him to know the truth, and by this song, which makes up our second Scripture lesson, we know that she was not being selfish. She was being faithful.

He had done nothing wrong. In fact, his mother knew that he would be about the work of setting the world right.

She hadn't left him alone, for we are never alone. Even when we feel the most abandoned, our Lord is by our side, if we only have the eyes to see. Yet, we don't always see. As we struggle to understand, most of the time in this crazy world, we are left to despair. No mother is always there to take you in her lap and to tell you that there might be another way to look at our situation. That makes being a teenager hard but being anyone at any age is hard.

Every time we read the paper, the reality of our world and our place in it is hard to grasp because we're always having to wonder what all this means.

Like Samuel growing up in the Temple, we're always tempted to ask: "Is the world falling apart or being put back together?"

Is the President about to be impeached, or is he about to Make America Great Again?

Is that caravan walking north through Mexico a band of women and children who need our help, or are they a horde that we must defend ourselves against?

In each circumstance, we're all looking at the same data. However, we're all seeing different things. Misunderstanding runs rampant in our minds, just as it does in the mind of every child, and just as it did with Samuel. To make any sense out of our world, we can't just turn to Fox or CNN, to one side of the aisle or the other. That's because it's love that reframes everything, and it's the love of God that so truly offers us the only way to truly understand what's really going on.

Just as young Samuel, in order to understand, needed to remember his mother's song, so today I call you to listen to Hannah's song as well.

For what people are saying today is doom and gloom. Either way you look at it, no matter which side of the aisle you're on, they'll tell you that chaos is on the horizon. They'll claim that if you don't give them the reigns, then the foundations of civilization are going to shake, but is there not more in heaven and earth than human philosophy?

Is there not more at work in our world than the will of partisan men and women?

Is there not something else going on all around us?

These days that we find ourselves living in are not nearly so pivotal as the self-important wish you to believe. For as it was true ages ago, so it is true today: the future rests, not in the hands of mortals who manipulate us or bullies who push us around, but in the hands of our God who is full of love for His children.

We have to reframe the world around us by hearing Hannah's song.

> The Holy One of Israel, He is a Rock and there is none like Him.

> And the proud: let them not talk so very proudly, and let arrogance not come from their mouth, for the Lord is a God of knowledge and by him actions are weighed.

> The bows of the mighty are broken, but the feeble gird on strength.

> The Lord makes poor and make rich; he brings low, he also exalts.

> He raises up the poor from the dust; he lifts the needy from the ash heap,

We had better stop our hand wringing and our worrying, for the future is not so uncertain. The pillars of the earth are the Lord's and on them he has set the world.

We must be bold enough to think again, trusting in the love of God that changes everything that we might sing:

> My heart exults in the Lord;

> My strength is exalted in my God.

> My mouth derides my enemies,

> Because I rejoice in my victory.

Amen.

Are You a King?
Revelation 1: 4-8 and John 18: 33-38a
Preached on November 25, 2018

Sara and I celebrated our 16th wedding anniversary last week and were able to get away for a couple days to North Georgia, up near Helen. Helen is a funny place. The names of roads up there will make you laugh. On our trip, we passed by Scorpion Hollow and Booger Hollow.

I wonder if the people who live there are ever self-conscious about reporting their addresses at the DMV. I knew a lady back in Tennessee who lived on a road called Sheep's Neck, and when she told someone her address, she answered two questions before they even had a chance to ask:

1. Yes, I am serious.
2. And, yes, that is out in the country.

The best street name we passed up in North Georgia last week was Nonchalant Lane. Now that was a place that I'd like to live. I can just imagine what life is like up there. I bet on Nonchalant Lane on Thanksgiving; everyone shows up to dinner wearing pants with an elastic waist band. I can imagine that no one feels self-conscious about falling asleep on the couch watching football after dinner, and anyone who would dare interrupt Thanksgiving by trying to force his family into matching outfits for a Christmas Card photo gets exiled over to Cares Too Much What Other People Think Avenue.

I imagine most of us live somewhere in between these two places.

Christ was more secure in His identity than most of us would dare be. He was more willing to take stands than most of us are. From the Scripture lessons we've just read, it's easy to gain a sense that our Lord was so secure in His identity that He would not deny who He was or back away from what He came to do. He was Himself even when His life hung in the balance.

Reading from the Gospel of John, we remembered when Pilate asked him, "Are you the king of the Jews?"

You can tell from this interchange that Pilate didn't really want to trap Jesus. He wasn't cross examining Him or trying to trick Him into incriminating Himself. In fact, it's as though Pilate was trying to do everything, he could to set Jesus free.

All Pilate needed Jesus to do was just compromise a little bit. He was only asking that Christ deny who He was slightly. Jesus wouldn't do it, though. He was determined not to hide or deny.

That's a superhuman quality then, for if there's anything we humans are good at, it's hiding who we really are.

Whether it's getting off the school bus a few stops early, embarrassed by where we really live, pretending to be the perfect family for the Christmas card, putting on a toupee or too much makeup, telling white lies, or keeping our real opinions to ourselves, for mere mortals it takes a profound level of trust before most of us are willing to just come right out and be who we really are, warts and all.

None of us really lives on Nonchalant Lane when you get right down to it.

There's a wonderful story I once heard about a wise, old Rabbi giving a sermon based on the story of Adam and Eve. Genesis chapter 3 tells of the first sin and its punishment, the story of the serpent who tempted the man and the woman to eat the forbidden fruit of the tree of the knowledge of good and evil.

After they ate this forbidden fruit, their eyes were opened, but soon after their eyes were opened, "they heard the sound of the Lord God walking in the garden at the time of the evening breeze, and the man and his wife hid themselves from the presence of the Lord God among the trees of the garden."

"Where are you?" the Lord asked, which is a funny question for the Lord to ask, the old Rabbi noted, considering how God already knows everything. "But you see," the Rabbi said, "the Lord God knew. He always knew where Adam was. But did Adam know? Adam was not lost to the Lord, but in hiding, was Adam lost to himself?"

In what is considered by some to be one of the most important philosophical works of the last quarter of a century, *Sources of the Self*, Dr. Charles Taylor claims that we are always in search of ourselves and always wrestling with the question of identity.

"Who am I?" we ask, "but this can't necessarily be answered by giving name and genealogy. What does answer this question for us," according to Dr. Taylor, "is an understanding of what is of crucial importance to us."[7]

---

[7] Charles Taylor, *The Sources of the Self* (Cambridge: Harvard University Press, 1989) 27.

What was of crucial importance to Adam and Eve? Well, the story of Genesis tells us that this shifted under the shade of the tree of the knowledge of good and evil. While in the beginning, all that mattered to the first man and the first woman was enjoying God's creation within the limits God ordained, tempted by the serpent, something shifted. Then, as the Lord God walked through the garden calling out to the man, "Where are you?" that same shift happened again. While once they had the kind of relationship where Adam and Eve walked through the garden together with God, in that moment of falling from grace, Adam and Eve thought it more important to hide.

That's human enough, but there's something in Christ that wouldn't let Him. In His refusal to ever deny His true identity, we see not only His integrity, but what is of crucial importance to Him: namely, to be Whom God created Him to be, and to do what God created Him to do.

We mere humans, on the other hand, are always tempted to hide.

When at the DMV, if we live on Booger Hollow, there's a temptation to hide.

When riding home on the school bus, if our home is on the poor side of town, we're tempted to get off the bus early.

When sending out Christmas cards, we want to project a certain image of functionality, as though we always dressed in color-coordinated outfits, and our lives were but one, long family vacation to Europe.

When going on a first date, there's the temptation not to be who you are, but who you think your love interest wants you to be. That's why I'm amazed by a man I met who always drives a dirty, old pickup truck when he takes a girl on a date. "If she'll take me like this, then she's seeing the real me" he says.

When Pilate summoned Jesus, he asked Him, "Are you the King of the Jews?"

We know how Jesus answered, but what about me? What about you?

Who am I? That's no easy question to answer. It's not something set in stone or fixed in history. Instead, identity is more like a ship pushed by the wind of peer pressure and circumstance. To maintain a sense of who we are, we must stand firm, holding close the commitments that matter most.

For some people, this is easier than others, I'm sure.

The country music legend Johnny Cash sings a song about a boy named Sue who had to fight every day of his life for his identity:

"Some gal would giggle, and I'd get red

And some guy'd laugh, and I'd bust his head,

I tell ya, life ain't easy for a boy named Sue."

The same must have been true for a woman remembered by the 1880 census of Maury County, Tennessee. The county historian there once called me over to show me that among all the citizens of that great county was a 35-year-old widow. Her last name was Mcville; first name, Parrollee.

Now a boy named Sue and a girl named Parrollee learn the same lesson: if you want people to really know who you are, you have to learn to stand up for yourself. The world asks us day and night, "Who are you?" and we answer through our commitments, our promises, and the stands we are willing to take.

It's not just what we are willing to say that matters, but the character we are willing to embody.

It's not just the words printed on the wall, but the words that guide our decisions.

It's not just the sermons we listen to or preach, but the sermons that we live.

> Give me your tired, your poor, your huddled masses yearning to breathe free,
>
> The wretched refuse of your teeming shore.
>
> Send these the homeless, the tempest-tossed to me,
>
> I lift my lamp beside the golden door.

These are the words engraved on our Statue of Liberty, stating one of the ideals that we hold close. Yet, are these ideals that we are willing to stand for?

"We hold these truths to be self-evident, that all men are created equal."

For all the years since these words were first written, our nation has been working to embody them.

Then, there's the greatest commandment: "Love the Lord your God with all your heart, soul, mind, and strength, and love your neighbor as yourself." That one's easy to say, but it's hard to do, so remember it's not what we say that matters. More important are the stands we are willing to take, and, unfortunately, when it comes to embodying the ideals of our nation or the ideals of our Christian faith, too many of us get off the bus two stops too early.

Our Lord is different, though, isn't He?

He stood trial before Pilate, the governor, the man who held our Lord's fate in his hands. In our second Scripture lesson, an event that ironically occurs just after Peter denied Jesus three times, our Lord stood trial and refused to deny the truth of His identity.

The Lord embodied the truth in His every breath.

He lived it in His every action.

He is Jesus Christ, the One that Revelation calls "the faithful witness, the firstborn of the dead, and the ruler of the kings of the earth."

It is by His love for us and His determination not to deny us but to face death on the cross that we are freed from our sins and made citizens of the Kingdom of Heaven.

That's the Good News. It's profoundly Good News that while Peter denied him three times, and while we are guilty of the same, the Lord refused to deny us.

"I am the Alpha and the Omega," says the Lord God, "who is and who was and who is to come, the Almighty." While we sometimes hide in the woods, relying on the most convenient truths rather than the real truth, rejoice in this: Christ won't hide from us, nor will He deny us, and we don't need to hide from Him when He comes again.

Amen.

The Days Are Surely Coming
Psalm 25: 1-10 and Jeremiah 33: 14-16
Preached on December 2, 2018

Neither our first nor our second Scripture lesson sounds particularly Christmassy on first reading, so now that it's December 2nd, let me read you this:

> 'Twas the night before Christmas, when all through the house
>
> Not a creature was stirring, not even a mouse;
>
> The stockings were hung by the chimney with care,
>
> In hopes that St. Nicholas soon would be there;
>
> The children were nestled all snug in their beds,
>
> While visions of sugarplums danced in their heads.

That's a good one, and it accurately describes what I remember feeling all the nights leading up to Christmas morning throughout my childhood. I remember falling asleep thinking about what Santa Claus would leave under the tree. The anticipation, the hope, and just the act of imagining what was to come brought me joy.

Is there anything in a lifetime that a person looks forward to as much as she did as a child looking forward to Christmas morning?

I hope so, but there are days when you wonder about that.

When your Georgia red is replaced with black for mourning last night's loss to Alabama, you have to wonder about that. Does it seem to you like hope has died?

Being hopeful about the future is hard sometimes.

I remember days when I couldn't wait to get older because I felt like you have to be older to have any fun, but that stops. No one has a fake ID so he can get a senior citizens discount early, does he?

At some point, rather than looking forward with optimism, we want to turn back time, fearing that the best days are in the past. We push the sugarplums of Christmas-morning-to-come out of the way to imagine turning back time so that we wake up with a full head of hair again.

107

So it goes that, as children, we rush down the stairs and into the future, only to turn into adults who mourn the passage of days.

One preacher said there's a reason the windshield is so much bigger than your rearview mirror. It's because while we must be mindful of what's behind us, our focus must always be primarily on what's ahead.

The season of Advent comes onto the scene as a reminder to change our perspective.

To reframe our reality, Advent turns our attention toward what's ahead.

This time of year is all about the future, and what is it that we have to look forward to?

If we truly consider what's ahead, then we'll be filled with more joyful anticipation than a young child who rushes down the stairs on Christmas morning, for during this time of Advent, we remember that what is promised us is the fulfillment of hope,

> The dawn of dreams,

> The beginning of joy,

> The rising tide of justice,

> The reign of love,

> The end of death,

> The coming of Christ.

Jesus, whose birth we anticipate during this season of Advent, is symbolized this morning as a "righteous branch to spring up for David."

"The days are surely coming, says the Lord, when I will fulfill the promise I made to the house of Israel and the house of Judah. In those days and at that time I will cause a righteous Branch to spring up for David."

Now, a righteous branch that springs up from a tree stump is a significant symbol, but this symbol is different in powerful ways from so many of the symbols that represent Jesus and His birthday this Christmas season.

Think of the Christmas tree.

I love the Christmas tree as much as I love the Thanksgiving turkey.

In fact, later today, we're planning on doing one of my favorite family rituals of the whole year. We're going out to pick our family Christmas tree.

Perhaps after some negotiation, a little compromise, and a bit of debate, we'll settled on a tree. Then, after it's packaged up in plastic mesh, tied to the roof of the car or stuffed in the trunk, a beautiful tree, cut fresh from its roots, will stand prominently in our living room. I'll bring down the Christmas boxes from the attic and will be in charge of the lights. Sara and the girls will finish it with decorations, some of which have been in the family since Sara and I were little. Yet, as much as I love a Christmas tree, it can't last forever.

In a month or so, I'll haul it out of the living room.

The tree will be so dried out that I'll leave a trail of pine needles behind me. At that point, regardless of how much it cost, the only thing to do with this symbol of Christmas once it's dried out is to toss it to the curb, over the fence into the neighbor's yard, or give it to an old farmer, who will use it to fill gullies that the rain has washed out around his farm.

When you think about the lifespan of a Christmas tree, it seems as though a Christmas tree represents, not the way our faith celebrates Christmas, but the way our culture does.

What does our culture suggest we do? Prepare for weeks, maybe months, while, for all the hard work, those presents get opened in about thirty seconds. Then, it's over. Our culture is all about leading us up to this grand celebration that comes and then goes. What do we have left on the afternoon of December 25th but a trashcan full of wrapping paper?

Our secular culture celebrates Christmas by anticipating, by dreaming of sugarplums. Then, once it's over, what do we have besides a dried-out tree to be dragged to the curb?

To truly embody the kind of hope that we should celebrate during Christmas, we need something different. Maybe we need the words of Jeremiah:

"The days are surely coming, says the Lord, when I will fulfill the promise I made to the house of Israel and the house of Judah. In those days and at that time I will cause a righteous Branch to spring up for David…"

Now Jeremiah tells us about this righteous branch right after Jerusalem was destroyed, right after the Holy City was cut down like a tree by the Babylonian army, who invaded in the year 587 BCE. This invasion was so massive, so complete, that the Temple was demolished, the king deposed, and so many of the survivors shipped off to live in exile. According to the Prophet, Israel was a tree, a great tree rooted in a place, among a people, nurtured by God, floored by the ax of Babylon.

All around the Prophet, people were looking back to the past, while fearing the future. What kind of future is there for a people whose nation has been reduced to rubble like a tree cut down to a stump?

It's like an empty house that was once full of life but is now emptied of its contents, sold to the highest bidder because divorce split the family in two.

It's like the cleaned-out desk. All the contents were placed in a cardboard box because the economy slowed and brought cutbacks and layoffs and early retirements.

It's like the memories we made with the person we lost, and now the place she's left in our lives is like a gully washed out by the rain. We know always that something's missing.

In the same way, Babylon invaded Jerusalem; the siege is said to have lasted for thirty months. When the armies finally left, nothing remained but a stump.

Only a stump was left: a stump and the memory of a tree that they looked back on like old wedding pictures. It was an account of bygone days, memories of how good things used to be, turned bitter with the fear that now life is only going to get worse. However, as the smoke lifted and the dust settled, this great prophet saw a shoot spring forth.

Now, there's a symbol of hope.

It's not so unlike the phoenix who rose from the ashes of Atlanta. While Sherman wanted her destroyed, reduced to dust to be swept away by the wind, the city rose again to become the traffic nightmare that it is today.

Joking aside, if you want a symbol of hope, a symbol to represent our Jesus, look not to the tree that's been cut down, but to the stump that was left only to rise again.

That's how God works. That's what God does when life cuts us down.

When everything that was supposed to happen never did, and everything that wasn't supposed to happen kept on happening until everything we worked for is gone, and the life we've been building looks like an old, worthless stump in the ground, keep looking at that stump and just wait. Watch and wait, for our God is in the business of bringing hope back to the hopeless.

That's Jesus.

He is a new branch growing out from an old stump.

He is a new baby growing inside an unmarried virgin.

He is a hope that grows from nothing at all but rises to rule the world.

This is what Christmas is really all about.

Christmas is not the dried-out tree drug to the curb, or the trash can filled with crumpled paper.

Christmas is the righteous branch that springs up from David.

"And he shall execute justice and righteousness in the land.

In those days Judah will be saved, and Jerusalem will live in safety.

And this is the name by which it will be called: 'The Lord is our righteousness.'"

Now, as Christmas approaches, go buy a tree to celebrate. Yet, when it's all over, once winter is passed and spring comes again, go out to the yard, find that Bradford pear tree you cut down last fall and left for dead and look at how death will not have the final word.

That's hope. That's Christmas. New shoots rising from an old stump.

That's our Lord. He is persistent life even in the midst of what appears to be death.

Thanks be to God.

Amen.

A Refiner's Fire

Malachi 3: 1-4 and Luke 1: 68-79

Preached on December 9, 2018

Last Tuesday, your church staff was honored to be welcomed into the home of Paul and Janice Phillips for the annual Church Staff Christmas Party. This was my second staff party there, and this one was just as extravagant as the first I attended. They served us hot apple cider and cheese straws as we gathered. Sitting at dining tables, we had three sauces to adorn our entrée: mango salsa, horseradish, or Jezebel Sauce. We had our choice of grilled salmon or smoked prime rib. I chose both.

Members of our Administration Council served as waiters. Bill Pardue even wore a bow tie. It was an outstanding experience, and we all couldn't help but give thanks for the gift that it is to work at and serve a church where we're so appreciated. It truly was wonderful, and then Santa showed up. I'm not kidding. He delivered some gifts, financial and otherwise, and he let me in on a little secret. In reference to Rev. Joe Brice's behavior at the party, he whispered to me: "Maybe Rev. Brice thinks he's in the clear, but I'm still watching. Bad behavior counts, and anyone could lose his place on the Good List, all the way up to Christmas Eve."

I know that by this point in the month of December, all children have already prepared their lists. In some way or another, I know that they've also prepared their reputations, believing that the old song has some truth:

"You'd better watch out, you'd better not cry

You'd better not pout; I'm telling you why

Santa Claus is coming to town"

You know the rest. You can sing it with me if you want to:

"He's making a list and checking it twice

He's gonna find out who's naughty and nice

Santa Claus is coming to town"

That's what kids are worried about this time of year. They're thinking about behavior. They're thinking about what list they're going to end up on and who's coming to town.

Adults, on the other hand, we're just worried about guests coming to town.

We're thinking about the beds to be made, the turkeys to be defrosted, and getting the eggnog nogged.

Even if it's that Cousin Eddie's coming over to do you know what in the storm drain, still there are ways that we adults must prepare for Christmas. On the other hand, children prepare in a different way. They prepare with a time of spiritual purification; you might call it. For them, this is a time of moral redirection and reputation redemption. This time of year, they are mindful of their behavior knowing that good children will receive gifts and bad children, coal. For them, the only imminent guest who matters is Santa Claus, and because he's coming to town, his arrival must be prepared for. A child prepares for Christmas by getting her life in order and not her house.

That almost sounds like the Prophet Malachi.

Do you know about the Prophet Malachi? Not many people do.

Even Bible scholars don't know much about the author of this book or the historical events that prompted this prophet to write. What is clear is that Malachi knows that Someone is coming to town and knows that with His coming, preparation is necessary.

However, the preparation that Malachi calls us to is not the kind of preparation that we see on the eve of the arrival of guests or relatives. We don't prepare for His coming by putting up lights or decking the halls. Rather, we prepare for His coming by recognizing the need for purification in our hearts, minds, and souls, for the One who is coming is "like a refiner's fire and like fuller's soap."

According to Suzanne Richard, Professor of Old Testament at Drew University in Madison, New Jersey, a fuller, or one who used fuller's soap, was the ancient world's version of a dry cleaner. Clothes soaking in lye were stomped as you might imagine a group of people would stomp on grapes to make wine. The clothes were then spread out on the ground to be bleached by the sun in what was called a fuller's field, which was always outside the city or town.[8]

If the One who is coming is like "fuller's soap," don't imagine one of those Dove Soap commercials where the soap is so gentle as not to irritate the skin or the kind of shampoo that makes washing your hair a pleasurable experience. The sales pitch for fuller's soap would be that it is so abrasive that it will bleach that skin right off.

---

[8] Paul J. Achtemeier, gen. edu, *HarperCollins Bible Dictionary* (New York: Harper One, 1996), 353.

The book of Malachi is about a messenger whose sole purpose is to say, "He is coming. The Lord is coming, so get ready. Be prepared, for He will be like a refiner's fire and like fuller's soap to all who are defiled and impure."

The messenger is John the Baptist, of course. He's the one whose birth is celebrated in the song his father, Zechariah, sang at his birth, which made up our Advent candle lighting liturgy and our second Scripture lesson for today. Zechariah sang, "You, child, will be called the prophet of the Most High; you will go before the Lord to prepare his ways," but what should we be preparing for?

A dinner party?

No. We should be preparing for a Savior who will purify our souls, and purification is no pleasant experience, according to Malachi. This fuller's soap is disturbing enough with its imagery of harsh cleaning agents, feet stomping, and being left to dry out in the sun, but have you ever seen a refiner's fire?

I had the opportunity to tour an aluminum recycling plant because my friend Brandom Gengelbach worked there.

A recycling plant is an incredible place. It's amazing really.

Before you go in, you have to put on these safety glasses, a helmet, and a protective coat.

Then, the tour begins with a look at the finished product, a great big slab of refined aluminum, called an ingot. To make an ingot, you have to start with used or unrefined aluminum, so the next part of the tour is looking at these big piles of car parts, old computers, bicycles, soft drink cans, and old wire.

All of this junk is placed in a furnace, and the furnace building is one of the hottest places I've ever been. It's one of those places where it feels like your eyeballs are sweating. It's so hot in there, you can almost see the heat. Then, we went up in the control room to watch as the junk is melted until the impurities, like the paint from the drink can or the plastic casing on the wire, are burnt off to create something new and pure.

I think of that when I read, "He will sit as a refiner and purifier of silver, and he will purify the descendants of Levi and refine them like gold and silver."

It doesn't sound pleasant, but here's something interesting. The Bible uses silver and gold, and I've been telling you about aluminum. Both silver and aluminum are two of the most reflective of all the metals. When aluminum is heated and purified, something called a "lighting sheet" is created so that the metal has a mirror-like quality. Apparently, that's also true for silver. When it's heated, the silversmith knows that his metal is pure because he can see his reflection in it.

Think about that.

The metal is refined when it reflects the Maker's image.

We were created in God's image, but, easily enough, we gathered impurities the way a white sweater gathers stains, or the way metal is painted and wrapped and treated. The human condition is one of starting out pure in the Garden of Eden. Then, because our Creator instilled in us a capacity to choose for ourselves, our decisions, our circumstances, and our world has corrupted and defiled what was once pure.

Refining is what we need, and you know it as well as I do.

It doesn't sound like a relaxing process, but when you look out on the world, can you really think for a moment that everything is as it should be?

Consider the corruption, disease, pollution, and genocide.

Then, there's oppression, poverty, cancer, and slavery.

Greed creeps into our hearts, and so many try to buy their way to happiness that we have to rent units to store all the junk that we went into debt buying.

Desire guides our thoughts, keeping us from being satisfied with the gifts that we've already been given.

Violence walks the streets, as the innocent are killed, and all are inspired to fear and worry.

We are confined to our houses and suspicious of our neighbors.

We are distracted and stretched.

We are overworked, yet still struggling to make ends meet, surrounded by people, yet often feeling all alone. We have too much to eat, yet there is an emptiness we can't fill. All around us is conflict, war, famine, and discord.

The primary focus of this morning's Scripture lessons is not a warning to change our ways. It's not an assessment of who's to blame, nor is the point that we must rush to do something about all that's wrong in our world. Instead in these two Scripture lessons, is a promise that the One who is coming will.

He will not tolerate the kind of denial that distracts us from the real issues.

He will not accept the half-hearted apology or the lie that masquerades as truth.

"Who can endure on the day of his coming?" is one question that Scripture asks, but "will we endure if he doesn't come?" is another.

A new day is dawning, and Scripture is clear that getting to that new day is as painful as being washed with fuller's soap or being refined in the fire. It's like a mother giving birth to a new child, the Apostle Paul said, for indeed, there is moaning before the shouts of joy, confession before forgiveness, and purification before redemption.

John the Baptist, born of Zechariah the Priest, is the one who was born to tell us to get ready for it, rejoicing in the promise of what's to come:

"The dawn from on high will break upon us,

To give light to those who sit in darkness and in the shadow of death,

To guide our feet into the way of peace."

For we have yet to learn the ways of peace. He is coming, though, and He will teach us.

Thanks be to God.

Amen.

Their Shame into Praise
Zephaniah 3: 14-20 and Luke 3: 7-18
Preached on December 16, 2018

It's funny how that second Scripture reading ends. John the Baptist "proclaimed the good news;" only it's not immediately obvious why this news is good. It seems like a strange ending until you step back and consider Christmas cards. I love Christmas cards. I bet that you love Christmas cards, too, and I hope that you receive a lot of them because they're so nice to get.

One of the things that I love the most about Christmas cards is when the card is a picture. When the card is a picture, I can see how my friends have changed. Some of the Christmas cards that we get in the mail come from people who, when I first met them, weren't nearly as respectable as they appear to be now.

It's so good to see them looking good and doing well.

The kids grow each year.

Dad's hairline recedes more each year.

Mom's getting better and better at maintaining that smile, while saying, "sit still" to her children through gritted teeth.

These cards bring a lot of Christmas cheer, don't they? Sometimes, though, the pressure to get them out gets to us. Every once in a while, I'll overhear a conversation where one parent says to another: "I'm thinking that this year, we'll just send out a Happy New Year card."

Some people are serious about Christmas cards. They feel good if they got them out early. They feel guilty if they didn't get them out at all. We felt ashamed one year because one year we received our first Christmas card the day after Thanksgiving. These friends of ours had it so together that they basically sent out a Happy Thanksgiving card. If that doesn't make you feel bad for not getting your Christmas cards out by Christmas, I don't know what will.

Plus, with that over-eager Christmas card came an announcement that Mom got a promotion at work, Dad's been running marathons, youngest Son is three but has learned to read, and oldest Son is five but is going off to medical school in the spring.

I remember one Christmas years ago when my grandfather made a point of reading us one of those Christmas letters that came with the card. You know what I'm talking about? Those are usually really nice to receive because they give an update of what all has been going on, who's been to camp and who's playing the piano, and all that stuff. My grandfather took offense to this one, though, so he took it off the refrigerator to read it to us. He read the sentence about this family's extravagant vacation, and he said, "Well, this is so full of braggadocio, I don't want to read another word."

At that time, I wasn't too sure that "braggadocio" was even a word, but you know what he means.

The point of the Christmas letter, just like the point of the Christmas card, is just to say, "Merry Christmas" and, "Let me tell you how we've been doing." If you open your mailbox to find a Christmas card in there, you can be certain that you are only receiving one because you are loved, but sometimes these things inspire a little bit of shame or envy.

The wife puts down the Christmas letter and says to her husband, "Would you look at that; the Johnson family has been to Paris," and he knows exactly what she's trying to say.

In the same way, the husband puts down the Christmas card from the out-of-town friends that includes a picture of all of them and says to his wife, "Would you look at Sally. Doesn't she look great? I wonder if she's been working out or something?" That sounds like an innocent question, but his wife looks into his eyes and wonders what this picture, meant to say nothing more than "Merry Christmas," has inspired in her husband's mind.

Christmas cards! It might be that one of the Christmas cards you receive brings with it, not Christmas cheer, but envy, desire, and longing for what you don't have.

Since it was already pretty hard to keep up with the Joneses before we found out their 5-year-old was going to medical school, John the Baptist reminds us to quit worrying about what they have and be satisfied with what we have.

There he was at the River Jordan. First, he calls the whole crowd a "brood of vipers." Not many pastors would think it wise to begin the sermon that way, but that's what John does. Then, the crowds asked him, if that's who we are, "What then should we do?"

To the crowds, he said, "Whoever has two coats must share with anyone who has none; and whoever has food must do likewise."

To the tax collectors, he said, "Collect no more than the amount prescribed to you."

To the soldiers, he said, "Do not extort money from anyone by threats or false accusation and be satisfied with your wages."

It's as though John the Baptist cuts right to the chase to say, "Be careful about wanting more; it's dangerous! It can lead you to do questionable things. Plus, wanting more can keep you from being satisfied with what you have already."

That's timely advice, for you know a man who, today, feels enormous pressure to provide for his family their every want and desire. You know a mother who keeps giving herself away so that there's nothing left. You know the feeling of showing up to a kid's school Christmas party with a box of cookies you picked up at Kroger, only to find that, by the looks of things, every other kid's mom must be Martha Stewart.

Life is such a competition, so listen to what John the Baptist came to say.

He came to say, "Enough."

Don't ask Santa for another coat. Instead, go in your closest, and if you're lucky enough to have two, then give one away.

Don't work so hard for more money. If you have $1,000 in your bank account, then you're better off than the majority of people in this country already.

And stop striving for so much because what you ought to be doing this Christmas season is sitting back in satisfaction with what already you have.

"Be satisfied," he said.

This remarkably countercultural message reminds me of a story that Dr. Fred Craddock told.

Dr. Craddock is one of the truly great preachers. He taught at Candler School of Theology on the campus of Emory University, then went to live up in Ellijay, Georgia. He used to like to eat at Waffle House. He said, "The Waffle House is a good place to go get a BLT. You have to take a shower after, but it's a good place to get a BLT."

Well, once he was at the Waffle House. The waitress assigned to his table asked for his order, and he requested a cup of coffee. Dr. Craddock asked for cream, and she patted down her apron and said, "I can never find anything in this capricious apron."

"Capricious?" Dr. Craddock repeated.

Then, she threw out six creamers on the table. He took two and pushed the four back toward the waitress, but she pushed them back towards him, saying, "Better to have and not need than need and not have."

Thinking to himself, "first capricious and now this," he asked, "Well, are you a waitress or a philosopher?" Then, he said, "But best is to take what you need and give the rest away."

There have always been people who have more.

There have always been people who look younger than we do.

There have always been nicer houses than the ones that we live in.

There have always been families that seem to have it all together.

There has always come a time when what you have to do is stop looking at what they have to see what God has already given.

What, then, has God given?

A Son.

Slow down for a minute and listen to God's promise from Zephaniah one more time:

> I will save the lame.

> I will gather the outcast.

> I will bring you home.

> And will change your shame into praise,

for the work that we've all been doing to ensure that ours is the perfect Christmas has already been done.

Thanks be to God.

Amen.

There's a Story Behind the Song
Micah 5: 2-5a and Luke 1: 39-45

Preached on December 23, 2018

I hate to start a sermon with complaining, but I want to tell you that I've been catching a little grief over our hymn choices lately. In fact, one woman poked me with her cane, she felt so strongly about it. It's true, and I'm to blame. I pick out a lot of the hymns we sing. In fact, you haven't even seen the worst ones because the worst ones that I've picked out over the last year, our Music Director, Dr. Jeffrey Meeks, talked me out of.

I do have a habit of choosing some hymns that maybe you've never sung before. Let me go on record saying that I'm completely unapologetic about this, but if you think it's bad now, ask Sara how bad it used to be.

A few years ago, I was approached by a church member named Robin Watson about a fundraiser. This was back in Tennessee, and Robin knew that some people were tired of singing some of the hymns that I'd picked out. She was trying to raise money for this organization that worked to renovate existing homes owned by elderly members of the community who have trouble doing the renovation work themselves or paying someone else to do it.

This was a great organization. The church wanted to support it. I wanted to support it, and Robin suggested a fundraiser where church members could select their least favorite hymn from the hymnal, and for $100 they could ensure that it would not be sung again for a full year.

I wasn't worried about whether or not this campaign would be successful. Judging from some opinions of my hymn choices, I worried that the campaign might be too successful. Had we decided to start the campaign during Advent, we probably could have funded renovations for half the houses in the city.

I know that some of the hymns that we sing during this season of Advent are unfamiliar. I've heard that one Sunday a couple weeks back, some folks only recognized one out of the three hymns we sang. I also know that everyone this time of year is excited to sing Christmas carols, but remember, there's more to a song than whether or not you like the tune.

Consider Hymn #84, verse 2:

> When this old world drew on toward night, you came;

but not in splendor bright

Not as a monarch, but the child

Of Mary, blameless mother mild.

That's beautiful, right?

Or Hymn #97, verse 3:

Watchmen, tell us of the night,

For the morning seems to dawn.

Traveler, shadows take their flight;

Doubt and terror are withdrawn.

Watchmen, you may go your way;

Hasten to your quiet home.

Traveler, we rejoice today,

For Emmanuel has come!

Those are powerful, poetic words. While maybe they're not as fun to sing as "Jingle Bells," they say a whole lot more.

There's more to a hymn than the tune. There's even more to a song than the words because sometimes it's the story behind the song that makes the hymn worth singing.

Sometimes, it's the circumstance that caused the writer to write or the hardship that inspired the poet to put his feelings to paper.

That's the case with many of these hymns we sing, and it's most obviously true for one of the most popular hymns of all time, "Amazing Grace."

You know this one well. It's been sung by everyone from Elvis Presley to President Barak Obama, who sang it himself during the memorial service for Reverend Clementa Pinckney, who was shot in Charleston, South Carolina.

This song is embraced by white and black, rich and poor. In our hymnals, it's printed in English, Choctaw, Creek, Navaho, Cherokee, and Kiowa. It's been a tool for racial reconciliation, and it's inspired many a sinner to kneel before his Redeemer, which makes sense because this hymn was written by a slave trader.

The details are foggy, and the story is probably much more legend than fact, but the story behind the song only adds to its strength. The details generally agreed upon are that "by 1745, [John] Newton was enlisted in the slave trade, running captured slaves from Africa to Charleston, S.C.

After he rode out a storm at sea in 1748, he found his faith. He was ordained an Anglican priest in 1764 and became an important voice in the English abolitionist movement. [And] at that time he wrote the autobiographical 'Amazing Grace.'"[9]

Our own Tracy Knapp loaned me a book all about the backstory of this hymn, knowing that backstory brings strength to the words because the blind man who now sees is a living, breathing man.

The wretch who's been saved, you now know in what way he was a wretch, and you know Who it is that saved him.

The lost one who's been found, he's no different from you. He's no different from me.

Knowing the story behind the song gives the words some new strength, and that's the case with all kinds of music.

Behind so many Taylor Swifts songs are the memories of breakups.

When Beyoncé sings about an unfaithful husband, we know who she's singing about.

All that force behind Aretha Franklin's voice when she demands some R-E-S-P-E-C-T, all that passion, comes from her true desire for equality, dignity, and respect in a society of segregation, sexism, and discrimination that she experienced first-hand.

So also, the songs that we sing this time of year are the same in that many of them, all of them, surely, have stories behind the songs.

You may already know that William Dix, who wrote, "What Child Is This?" was a manager for an insurance company. In 1865, he asked the same question of Joseph and Mary that he asked himself when he held his own newborn children: "What child is this, who, laid to rest, On Mary's lap is sleeping?"

That's the same question that every father and mother ask: "Who is this little miracle that's just been handed to us?"

I remember all too well the night our oldest daughter was born. The nurse brought her into our hospital room, handed her to us, and then turned to leave.

---

[9] http://time.com/3939193/amazing-grace-history-john-newton/

"Wait a minute!" we said, "Are you just going to leave her with us?"

The responsibility was overwhelming.

The honor and the burden of being entrusted with a newborn child were already big enough, so can you imagine being entrusted with the Son of God?

> This, this is Christ the king,
>
> Whom shepherds guard and angels sing;
>
> Haste, haste to bring him laud,
>
> The babe, the son of Mary!

There's a story behind the song, and, likewise, behind the Scripture lesson for today stands a story that you know but that we didn't read.

These verses makeup the very first Christmas carol ever sung, the song that Mary sings. The Magnificat, it's called. You know most of it because it's ancient and it's beautiful, and with this song, she says what we all want to say if only we had the words:

> My soul magnifies the Lord,
>
> And my spirit rejoices in God my Savior,
>
> For he has looked with favor on the lowliness of his servant.
>
> Surely, from now on all generations will call me blessed;
>
> For the Mighty One has done great things for me,
>
> And holy is his name.

You know the song, and it is powerful. Just the words alone are powerful. It is even more powerful when set to music, but did you ever notice that Mary doesn't sing in the presence of the angel Gabriel? Neither does she sing this song after hearing that she would be the mother of the Child who would assume the throne of His ancestor David.

The story behind the song is that Mary sings in Elizabeth's house.

Maybe you know already why that's the case because it would have been the same with you.

Maybe you heard that you got the job you were hoping for. The phone rings with the news that you wanted to hear. When you answer, you can't help but smile ear to ear. You're excited because you got the job you wanted, but you don't sing for joy until you tell your mother.

What about when your heart breaks, but you don't cry. You don't really cry until you find your way home through a fog of disappointment to that safe easy chair in your grandmother's living room. She pours the tea and the speaks the words, "Honey, what happened?"

To tell someone the news, good or bad, makes it all real.

It's when you're finally safe in the presence of someone you love that you let yourself feel all the emotions that you've been guarding yourself from. It's with your mother, your sister, your wife, or your best friend that you really laugh or cry, sing or wail.

That's how it was with Mary. That's the story behind her song.

Elizabeth was her relative, and as scared as she must have been, pregnant Mary set out and

> went with haste to a Judean town in the hill country, where she entered the house of Zechariah and greeted Elizabeth. When Elizabeth heard Mary's greeting, the child leaped in her womb. And Elizabeth was filled with the Holy Spirit and exclaimed with a loud cry,

> "Blessed are you among women and blessed is the fruit of your womb.

> And why has this happened to me, that the mother of my Lord comes to me?"

Do you know how good it must have felt to hear those words?

It must have felt as good as sitting on her mother's lap, safe and warm.

It must have felt as good as resting her head on her father's strong shoulder, reassuring, steady, and present.

It's hard when these people are gone because flesh and blood does us so much good.

That's part of the story behind the song, but there's more to it than just that because Mary's song isn't about Elizabeth, it's about Jesus.

What it is about Jesus exactly that Mary knows and is trying to tell us makes me think of one of those old preacher stories that gets told again and again.

Maybe you've heard it. A little girl calls out in the night for her daddy. He rushes into her room, and she tells him that she's afraid.

"Well, don't worry, honey. You're going to be fine; now let me go back to sleep," her father says.

"But, Daddy," pleads the daughter, "won't you stay here with me?"

You can imagine his face now, and so you know that it was more self-serving than faithful when he said, "You don't need me to stay with you. Don't you know that Jesus is always with you to protect you?"

"But, Daddy," the little girl says, "I need someone here with some skin."

That's a significant request: "I need someone here with some skin."

Yet, that's how it is with us all. We need someone with a lap for children to sit in, with a shoulder for the hurting to cry on, and with a hand to hold and a voice to speak and footsteps to follow in.

That's the rest of the story behind this song of Mary's.

The Lord is coming, and He's coming in flesh and blood.

Amen.

Part 5: Christmas is just beginning

My favorite time of year is Christmas. From the first opportunity to buy peppermint ice cream to the moment I have to take the lights down from the tree, I celebrate "the most wonderful time of the year." However, the Christmas Season isn't like a window that opens then closes, but a new reality that changes everything.

In the following sermons, which stretch from Christmas Eve to the beginning of Christ's ministry among us, I felt renewed by this new reality.

For a Child Has Been Born for Us
Isaiah 9: 2-7 and Luke 2: 1-14
Preached on December 24, 2018

This is a different kind of night, and tomorrow is a different kind of a day.

I assume that a majority of you who work have the day off tomorrow unless you work for an Ebenezer Scrooge who has yet to have a change of heart. However, if you're a parent of young children, even if you don't work tomorrow, there will be no sleeping in. Your kids will wake you up, possibly earlier than on a day when they have school. That is interesting to think about.

Have you been dragging your children out of bed in the morning for school?

Have you poked and prodded them until they rolled out of their beds, ushered them to their dressers to put on some clothes, forced them to make cereal decisions, made their lunches, then pushed them out the door while their eye lids are still only half open?

Why is it that they require so much assistance and act so tired on a school day, but tomorrow they'll wake up at 5:00 without so much as an alarm?

There's a difference, isn't there?

There's a difference between tomorrow morning and every other morning, just as there is a difference between doing something because you have to and doing something because you want to.

There's a difference between waking up for school and waking up for Christmas.

There's a difference between going to Bethlehem as Mary and Joseph did, because the Emperor told them to, and going to Bethlehem as the shepherds did.

Just think about that.

How many things do you do in a day, not because you want to, but because you have to?

I was at an estate sale a couple months ago.

Do you know about estate sales? That's what fancy people call yard sales. I was at this estate sale looking at all the tools in the garage with our daughters, and I heard a woman say, "I don't know what to do with any of the stuff in here, so I'm going to keep walking."

An old guy who was standing nearby said, "I know what to do with it and don't want to, so I'm going to keep walking, too."

What is it about life that turns so many of our moments into drudgery? When we were kids, anything could become a game. I know plenty of kids who think that there's nothing more fun than going to their mothers' offices. I remember a day when my dad convinced some of us that there was no better way to spend an afternoon than by stacking wood. Then something happened: he tried to pay us for it, and immediately, the fun was let out like air in a balloon.

I wonder what most days feel like to you. Do you wake up feeling like Joseph and Mary on the way to Bethlehem?

Are you like a mother, pregnant and uncomfortable, yet forced to ride for miles on the back of a stinking donkey? Are you like Mary and Joseph, already financially stretched before you were forced to take off from work to go on a long trip you can't afford to a place you have no interest in visiting because the Emperor said you have to?

For Joseph and Mary, it was the Emperor who was ordering them around.

They were citizens in his kingdom, to be moved at his will like pieces on a chess board. Most of the time, it was probably about the same for the shepherds.

History tells us that most shepherds at the time of Jesus' birth were slaves.

That must be true, for just think, who could you get to spend the night outside with a herd of animals? People who have no choice, that's who.

They were out in the fields, watching the flocks by night, not because they wanted to, but because they had been told to. Life in Israel, which was at this time a part of the Roman Empire, was for so many a life of harsh injustice and cruel hierarchies of class.

The great orator Seneca was once invited to a friend's house, and after casting a judgmental gaze at the slave at his friend's door, he said, "Where does this decrepit creature come from? You did well to post him at the door, for he seems on the verge of leaving this house for good and finding his way to [his grave]!"

The slave, hearing what Seneca had said, spoke up: "But Master, don't you recognize me? I am Felicio, with whom you used to play when you were little."[10]

A life of being told what to do and where to go will put miles on a body, so it was with this slave, and so it is with us all.

There's a poem about the difference between doing something because you have to and doing something because you want to. You've probably heard it:

Out of the mud two strangers came

And caught me splitting wood in the yard,

And one of them put me off my aim

By hailing cheerily "Hit them hard!"

I knew pretty well why he had dropped behind

And let the other go on a way.

I knew pretty well what he had in mind:

He wanted to take my job for pay.

But yield who will to their separation,

My object in living is to unite

My avocation and my vocation

As my two eyes make one in sight.

Only where love and need are one,

And the work is play for mortal states,

Is the deed ever really done?

For Heaven and future's sakes.[11]

Do you know that poem?

---

[10] Paul Veyne, *A History of Private Life* (Harvard College: First Harvard University Press, 1992), 136.

[11] Robert Frost, "Two Tramps In Mud Time," retrieved from poemhunter.com

It's by Robert Frost, and I used to hate it because an English teacher made us read it. Now I love it because I sought it out on my own.

It's so strange the difference between doing something because you have to and doing something because you want to.

You have to go to work.

You have to go to school.

You ought to feed your family.

You go to Walmart because it's cheap but going in there ruins your day.

You feel obligated to clean up around the house, only to watch it get messy again.

You can't get out of paying your bills, even though it's not any fun.

Then, at some point today, maybe you felt like you had to come to church, too, so you're here, but may this be different.

With this service, rooted in the Gospel of Luke's telling of the Christmas story, comes the reminder that whoever it is that is always making you get up out of bed and on the road to wherever, isn't really as powerful as he thinks he is.

It's on this night that we remember that, among all the orders and directives, memos and report cards, in the midst of all the declarations and legislation, speeches and power mongering, obligations and all the don't-want-to-but-have to's, it's the words that the Angles say that really matter:

"Glory to God in the highest heaven,

And on earth peace among those whom he favors!"

With that, the shepherds, who had probably been ordered around their whole lives, said to one another, "Let us go now to Bethlehem and see this thing that has taken place," so with haste they went, and it wasn't because they had to. It was because they wanted to.

It was because everything had changed.

It was because they were no longer slaves, but messengers of God.

They were no longer those who take orders but had become those entrusted with Good News.

They were no longer the downtrodden, but the hopeful.

130

They weren't to be looked down upon because the God of Heaven and Earth was born unto them.

Sometimes, life can seem like one long obligation, but not tonight.

Tonight, go to sleep like free men and women, entrusted with Good News, serenaded by angels, guests of the Christ Child.

Amen.

Following a Star
Isaiah 60: 1-6 and Matthew 2: 1-12
Preached on January 6, 2019

Today is January 6th, and in some ways, it feels to me like Christmas is a distant memory. We mostly put Christmas away a little more than a week ago. I feel like I heard somewhere that it's bad luck if you don't have all your Christmas decorations put away by January 1st, which pushes us to get it done. I hope that's not true because while we did take down our tree and put most of our special Christmas things back in the attic to stay until we take them out again next year, there's probably two or three things that are resisting our efforts. I wonder if it's that way with you.

You think it's all up in the attic, but then you go to unload the dryer and there are all your Christmas napkins, or you vacuum the carpet in the living room and come across a lost ornament. Maybe some bad smell emanates from the garage, and you say to yourself, "so that's where I put the turkey to defrost."

I know that at our house there's at least one Christmas ornament that refused to be put away; it's the star that I hung way up in the tree in front of our house. Friday before last, on December 28th, I managed to get all our other Christmas lights down, but I couldn't get that star out of the tree, so I decided I'd just keep it up there through Epiphany.

Maybe that's just an excuse, but I'm glad about it today.

I'm glad it's still up there because really, on this Epiphany Sunday, we acknowledge that Christmas is just now getting started. Even though the seasonal aisle at Kroger has completely changed its contents, Christmas is just getting started.

You can tell that's the case because, as we read in our second Scripture lesson, only just now are some of the most important guests arriving. Now, who are these people showing up late for Christmas? Tradition tells us that their names are Balthasar of Arabia, Melchior of Persia, and Gaspar of India, but none of that is in the Bible. Somebody just made that up. In fact, the wise men are never even numbered in the Scripture lesson that we just read from the Gospel of Matthew, only their gifts are.

That first Christmas, many years ago in Bethlehem, wise men sought out the baby Jesus and brought Him gold, frankincense, and myrrh. These were strange and valuable gifts, fit for a king. Bible scholars of the 21st century debate many things about them. They debate about the meaning behind the gifts, where these wise men came from, how many of them there were, and whether or not they were all even men. I wonder about their gender as well, considering how they stopped in Jerusalem to ask for directions.

Our Gospel lesson reads:

"In the time of King Herod, after Jesus was born in Bethlehem of Judea, wise men from the East came to Jerusalem, asking, 'Where is the child who has been born king of the Jews? For we observed his star at its rising and have come to pay him homage.'"

Now, that they stopped and asked for directions is interesting enough, but what's more is that Scripture tells us, "When King Herod heard this, he was frightened."

Isn't that an interesting reaction?

Why would King Herod be frightened?

Well, to understand this king's reaction, it's important to remember that the spirit of Christmas inspires most of us to give. Christmas so often brings out our very best. You can see it in the small and large acts of kindness, the general sense of goodwill that pervades each day of December, but there are still, in our world today, those who resist it all.

In the Christmas movie, "It's a Wonderful Life," there's George Bailey on the one hand, but Mr. Potter on the other. Just as George Bailey is always giving and always enabling others to do more and have more, Mr. Potter is always holding close what he has with one hand while reaching for what he doesn't have with the other: that miserly old man. The only thing colder than the winter weather in that small town of Bedford Falls is the state of Mr. Potter's heart.

It must have been the same with King Herod.

King Herod hears that there is a child born King of the Jews and immediately thinks to himself, "But I'm king of the Jews! Who does this Christ child think he is?"

When he hears the news that the wise men bring, unlike them, he doesn't think about giving presents or showing kindness. He only ever thinks about what he stands to lose.

Isn't that a pitiful way to be?

Because that's King Herod, what happens next is tragic. King Herod asks about the place of this child's birth, then "killed all the children in and around Bethlehem who were two years old or under, according to the time that he had learned from the wise men." So threatened was he by the Savior's birth, knowing that it would require that he step back from power, Herod massacres the infants of Bethlehem. That's nearly the opposite of what the wise men did. It's good to think of them as kings as the hymn "We Three Kings" does because some kings will hold onto power until it's pried out of their cold dead hands, but these kings show us another way. Unlike Herod, they let go of what is precious, offering it at the feet of the Christ child in His meager manger. That kind of generosity, that kind of letting go, is what Christmas ought to inspire in us. That's the appropriate response to what God has done, for at Christmas, we remember how the God of creation gives us the greatest of all gifts, His Son Jesus Christ. Such a gift inspires most of us to give of what we have. That's the Christmas spirit.

Despite that, too many have packed up that Christmas spirit into their attics, allowing self-interest to define their behavior. We have two options then. There are two kinds of people for us to be:

on the one hand, the wise give; on the other hand, the Herods horde.

The wise are filled with joy, while the Herods are filled with fear.

The wise encounter the Christ child and go home by another road, but the Herods stay on the same road that they're on and massacre anyone who'd get in their way.

In this season of New Year's resolutions, what will we do? Who will we be?

Will we live as though Christmas is just beginning? We will live as those who know that there are still gifts that we might generously give, or will we put away our decorations and get back to life as normal, forgetting that His birth has changed everything?

I heard a poem from Howard Thurman.

Dr. Thurman is considered by many to be the great theological mind of the Civil Rights Movement. He wrote this poem about the days after Christmas:

When the song of the angels is stilled,

When the star in the sky is gone,

When the kings and princes are home,

When the shepherds are back with their flock,

The work of Christmas begins:

To find the lost.

To heal the broken.

To feed the hungry.

To release the prisoner.

To rebuild the nations.

To bring peace among people.

To make music in the heart.

Imagine that.

Imagine if Christmas were not put away but only beginning.

Imagine that there is no rush to find the Christ child so that power might be maintained by those who have it already, but there is, instead, a rush to find Him that His birth be celebrated, and lives changed for the better.

Imagine what it would look like if the Mr. Potters of the world give up on hording to see that the only way for them to have what the George Baileys of the world have is to let go and be made new.

Imagine if Christmas was not put away but was lived.

Imagine the change that would take place if we all made the same pledge that Ebenezer Scrooge made at the end of "A Christmas Carol:" "I will honor Christmas in my heart and try to keep it all the year!"

Having seen Him, will you give up the road that you've been walking down to take another road?

Will you follow where He leads, though going where He leads means going someplace new?

Will you rest in the security of His powerful love, and receive the gift of peace that the true Messiah can provide?

Let us live each day as Christmas, always following His star.

Amen.

When Emmanuel Was Baptized
Isaiah 43: 1-7 and Luke 3: 15-22

Preached on January 13, 2019

There's a church bell in our steeple. It rang just a few minutes before this service started to call all of us to worship. It is the signal to get into our seats and to prepare our hearts, that we might focus our attention on the God of all creation. Considering that bell, I realize that it's one thing to hear that bell ring, and it's another thing to touch it.

Howard Swinford was kind enough to invite me up there to see our bell up close last week. Howard is one of those guys who has learned many of the secrets of our church. Before the renovation, he emptied the buckets that caught the Sanctuary roof leaks. He knows what to do if the pipes clang under our offices or if the air conditioner stops working in the summer. He stopped by my office last Wednesday morning and invited me to climb the ladders that lead all the way up to our church bell.

By telling you this, I imagine that I'm making some of you jealous and others of you nervous. Such emotions are not what I want to inspire, for what I want to emphasize is how different it is to see something up close and personal, just as it's different when someone sees us up close and personal.

Many of us are conditioned to think of God as a far-off heavenly being or to think of a God who lives way up in heaven or in purely spiritual, nebulous terms. It's in this season, during and after Christmas, that such misconceptions are corrected, for now we remember how God was born in a manger and how the Prophet called Him Emmanuel, God with us.

The Prophet did not call Him "God above us," but "God with us."

He is not "God in theory," but "God in flesh and blood."

Isn't that something?

On Christmas Eve, we remembered how He was born of a mother, just as we were.

We remembered how the baby Jesus cried out when He was cold or hungry, just as we did.

Then, last Sunday, we remembered how when He was born, people brought Him gifts. What we remembered last Sunday was something like the baby Jesus' baby shower.

136

Now, the wise men didn't bring Him a Pack 'n Play. He was like us, but also unlike us, so they brought Him gold, frankincense, and myrrh. The brought Him gifts for a king, a Heavenly King who came down to be with us.

At this time of year, we know that He didn't just listen to our prayers the way we hear the tolling of our bell. Our prayers were not words from some far-off and removed place. No, instead He came to earth to touch our faces, and to wipe the tears from our eyes.

Isn't that wonderful?

Then, today we remember how He was baptized in the Jordan.

Now, here's something to think about: why was Jesus baptized?

We often think of baptism being about the forgiveness of sins. We are washed in the waters and our sins are wiped away, but what sins did our perfect Lord need to be cleansed from? We know He was perfect, and so we have to consider what else baptism means. Considering His baptism, we can see that baptism is also about an initiation into a family of faith.

When a child is baptized in this church, she becomes a part of this body. We all promise to love and support her, to be there when she cries, and to pick her up when she falls. She becomes one of us, and so Jesus did as well.

I was baptized at Morningside Presbyterian Church in Atlanta. It's there in the Virginia Highlands Neighborhood. My mother was raised a Baptist and didn't think to have me baptized as an infant, so I was baptized there when I was seven.

My father sang in the choir.

My mother taught Sunday school.

A woman named Perky Daniels was the preacher, and a man named Jerry Black directed the choir.

You might have met Jerry Black. After serving Morningside Presbyterian Church, Jerry moved out here to the suburbs as we did. He was the Music Director at Covenant Presbyterian Church and then John Knox Presbyterian Church, and about twenty years ago, when my father had quadruple bypass heart surgery, Jerry Black went to visit him.

When my dad talks about it, if you watch his eyes, you can tell how much that visit meant to him. Those tears attest to the reality that there's a difference between hearing that you're loved and that you're being prayed for and having someone show up in your hospital room to do it.

It's the same as the difference between hearing a bell toll and touching it.

137

When we consider love, it's true that sometimes love needs to be "up close and personal."

Sometimes, love needs not just words, but flesh and blood.

Therefore, God takes flesh and blood, and, no, he didn't need to have any sins washed away, but He did need to be with us. He did need to identify with us and show us how deep is the love of God. Knowing all that changes things.

I was reminded of what all it changes when I read an article Fran Summerville sent me. Fran Summerville is a Stephen Minister here at our church. (She's also my fourth cousin. Isn't that amazing?) She sent me an article about the link between spiritual and physical wellness. The article came from *The Tennessean* (That's Nashville's newspaper.). In this article, Dr. Dale Matthews, an associate professor of medicine at the Georgetown University School of Medicine, says that "the mortality rate for people who attend religious services once a week or more is 25% lower in men and 35% lower in women than those who go to their house of worship less frequently."

I wish I had been able to cite that statistic Christmas Eve when all our "Christmas and Easter Only's" were here. "Doctors need to pay attention to these studies," Matthews said, "and to what's important to their patients. Some patients are just fed up. They're saying 'We're sick of being on the assembly line. I want somebody who pays attention to my personhood and even my soul, not just my liver or gall bladder.'" Can you relate to that? Of course you can because that's how we're treated most of the time. We call the office and end up talking to a machine. We want human contact, but all we get are emails. We go looking for real community and real connection, but it won't do anything for the true state of our souls unless there's some face-to-face and hand-in-hand, as there is here. That's Jesus, you see?

What was He born unto us for if not to make the love of God no longer distant, but tangible? Why did the wise men bring Him gifts if not to pay honor to the God of heaven come to earth? Why was He baptized in the Jordan by John if not to be a part of our lives and our families and to pay attention to our personhood and even our souls, not just our livers or gall bladders?

You see, if God was like the tolling of some distant far-off bell, in Jesus Christ, we touch His face as He touches ours.

That makes a difference, doesn't it?

However, we don't always get the chance to have that kind of contact because often our fast-paced lives prevent it. That's why I have a debate with myself whenever I check out at the grocery store. At the grocery store, there are some lines where you can check yourself out with the help of a computer and the other lines that actually have a person standing behind them. I was at Kroger years ago when those things were first introduced. That morning, I was in a hurry but not too much of a hurry. I thought about the self-checkout line, the one with the computer, because that line was empty. In the line with an actual cashier, there were a couple people already there, but I wasn't in too much of a hurry, so I went to the line with an actual Kroger employee. I remember that the man in front of me bought cigarettes, cat food, and a newspaper. I'm a nosy person. I was surprised that he started talking about a book he's reading with the woman at the register.

"It's a work of science fiction. It will probably take me six weeks to read it. You have to have a physics background to understand it. I have to sit and think awhile after I've only read five pages. Could you also give me change for a ten? Two fives, please," the man said.

She handed him the two fives, and he explained, "I'm taking my mother to get her hair done, and if I only have a ten-dollar bill, she'll want to tip the stylist the whole ten dollars."

"It looks like you got a haircut, too," the woman at the register said. "You look nice."

"Not too nice, though," he replied. "I lost another tooth, so I'm scared to smile because when I do, I look like I'm from Appalachia."

That was a mean thing to say about people from Appalachia, I thought, but I didn't say anything. I just kept eavesdropping.

"I'm getting a new tooth, though," he said.

The woman at the register looked pleased. "Come in here smiling once you do," the woman said. He covered his mouth, "I'm smiling now, but don't look; you may hear the theme song from 'Deliverance.'"

Then, he left.

The cashier looked to me. "I love seeing that man. He makes me smile every time I see him," the woman at the register said.

Profit drives stores to have those self-checkout lines. We like them, too, not just because they're convenient, for if they save a little money, the stores will save us a little money. Yet, there are more important things.

Self-checkout lines don't get jokes.

They can't smile.

You can't touch them.

They can't hold your hand as they pray.

They have no fingers to wipe away tears and no arms to hold you up when everything is falling apart.

If God were for you, like some far-off bell that you only ever heard tolling the hour, then know that Jesus Christ, Emmanuel, God with us, is God's love in flesh and blood that we can touch and see. Not only that, God in Jesus Christ is also the God who can touch and see us.

This truth demands something of me and you.

This Jerry Black, whom I mentioned before, the Music Director who visited my father in the hospital, died last week. His funeral was last Friday. Choir members from all the churches he served were invited to come and sing. Several members of our choir were there with them. His wife, Charlize, called and asked me to preach.

I had to think about that.

Life gets busy. Still, I called and told her I would, for how could I not show up in person to honor the man who showed up in person for my father? Not only that, who would I be, whom would I really represent, if in claiming to serve the God incarnate in flesh and blood who came down to earth to be with you and me, if I were too busy to show up myself?

The Lord didn't just say it.

He did not render those words of the Prophet Isaiah empty: "That I will give people in exchange for your life." No! He did it. He gave His own life, His own flesh and blood, for you and me. Then, how could we not show up in flesh and blood for each other?

Amen.

A Hometown Prophet
Nehemiah 8: 1-3, 5-6, 8-10 and Luke 4: 14-30

Preached on January 20, 2019

While completely inadvisable and totally ridiculous, there are times when congregations draw faint comparisons between their preachers and Jesus. Yet, that happened to me even before I began to serve a church back in my hometown.

Just weeks before we arrived in Columbia, Tennessee, where I would serve the First Presbyterian Church there, a woman named Wanda Turner found out my age. She called her friend Mrs. Cotham and asked her if she'd heard that their new pastor was only twenty-nine years old. Mrs. Cotham paused, then thoughtfully responded to her friend: "Well, Jesus was only thirty when he began his ministry, and, Wanda, let's just hope we don't crucify the poor boy before he turns thirty-two."

They didn't because I'm not Jesus.

Jesus was absolutely remarkable.

That great preacher William Sloan Coffin once wrote:

"Deserted by his disciples, in agony on the cross, barely thirty years old, Christ said, 'It is finished.' And thus ended the most complete life ever lived."

Jesus and I, we may both have been called to preach in the community we grew up in, but the comparison ends right there. For one thing, rather than try to throw me off a cliff, you have been far kinder to me than I deserve. You are too good to me, but the point I want to make here is that Jesus is different. You can't compare any preacher to Jesus, especially not the one standing before you now because Jesus offends preachers as much as anyone.

It's true.

Jesus is too honest to be polite all the time. He can be so blunt and plain-spoken as to cause offence. Not everyone talks about that, but it's clear from Scripture that Jesus was not all the time petting sheep and holding little children in his lap.

Jesus was tough.

He kicked over the tables set up in the Temple. He called the religious authorities of the time a bunch of "whitewashed tombs." Once, He even said

141

to his friend Peter, "Get behind me Satan! You are setting your mind not on divine things but on human things."

There's a great story from the writer Anne Lamott.

She tells this story of a women's Bible study, and they go around the circle prompted by the leader to answer the question: "Who has been like Jesus to you?" One told about her grandmother who lived next door to her growing up. Whenever she had a bad day at school, she'd go over there. She thought it must have been that somehow her grandmother could feel her coming because on those really bad days, she'd walk in, and her grandmother would be taking freshly baked chocolate cookies right out of the oven. "She was like Jesus to me," the woman said. Then another talked about her dedicated and faithful Golden Retriever, who lay by her side through her divorce. Around the circle they went. The last woman in the group had to speak. She had been thinking about the question deeply. As though this incident that took place when Jesus went back to his hometown were on her mind, she said, "This is a hard one to answer because I have to think about a person who has been so honest with me that I wanted to kill him."

Jesus can be not just comforting but offensive. That's because there are things that we do that He just won't tolerate. He stands not just beside us but along for the ride. So genuinely He wants what's best for us that He pushes us towards justice and righteousness and challenges us when we're only paying lip service to the Gospel. If He's the Word of God Incarnate, then facing Him demands that we face our sin and all the ways we fail to embody the love of God.

That's true, and it's not just true of Jesus. That's true of Scripture in general.

The event I read about from the Old Testament book of Nehemiah, where the Word of God was read, and it caused all the people to weep, may sounds strange, but if the Word of God is the truth, then it ought to cause us to wonder about how much truth we're really living.

Jesus, that Word of God Incarnate, tells us the truth as He did his hometown. Regardless of whether we're his mother, his brother, or the guys he used to play ball with, He gets down to the heart of things and says not what's polite, not what we want to hear, but what we need to hear. Picture the scene.

There He was back home.

They had heard about Him.

They knew who He was and what He could do.

They were probably hoping for what any of us would be hoping for: that this hometown boy would lift them up and out of their hardship, heal their wounds, and save them from affliction. Surely, their expectation was that He would bring a little prosperity to the regions, free them all from oppression, and make the changes that would benefit them and make their lives easier. They must have been asking, "Will you save us, Jesus? Surely, You are here to save us."

Jesus answers:

> The Spirit of the Lord is upon me,
>
> because he has anointed me to bring good news to the poor.
>
> He has sent me to proclaim release to the captives
>
> and recovery of sight to the blind,
>
> to let the oppressed go free,
>
> to proclaim the year of the Lord's favor.

This is a remarkable response, and in case what He was saying wasn't clear enough, He tells them exactly what He means:

> > The truth is, there were many widows in Israel at the time of Elijah, but who did God send him to? God sent him to save the out of town widow. And there were plenty of lepers among his own people at the time of the prophet Elisha, but who did God tell him to heal? God sent him to their enemy's general, Naaman the Syrian.

Of course, the citizens of His hometown want Him to help out His own; yet, He says He's been sent out to serve someone else's widows and their enemy's general.

How could that possibly go over well? Maybe now you're starting to understand why they wanted to throw Him off that cliff. It's as though you brought a pastor back to his hometown, and he walks in one Sunday morning and says, "It sure is good to be home, but I think I'll just go over to the Methodist church to preach today." Wouldn't that be something?

However, it's more than that even.

What Jesus is saying is far more than that because He wasn't saying that God was sending Him to the folks on the other side of town. He was saying that, "The Lord has sent me to serve the people on the other side of the wall you've been trying to build."

In Jesus Christ, it becomes so obvious that where we see difference: hometown and out of town, native and foreign, legal and illegal, us and them, God just sees His Children. But wait; there's more: He's calling us to see the same way.

This Sunday morning, we do one of the most amazing things that Presbyterians do; we will ordain and install the new leaders of our church, who are all of them called to be elders and deacons in their own hometown. As we do so, we must remember that while they were elected by you, they are called to serve in a way that honors our Lord and Savior Jesus Christ.

We might all think that they've been called to do what we want them to do and to follow our orders, but no. It is God who calls them, and it's God whom they must serve.

This God of ours, incarnate in Jesus Christ, calls them, not only to serve this church, but beyond these walls. He calls them not only to nurture the members of this church who have been here for years, but to welcome those who are walking in for the very first time, for all those who walk in these doors, whether they look like us or not, are God's children.

Officers of the church: your call is to bring honor, not only to those whom you know and love, but to those whom God loves. Therefore, you must be dedicated, not only to the survival of this church, but to the Gospel being proclaimed here and to the ends of the earth. Set your hearts on justice, that your ears be tuned to hear the cries of the poor and the oppressed. May your lives be lived, not only for us, but for the least and the lost. Remember, always, that you serve the Lord who served them all.

Amen.

When the Wine Gave Out
Song of Solomon 8: 6-7 and John 2: 1-11

Preached on January 27, 2019

Consider weddings.

When it comes to weddings, you plan, and you plan, yet something always seems to go wrong. At the wedding in Cana of Galilee it was the wine that gave out, but it's always something.

It's no wonder marriage is hard; just getting through the wedding is hard.

There's a great story I heard about a wedding back in Tennessee that took place in a Baptist church. The groom and his father walk out from the front of the church. During their processional, they somehow trip and fall into the baptismal font.

"I guess they got a two-for-one deal: married and baptized in the same ceremony," someone said. As a preacher, I'm proud to be a part of weddings. I'm proud to have had the honor of being a part of some of your weddings, but our own wasn't perfect. When planning our wedding, I only had one job: to secure a soloist. When a friend offered to sing at our wedding, I thought to myself, "That was easy." I just took him up on his offer, which took care of that, only I never thought to ask whether or not he could sing. The first time I heard him sing was when Sara and I were up there, just having made our vows. He was so bad we could hardly keep a straight face. My cousin asked if I had asked him to sing that way because I thought it would be funny, but I hadn't.

Weddings.

Something has to go wrong.

When I officiate, I get to stand right up front next to the groom as the bride walks down the aisle. I get to watch as he sees her walking toward him, which is a special thing to get to see, but there are other things that the preacher sees. Sometimes, I'm the person who knows the most about what's lurking below the surface of "the big day." Sometimes, I know where the bride's father is and why he's not there walking his daughter down the aisle. Sometimes, I know why the groom's grandmother can't stop crying. Sometimes, I know about the barely resolved crisis that caused the wedding to start five minutes late. Sometimes, I have an idea of the dysfunction that's been covered up and the pain that everyone has agreed to momentarily push aside. Sometimes, I know that this day is meant to be perfect, so I keep my mouth shut. If it can't be perfect, at least we can pretend it is, right?

Jesus' mother, on the other hand, she said something about it.

Did you notice that?

Mary, the mother of Jesus goes to her son and makes a big request that masquerades as a simple observation: "They have no wine."

At this wedding, we can imagine that no groom fell in the baptismal font, the soloist sang on key, the ceremony started on time, Daddy was there to walk the bride down the aisle, and grandma at least pretended to be happy, but the wine gave out. That's what went wrong with this wedding. Something always goes wrong. That's what went wrong at this one, and if you've ever been at a wedding reception when the drinks ran out, then you know that this would bring an embarrassing and abrupt end to the party.

No one wants that to happen, but no one wants anyone to know that something is going wrong either, so I can just imagine the mother of that bride discreetly rushing up to the steward in charge of the wine and loudly whispering or softly yelling: "Do something about this! Do anything! Go to the store! There must be one open. I think there's some Kool-Aid packets in my purse. Just mix them up with some water and add some vodka. Maybe no one will notice."

Do you know that feeling?

The wine has run out, but you don't want anyone to notice.

Something is going terribly wrong, but it's too hard to speak of it.

The appearance of perfection keeps you from asking for help.

All that denial is extremely dangerous because if we can't have a perfect wedding, if we can't "do perfect" even for one day, there's no chance of a perfect life, so we must learn to be vulnerable. We must learn to be vulnerable enough to ask for help when the wine gives out. Some people are better at that than others.

I grew up with a woman named Mandy Swartwood who's getting good at it.

Her parents are Bob and Judy Harper. On Facebook, I noticed that Mandy posted a picture of herself drinking out of a coffee mug that said on the side, "World's OK-est Mom."

I thought that was funny, and I told her so. She then pointed me toward an article from *The Today Show* website: "Moms, sometimes it's OK to be 'just OK.'"

146

It was a captivating article.

The journalist, Nicki Snyder, is a mother of three boys. Her oldest is 7, and she described one afternoon and evening with her children like this:

> Husband had to work late, so I had to pick up the boys from the babysitter. After arguing with one of the 7-year-olds on the sidewalk for what felt like 27 minutes about why his "pulled hamstring" (barely their bruise on his leg) should not be causing him to walk at the pace of a slug, we made it into the car. Everyone buckled, we survived the 6-minute drive home. Walked in the door, everyone is starrrrrrrving. Made 3 separate simple dinners for each of them because heaven forbid, they eat the same thing and I had about 10 minutes before someone over-dramatically "passed out" from hunger. Listened to one complain about why ketchup is too spicy and another yell at me for not signing his homework yet. Opened refrigerator door on 3-year old's head. Soothed screaming 3-year-old. Unpacked backpacks while they were eating, found nerf bullets and one shoe in one backpack. Decided not to ask why. Packed lunches for tomorrow. Listened to all 3 whine about tablets and Nintendo not being allowed at dinner table. Cleaned up dinner and dishes. Cleaned up the disastrous mess puppy decided to leave upstairs while boys were eating dinner. Stared at myself in the mirror and silently encouraged myself to breathe and just. keep. going. Finally changed out of my heels.

I can't relate to the heels part, but I do know this feeling.

Maybe you do, too.

It's like how you sanitized every pacifier that fell on the floor for your first child. For your second child you washed it off in the sink, but, for your third, you just stuck the thing right back in his mouth.

Of course, it's one thing to do that. It's another thing completely to let someone know about it. That's why my favorite quote to read at weddings comes from one of the great icons of Christianity, Ruth Bell Graham, who was married to Rev. Billy Graham. Someone once asked her if she had ever considered divorce. She said, "No, though I often considered murder."

How nice it is to know that even for her, the wine could go out.

How nice it is to know that even for her, there were hard days.

How nice it is to know that even for her, not every day was sunshine and roses.

The truth is that in the life of even the woman married to one of the greatest preachers in history, there was struggle and plenty of days when the best laid plans fell apart.

Of course, that's true for everyone, but we don't always talk about it.

Sometimes, we think, "Even if I'm not perfect, maybe I can appear that way." That's a true temptation, but I ask you:

Do the sick get healed by pretending to be well?

Do the broken get mended by pretending that they're not in pain?

Will the marriage get better so long as the couple suffers in silence?

Will everything be OK so long as no one knows?

You know the answer to these questions.

Divine guidance for our human condition in there in the Scripture lesson. Consider, why does Jesus turn this water into wine? Why does he save the wedding from disaster?

It's because His mother had the courage to tell Him.

It's because someone decided to stop covering up.

It's because she was bold to trust the One with grace enough to cover all our sins, power to heal the brokenness, and a voice to calm the storm.

He is the One who will come to our aid just as soon as we're ready to stop pretending that we don't need His help.

It might be hard to call out to Jesus.

It takes real courage to ask for help.

It might take everything we have to put up the white flag of surrender, but if we never tell Him that the wine has given out, then the One who can turn water to wine never has a chance to make a miracle happen.

Too often, we suffer in silence as the wine gives out.

We worry about making that appointment with the counselor.

We keep walking in pain afraid of the diagnosis.

We fail to lean on the everlasting arms of Christ our Savior, trying to stand up on our own two feet in the storms of this life, but we can't do it ourselves.

We can't even pull off the perfect wedding, so how could we possibly make it through life without some help?

When the wine gives out, call on Him and watch what He can do.

Amen.

Part 6: We all have a part to play

In the wake of the miracle of Christmas, we can't fail to notice the equally grace-filled miracle, that He calls us to play our part in the redemption of the world and the salvation of humankind.

This second miracle becomes all the more miraculous when you consider the headlines of 2018 and the very human events that they described.

In the following sermons, I saw the Gospel come alive in the disparaging pictures of Governor Northam, whose political career ended when pictures of him in blackface surfaced, a government shut-down, and in the realization that we are all unworthy of the grace that we have received.

Caught Red-Handed
Isaiah 6: 1-8 and Luke 5: 1-11

Preached on February 10, 2019

Today, we remember two beautiful and revealing accounts of how two faithful people, both pillars of our faith tradition, started out on their journeys to change the world as they knew it. From the book of Isaiah, we read about how this prophet was called. We learned again how he responded when he found himself standing in the presence of God.

In our second Scripture lesson, there's a similar account.

The Gospel of Luke told us the story of how the Apostle Peter, the rock that Christ's Church would be built upon, reacted when he realized one man aboard his ship was no ordinary man at all. Jesus told Peter, who was then called Simon:

> Put out into the deep water and let down your nets for a catch… When they had done so, they caught so many fish that their nets were beginning to break… They signaled their partners in the other boat to come and help them but when they came and filled both boats with fish, the boats began to sink.

How does Peter respond?

"He fell down at Jesus' knees, saying, 'Go away from me, Lord, for I am a sinful man.'"

This is the picture of repentance and humility.

It's a picture of complete vulnerability and confession.

His boats are sinking, his livelihood is disappearing before his eyes, and yet, "He fell down at Jesus' knees, saying, 'Go away from me Lord, for I am a sinful man.'"

Can you imagine?

This place that Peter finds himself in is a humbling place to be. To be in the presence of God and feel your sinfulness become fully revealed is a most humbling place to be. Do you know what that's like?

I do. I'm a parent.

Most recently, it was Lily who made it happen.

She's our nine-year-old daughter, our first born. She was with her basketball team, and because she's playing in the church league over there at Roswell Street Baptist Church, the coach was admonishing them to memorize their weekly Scripture verse, Hebrews 11: 1.

"Girls," he says, "I want you to have that verse memorized by next practice."

Lily says, "But we don't have a Bible at home."

Do you know how the other parents looked at me? I wanted to shield my face; "Go away from me, for I am a sinful man." Of course, we have a Bible. We have a hundred Bibles, but this moment last Monday reminded me of that place of humility in which Peter found himself. In light of our Scripture lessons for this morning, that experience made me wonder: what should we faithful people do when we are caught red-handed and our sin becomes obvious?

This morning we have two good examples of what to do from Scripture.

We can contrast these two examples with what we see on the news and in the paper, for out in the world today, we have at least one example of what not to do when we're caught red-handed. I'm talking about one Governor's yearbook photos this morning, of course, but before I name his name, let me first make the obvious statement that should anyone have a copy of the 1998 Marietta High School yearbook from my senior year, I'll pay top dollar if it never sees the light of day.

The thing about yearbooks is that even if you weren't pictured in yours wearing a racist Halloween costume like the Governor of Virginia was, the person you were then probably doesn't resemble the person you are now.

Whether you were a long-haired, rebellious, class clown like me with a distaste for respectable citizens and authority, or a medical student with a lack of empathy for his African-American neighbors like Governor Northam, I am sure there are parts of who you once were that you are now embarrassed of.

I am sure that there are things that you once did that you now regret.

There may be photographic evidence that you, too, are or once were "a sinful man" or woman who would feel ashamed to be in the presence of God because that's part of being young and because that's just part of the human condition.

I was reminded of that last weekend.

Last weekend I was out of town.

I hated to miss Youth Sunday.

I watched the service last Sunday afternoon, and I'm so proud of our youth group. I'm proud of Melissa Gilbert who was given the Jimmy Scarr Award for all the work she's done to make our youth group so strong. I missed being here because I've made a commitment to my college roommates.

Every year, we get together for one weekend in February, and if I miss it, then I'll be the one they talk about. Actually, none of us ever misses it. When we get together, it's as though, for that short time, nothing has changed.

Our friendship is timeless.

I was playing horseshoes with my old friend Sam, and I asked him, "Does being together like this make you miss college?" Sam said, "I miss all of us having the freedom to spend so much time together, but I don't miss being as stupid as we were then." Neither do I; however, I still make mistakes. I'm human, and you are, too, so we all need to look to Peter and Isaiah to see what it is that we should do when we're caught red-handed.

We need their guidance to know what we should do when the people we aspire to be and the decisions we've made don't match up, the ghosts of the past rise up to haunt us, and the skeletons won't stay in the closet. We need their example to know what we should do when Jesus comes to see us, and we are ashamed to stand in His presence.

What should we do then?

Look to Isaiah.

When he was in God's presence and the doorways shook and the house of God filled with smoke, he didn't dare double down on his lie or make up excuses. Instead, he was bold to say, "Woe is me! I am lost, for I am a man of unclean lips, and I live among a people of unclean lips."

Likewise, look to Peter.

He didn't deny that he was the man in the hood. He didn't pretend he didn't recognize himself in the picture. Rather, he fell down at Jesus' knees, saying, "Go away from me, Lord, for I am a sinful man."

Do you know how faithful you have to be to do something like that?

Do you know how courageous you have to be to do something like that?

In our world today, too many see confession as failure.

Too many see needing forgiveness as weakness, only consider the reality of human imperfection. As imperfect people, how are we ever to stand before God as we truly are if we deal with being caught by pretending that we aren't guilty?

I think about my grandfather.

My grandfather was bold to tell me that even way out in the wilderness of the Caw Caw Swamp where he grew up, the lines of race were drawn so severely that when a group of men came to work at his family's farm, the white workers were welcomed into the house to eat in the kitchen, while the African American men were served lunch on the back steps of the house.

He once told me, "As a young adult, I resented everything that Martin Luther King, Jr. said, but he saved us from ourselves, Joe; he saved us from ourselves."

If only we, too, can be bold enough to fall at His feet when we've been caught red-handed, rather than double down on the lie that we've been telling.

If only we, too, can be bold enough to confess our sins and name them out loud, rather than pretend that we're not guilty.

If only we, too, can say, "I am a sinful man," rather than say, "The man in the picture, he's not me."

I know it's hard.

Of course, it's hard.

Sometimes, it seems as though the world doesn't believe in forgiveness anymore. So often, it seems as though the world is running short on grace because the world will take your vulnerability and will post it on the headlines for everyone to see.

Still, I tell you this: that's not so with Jesus.

In me, there's unworthiness, but in Him, there's grace.

In me, there's sin, but in Him, there's forgiveness.

In me, there's regret, but in Him, there's the invitation to live a new life.

That's what I want.

Is that what you want?

Of course, it is. It's not only the thing that we want, it's the thing that the world needs, so the Lord took that Peter, picked him as one of His disciples, and said to him and his friends, "Do not be afraid; from now on you will be catching people."

At first, that must have sounded funny. They must have asked among themselves, "Catching people? I don't know about you, but once I catch a fish, I gut it then I fry it." That doesn't sound so good to me, either, so listen

156

to this; imagine, instead, that what Jesus means here is that we are a people, drowning under water, and He called on Peter to start pulling some people out.

A Bible scholar named Gay L. Byron said that's what Jesus is really getting after here. I believe she's right because I know that Jesus isn't like the media who is prone to capitalize on weakness in order to sell more papers. He's not interested in that, and we know He's not because we've heard it said, "God did not send the son into the world to condemn the world, but in order that the world might be saved through him."

Do you know that one?

That's a good one to memorize, but you might not have a Bible at home, so write it down before you leave today.

My poor Lily.

Ray Fountain posted on Facebook the other day, "It's dangerous to live with a preacher because anything you do might be used as a sermon illustration." That's true. I'm always looking for sermon illustrations. In fact, I can't help but see them.

Everything that I see in this world is either proving to me that God is at work or that something has to change. Today, what I know has to change are you and I. You and I, sinful men and women who have fallen at the feet of Jesus and found forgiveness, must now get to work pulling up drowning people. We are called to a vocation of fishing for people, pulling up those who are drowning in the past by letting them know that a past of racism need not result in a future of it. We must let them know that a past of ignorance, failures, or mistakes are not a Scarlet Letter ensuring condemnation, but the proof that what Christ offers is exactly what we need.

We must go fishing.

We must go fishing for people so that all those who are drowning in shame and regret or the fear of condemnation might come up for air to feel the Holy Spirit blow, the warm rays of forgiveness and acceptance that shine forth from the Son of God, and the brother and sisterhood of all people regardless of race, creed, nationality, orientation, gender, or language.

Every one of us is red-handed, but to every one of us, He issues this call: go and fish for people, letting them know that we're just a bunch of forgiven sinners, and they can be, too.

Amen.

From Whom All Blessings Flow
Jeremiah 17: 5-10 and Luke 6: 17-26

Preached on February 17, 2019

Isn't it amazing how things can change?

Our two Scripture lessons deal with change.

Jeremiah reminds us that those who put their trust in their own strength are cursed. Why? It's because human bodies change, and human strength may be here one day but gone the next. Jesus reminds us of the same thing, saying that those who are blessed now will not be forever, and those who are poor today may not be tomorrow, for no one but God can completely control the way things are. That's more obvious sometimes than others.

Last Tuesday, it was obvious.

That's because last Tuesday, I got caught in the rain, and it became obvious how things change and how little control I have over them. Do you remember how much it rained last Tuesday? Back in Tennessee, they'd call it a gully washer.

In South Georgia, they call it a frog strangler.

Justis Brogan and I were walking back from lunch at Stockyard: that place with the really good hamburgers on the Square. Neither of us had an umbrella or anything. We just ran to take cover. The first place safe to stand was under an awning at Jane Pratt's office. Jane Pratt works right on the corner there, and she has great big windows in front of her office. She saw us standing out there looking pathetic. She invited us in and gave us both plastic bags.

That was the best she could do, but at least our perms wouldn't go flat.

Jane was very helpful and kind, only there wasn't really anything she could do. It was raining too hard, and sometimes, that's how it is. We don't always have control over these things. One might be dry one minute but wet the next.

We don't have control over all our blessings or our woes.

"Blessed are you who are poor, for yours is the kingdom of God," is what Jesus said. It only makes sense to say that the poor are blessed. We all must recognize that the way things are now isn't how they'll always be. We don't always recognize that.

Instead, we tend to take blessings for granted and feel stuck in our woes.

Natalie Foster was nearby working the car rider line for our preschool when Justis and I ran up soaking wet. Natalie notices every time I go out to lunch because she never gets to. She works at our preschool as their Assistant Director, so she has to eat lunch here. Her lunch probably always gets sneezed on by preschoolers, so she looked at me all wet, like a drowned rat and said, "You might expect me to feel sorry for you, but I don't."

I mean we were soaked.

I was so wet, but Natalie Foster said, "Ate lunch out again, I see. Even if you're all wet, that's still better than some people's lunch hour."

I thought I had it pretty bad, but sometimes you don't know how good you have it. It's easy to take your blessings for granted and to get stuck in your woes. That's true.

There have been plenty of times when I was ignorant as to just how good I have it. I learned over lunch that Justis works at the airport. That means he has a forty-five-minute commute. I can ride my bike back and forth from our house to here seven or eight times in the amount of time it takes him to get to work once. Sometimes, you don't know how good you have it until you look around and see what it's like for other people.

That's one of the things that happened to me when we went to Mexico on a mission trip with this church back when I was in high school. I'd gone my whole life thinking that I was born into a middle class, average American family. Every day of my life, we had two cars in the garage, running water, heat in the winter, and AC in the summer. My biggest problem was teenage acne, and I'd gone my whole life thinking those things made me average.

In Mexico, I went to a neighborhood that made me realize just how lucky I was.

To get water in that neighborhood we went to, not unlike the neighborhood in Mexico where we go and build houses now, we walked to the store to buy it. That's what the people in that neighborhood did every day without running water. This act of buying water at the store wasn't like us buying fancy drinking water in twelve packs at Kroger. We buy water at the store by choice. They have to buy water at the store because clean drinking water piped into the house is a luxury not available to all God's children.

One of the many problems with our society today isn't just that some have and others have not. It's also that many of us who have are blind to how good we have it.

159

The problem with that can be obvious after watching the news.

The government shut down recently. It may be shutting down again, and maybe that has to happen every now and then. Maybe it's too much to ask that politicians deal with controversy in a decent and civil manner, but it's not too much to ask that wealthy politicians be empathetic to those government employees who live paycheck to paycheck.

"Let them take out loans," someone said. That sounds too much like Marie Antoinette saying, "Let them eat cake." What they don't realize is that at any second, everything could change. They could end up in the same boat with those employees who are losing their homes. In our world today, many wealthy people suffer from a certain kind of arrogance and ignorance.

Some suffer from an absence of empathy, unable to understand what it's like when you're working 9 to 5. Dolly Parton understood:

"Tumble out of bed and stumble in the kitchen

Pour myself a cup of ambition."

You know that song?

It's catchy, but it's also pretty radical.

"It's a rich man's game no matter what they call it

And you spend your life putting money in his wallet."

Then, she keeps going:

In the same boat with a lot of your friends

Waitin' for the day when your ship'll come in

And the tide's gonna turn

And it's gonna roll your way.

That sounds like the Beatitudes. That sounds like the whole Gospel of Luke, as a matter of fact. Mary sang about it in the Magnificat way back in Luke chapter 1:

He has scattered the proud in the thoughts of their hearts.

He has brought down the powerful from their thrones,

And lifted up the lowly;

He has filled the hungry with good things,

And sent the rich away empty.

160

Throughout this whole book of Luke runs the theme that Dolly sang about:

"But the tide's gonna turn

And it's all gonna roll your way."

Why? It's because God's in charge. Jesus said,

> Blessed are you who are poor for yours is the kingdom of heaven.

> Blessed are you who are hungry now, for you will be filled.

> Blessed are you who weep now, for you will laugh.

> Blessed are you when people hate you, for surely your reward is great in heaven.

In the Gospel of Luke, He said these things to a crowd assembled on a level place, not on a mountain, but in a place where all people sat on one level. No one was higher than the other. There was no partiality. There was no Jew or Gentile, no slave or free. Instead, there was just one people sitting before the Son of God hearing the truth. They heard the truth that those who have nothing now have everything to gain, but those who have everything now have everything to lose.

"Woe to you who are rich, for you have received your consolation.

Woe to you who are full now, for you will be hungry.

Woe to you who are laughing now, for you will mourn and weep."

These are harsh words for those of us who go out to lunch on the Square every day of the week to eat ten-dollar hamburgers. These are harsh words for most all of us, but they're important to hear. They are important to hear because too many of us have forgotten that we're only doing just fine because it hasn't started raining. Then, once the rain has started, we forgot how to see rain for the blessing that it is, and we're too slow to give thanks to God Who is the source of it.

Rev. Joe Brice, the Sage of Paulding County, told me that last year on Father's Day, his son called him up, and he said, "Dad, since it's Father's Day, I'm wanting for us all to come over to your house, so you can cook us anything that we want, and, while you're at the store buying the food, why don't you pick yourself out a card from all of us. Something real nice."

C.S. Lewis once wrote that we're all like Joe's kids.

Our Father in Heaven gave us ten dollars so we could go to the store to buy Him a birthday present, but we spent nine on ourselves and only one dollar on the present. That's if we're tithing.

161

The truth is that we don't know how good we have it, and we're ignorant as to where our blessings came from, as though wealth and blessings just fell from the sky. What's more entitled than that?

"Blessed are the poor," Jesus said, but "Woe to you who are rich, for you have received your consolation" and you never even stopped to thank God for it.

Jeremiah said it like this:

> Blessed are those who trust in the Lord.
>
> They shall be like a tree planted by water, sending out its roots by the stream.
>
> It shall not fear when heat comes, and its leaves will stay green;
>
> In the year of drought, it is not anxious.

Why? It's because they know from whom all blessings flow.

Let us live as those who daily thank the Source of all our blessings, who put our trust in the Lord, and who daily live caring for our brothers and sisters who have less, knowing that any minute we could be in the same boat with them.

Amen.

It's Not Fair
Genesis 45: 3-11 and Luke 6: 27-38
Preached on February 24, 2019

You know what's not fair? I'll tell you what's not fair. It's not fair that some people never get what they deserve, and it's not fair that Jesus tells us to keep being nice to them anyway.

It's not fair.

For as long as I've lived such injustice has burned me up.

It began with the unearned attention lavished upon my cute little sister.

There are some big brothers and big sisters in the congregation this morning who know exactly what I'm talking about. I'm just going to say it. It's not fair.

It's just not fair how everyone thinks they're so cute.

I remember when my dad came home with a camcorder. It was the big kind, and by the time this technology was inexpensive enough for him to buy one, I was an awkward pre-teen who wanted to hide from the camera, while my sister was little and really cute, with curly, red hair. Today, if you watch our family's old home movies, it's basically just one long tap dance routine featuring Elizabeth Evans.

Everyone thinks little sisters are so cute.

It's not fair.

You know what else isn't fair? Not only do little brothers and sisters get all the attention, they also get to do everything sooner. Some big sister here remembers how her little sister got her ears pierced sooner than she did. Some big brother resents how his little sister didn't have to wait as long to get a cell phone. I remember how I wanted to go see a PG movie, *Indiana Jones and the Temple of Doom*. It had bad words in it, so my parents said I had to wait to see it until I was twelve. Do you know when my little sister got to see it? The day I turned twelve and she was eight because my mom couldn't take us to two separate movies.

It's just not fair, and it would burn me up. The injustice of it all would drive me crazy! Maybe you can imagine what my mom would say: "Life's not fair, Joe."

That's what she would say, and believe it or not, that didn't make me feel any better.

For generations this has been the case.

The youngest gets special treatment.

The consolation from Scripture for those of us who are older siblings this morning is twofold:

> 1. No matter how much favoritism our little brothers and sisters received; it probably wasn't as much as the favoritism little Joseph received from his father Jacob in the book of Genesis.

> 2. In the book of Genesis, we get to see this favored little brother get what he deserves.

That's right. I said it, and if you never had the urge to sell your little brother into slavery, then clearly your sibling experience was not the same as mine.

Little Joseph was their father's favorite, and old Jacob didn't even hide this fact. In fact, he broadcast it for everyone to see. You've heard about Joseph's multi-colored coat that his daddy gave him. If you look that up in our new Bibles, which are the New Revised Standard Version, you'll see that scholars now believe, based on better translations of the ancient scrolls, that the special robe was not multi-colored but long-sleeved. This detail may not seem so important until you think about how much work people do in short sleeves compared to long sleeves.

It's as though all the sons of Jacob were lined up as a work crew. Jacob, their father, handed all the brothers a shovel, but gave to young Joseph the clipboard. Do you know what I'm talking about? It gets worse. It gets much worse!

Joseph dreamed. Young Joseph, at the age of seventeen, told his brothers:

"Listen to this dream that I dreamed. There we were, binding sheaves in the field.

Suddenly my sheaf rose and stood upright; then your sheaves gathered around it and bowed down to my sheaf."

How do you think his brothers responded to that?

Scripture tells us that "they hated him even more because of his dreams," but after that one, he had another dream involving eleven stars bowing down to Joseph, center of the universe. Then, his brothers decided to get rid of him.

They were all out watching the flock. Jacob sent Joseph out there to check on them (Of course, he did). When they saw him coming, they decided to kill him, throw him into a pit, and tell their father that a wild animal had devoured him. Fortunately, Reuben spoke up: "Let's just throw him in the pit and teach him a lesson."

Before Reuben could do all that, Judah, another brother, saw a caravan of Ishmaelites coming from Gilead with their camels, on their way down to Egypt. They pulled Joseph up from the pit and sold him to the Ishmaelites for twenty pieces of silver. From this point, the story gets worse, of course. It all gets worse for Joseph before it gets better.

Once the Ishmaelites make it to Egypt, Joseph is sold to Potiphar, whose wife tries to seduce him and then accuses him of forcing himself upon her after he refuses. Despite the baseless nature of the accusations, like many powerless people, he's thrown into prison. Can you imagine how nasty that prison must have been?

There was no TV for him to watch.

There were no weights for him to lift.

I can just imagine Joseph spending all his time drawing pictures on the cell wall of all the horrible things he would do to his brothers if he ever got back home.

Vengeance gives us something to occupy our minds, but it rots our souls, so it's a good thing his new cell mates started dreaming. At this point in the last service, while I was telling this story, I noticed that a couple men on the back row started dreaming, too.

This is a long story, I know, but we have to know it.

Knowing and understanding this story will change our lives, so let me keep going.

Folks began to seek Joseph out, and eventually, his ability to interpret dreams reached Pharaoh. Pharaoh kept having these bad dreams, so he sought out the young man locked up in prison. Pharaoh dreamed that he was standing on the bank of the Nile. Seven cows, fat and sleek, came up out of the Nile and fed in the reed grass. Then seven other cows came up after them, poor, very ugly, and thin. The thin and ugly cows ate up the first seven fat cows, but when they had eaten them, no one would have known that they had done so, for they were still as ugly as before. Joseph said to Pharaoh:

This is what your dream means.

There will come seven years of great plenty throughout all the land of Egypt. But after them there will rise seven years of famine, and all the plenty will be forgotten in the land of Egypt; the famine will consume the land. The plenty will no longer be known.

This is a bad dream, but fortunately, Joseph also has in mind a solution. He says to Pharaoh:

"So, during the years of plenty, let Pharaoh select a man who is discerning and wise and set him over the land of Egypt, that he might take one fifth of the produce of the land during the seven plenteous years. That food shall be a reserve for the land against the seven years of famine." Pharaoh thinks this is a good idea, and so he said to Joseph: "Since God has shown you all this, I will set you over the land of Egypt to do it."

Imagine that! Instantly he goes from the jail cell to the corner office.

He goes from plotting revenge to saving an empire from famine.

In one moment, he's consumed with his bad luck, but in the next, he's amazed by his good fortune, only he's also faced with the difficult reality that none of it ever would have happened had his brothers not sold him to the Ishmaelites in the first place.

What do you do with that?

What do any of us do with the reality that, despite whatever unfairness we've faced, still we receive God's blessing?

What do we do with the truth that, even when we walk through the valley of the shadow of death, we will fear no evil?

How, then, will we treat our enemies and all those who have wronged us, once we realize that in all things, God has done wonderful things for us and for our salvation?

Joseph is about to find out what he'll do, for while Joseph goes from slave to prisoner, then to high office in the Empire, life for his brothers has been difficult. The first two of those seven years of famine have come, and the only nation anywhere who has any food is Egypt. In desperation, the brothers make their way to Egypt and bow their heads before Pharaoh's right-hand man. In this moment, Joseph's dream that his brothers would bow down before him like sheaves in the field or stars in the sky comes true.

What will Joseph do?

What will he do when his brothers, once so much bigger, now bow before him?

What do any of us do to those who have hurt us, considering how God provides us, not with just punishment, but with a cup of blessing?

Certainly, Joseph doesn't kill them.

How could he?

That's what they expect, but that's not what Joseph could possibly do, for God's love has changed things. God's love has changed the definition of fairness for evermore, so Joseph says,

> God sent me before you to preserve for you a remnant on earth.
>
> It was not you who sent me here, but God;
>
> he has made me a father to Pharaoh, and lord of all his house and ruler over all the land of Egypt.

Do you see what happened?

All our lives, we've been demanding fairness, so we naturally want to see the bad guys punished and the bullies get a return on the abuse they've dished out. We might naturally say that it's not fair that these brothers, who threw him into a pit, aren't thrown into a jail cell. We might say that it's not fair that these brothers, who sold him into slavery, aren't sold into slavery themselves. We might say that it's not fair and that these brothers deserve exactly what they subjected Joseph to, namely, many long days lived away from their family, forced to survive in a foreign land, followed by long, dark nights wondering if they'll ever make it back home again or if they'll even survive until the next day.

However, for Joseph, in all of that suffering, some other power was at work, some other hand was making a way by placing Joseph in a seat of power that he might not only save himself, but his entire family. Based on human definitions of fairness, these brothers deserve punishment, but in all those long years leading up to this moment, Joseph learned that there's another definition of fairness at work in our lives.

God's grace, which defines us, isn't what we call fair.

My mother was right. Life isn't fair, and we Christians know it, for instead of punishment for our sins, what do we receive from God?

Forgiveness.

Rather than judgement, we receive grace.

God's fairness isn't like our fairness, for God's grace isn't fair.

God's grace takes the sin of jealous brothers and saves them from themselves. It takes broken men and women and ends their suffering by putting them back together. God takes us, in all our depravity, and provides us with life and love and light. God's idea of fairness is embodied in Christ upon the cross who looked down on those who put Him there and said, "Forgive them, for they know not what they do." That's why we can't be surprised that He says, "Love your enemies," for God hasn't stopped loving them any more than God has stopped loving us. Our God "is kind to the ungrateful and the wicked," and we must be merciful, just as our Father is merciful to us. It's so easy to say, "that's not fair," but grace isn't fair. Once we've received it, we must not nullify it by failing to pass it on.

Amen.

Part 7: From Ash Wednesday to Easter

Ash Wednesday, while ancient, in a new tradition for many. In the following sermons, marked by the ashes of our own sin, we journey to the cross and beyond it.

What Will We Leave Behind?
Isaiah 58: 1-8
Preached on Ash Wednesday, March 6, 2019

As Rev. Joe Brice said at the beginning of this service, you've all been given paper crosses. On those crosses, we are all invited to write something. We're all invited to write either what we are going to give up for Lent or what spiritual practice we're going to take on.

We'll set these crosses with our Lenten discipline written on them on top of the communion table, dedicating them to God, just before we receive the ashes on our foreheads.

While you are welcome to take something on, I encourage you to give something up as a spiritual discipline because I'll bet you have too much already.

That might not be true.

Maybe you don't have nearly enough or maybe you don't have nearly enough to do, and you need more, but I doubt that's the case. My suggestion to you and to myself is that you use that little paper cross as an opportunity to do a little bit of spiritual KonMari.

Do you know what KonMari is? (I might be saying it wrong.)

KonMari is something that people are doing now. It's new, but a lot of people are into it. It's all based on the book titled, *The Life-Changing Magic of Tidying Up.* The book is a bestseller. There's even a show on *Netflix* about it. In fact, because of this KonMari, so many people are tidying up their homes and getting rid of their junk that the Salvation Army and other thrift shops claim they're being over-run with donations from people whose lives are being changed because of the *Life-Changing Magic of Tidying Up.*

The author of the book is a Japanese woman named Marie Kondo. I read a little bit about her, and what got my attention was a line a journalist used. She wrote, Marie Kondo "doesn't want merely to reorganize your closet. She wants to transform your soul."[12]

Now, how could that happen and what does this have to do with Lent?

---

[12] Kathryn Reklis, "What makes KonMari different," *The Christian Century,* February 27, 2019, 44.

Well, the commonality struck me when I read about a man who couldn't part with an old mailbox. He thought it might come in handy someday, but Marie Kondo was there with him, trying to help him part with some of his stuff. She gently asked, "So you have decided that this is an object you want to bring into your future?"

It was a mailbox.

You can imagine that when she helped the man see the mailbox in the context of taking it into his future, the choice became easier to make. Immediately, the man relaxes. "No," he says, "When you put it that way, I definitely don't need this in my future."

The question I have now is: how much junk are we carrying with us into ours?

Ash Wednesday gives us a unique spiritual opportunity. Tonight, we are given permission to take an inventory of all our habits, goods, patterns, and relationships. Ash Wednesday invites us to examine what we are walking around burdened by.

We are asked to take a look at things like social media, smoking, drinking too much, gossiping, complaining, or eating fried foods to ask the question: is this something I want to carry with me into my future?

If the answer is "no," then give it up. Try going without it for these forty days of Lent, for you see, there's more to Lent than doing without chocolate.

Do you think God really cares about chocolate?

From Isaiah we read,

"Is such the fast that I choose?

To bow down the head like a bulrush, and to lie in sackcloth and ashes?"

What good does that really do for you or anyone else?

Don't let Lent be just doing without something until Easter. Lent can be more than that, and it doesn't even have to be any harder.

For the past several years, I've been ashamed to admit that I've only given up milk in my coffee.

That hasn't sounded like much to a lot of my more hard-core Christian friends, some of whom have given up something like flour, so one Lent, in an effort to truly observe Lent, I gave up red meat. It was really hard, which says something about my diet, but is that what the Lord requires?

172

Is not what the Lord requires exactly what we read in Isaiah, "To loose the bonds of injustice, to undo the thongs of the yoke?"

If that's the case, then why would we shoulder such a heavy load of hardship when what the Lord wants us to have is freedom?

Rather than deprive ourselves for the sake of hardship, it is better to ask ourselves, "What might we leave behind to have a better future and a closer walk with our neighbor and our God?"

What might we lay down in order to carry a lighter load?

What habit might we drop to have a more joyous existence?

That's what Lent is about. On the other hand, I remember so well one season of baseball. A teammate had been fasting. It was a complete fast. He hadn't had anything to eat all day. He was so hungry that you could see it in his face.

Then, it started raining, which meant that we had to cover up the infield with tarps. The two of us were working on the pitcher's mound, and I said, "Todd, what about that stake?"

He said, "Real nice, Joe. Here I am starving, and you ask me about a steak." I said, "Not steak. Stake. The stake by your foot to secure the tarp."

"Look," the Prophet said, "You fast only to quarrel and to fight and to strike with a wicked fist. Such fasting as you do today will not make your voice heard on high."

If all you do is argue about politics, if you can't understand how anyone could ever think that way, and if you constantly wonder what's the matter with young people, or old people, white people, or democrats, then give up watching the news on that same channel you've always watched where they never say anything that you don't already agree with.

For Lent, give up reading the columns in the paper that tell you just what you want to hear.

Abstain from the radio show that fuels your self-righteousness and tells you how those people you disagree with are a bunch of idiots.

If you were to leave partisanship behind this Lent, might you be a happier person, and might our country be better off?

There is so much junk that we carry that does us far more harm than good, and that's the kind of sacrifice that God is after. God's not after suffering, hardship for the sake of hardship, weeping or gnashing of teeth. No. What God wants of us this Lent is what God always wants: to loose the bonds that are suffocating His people, to undo the heavy yoke that is holding us down,

173

and to set us free from all these habits that confine us to death and destruction.

We must always remember that God doesn't want us punished. Instead, God wants us redeemed, but that can be hard to remember, which is why what Bebe Adams said last Sunday morning is so important to me.

You might remember last Sunday morning when he was up there during the worship service, not doing anything that on the surface seems so extraordinary. He was just leading us in reciting the Apostles' Creed, but before doing so, he said,

> The Apostles' Creed that is in the bulletin this morning is one of eleven that are found in our Book of Confessions. A lot of times, the word confession indicates an admission of guilt for some sort of wrongdoing. We're taught by that book that our confession is for us to admit to something that everyone in this room believes in.

That's what he said.

A lot of times, confession is an admission of guilt, just like how a lot of the time people think of Lent as penance for what they feel guilty for, but Bebe said that to confess is also to admit to something that everyone believes in. In saying that, what hit me so hard is that to properly confess our sins, we have to believe in God's love.

To confess that we've done wrong, we must first confess that we believe in a God who won't strike us down but will renew us.

To observe this season of Lent the right way, we must be sure that we know who this God is, so listen to me when I tell you that Lent is about giving something up, but not to punish yourself. That's not what God ever wants. All God ever wants for us, His children, is that we might have a brighter future unencumbered by the habits that are holding us back from joy.

So often, we're afraid to even think about such things.

Someone who loves us finally gets the courage to mention the problem, forces us to face the music, or helps us see our bad habits for what they are, but we can't hear them because we don't see our defects as things that are hurting us. We have to push their words away because we see bad habits as things that will disqualify us from being loved.

You hold up a mirror, and all some people see are the wrinkles, and then they conclude that they're flawed.

174

You can talk to someone about harmful patterns, but until they know how much you love them, they'll see their harmful patterns as what defines them, not as what holds them back.

We all make mistakes, and we all have things we ought to leave behind, but too many of us believe that we are mistakes. Should that be the case, before you give something up, get to know who God really is.

It's tempting to think about the ashes that either Joe or I will put on your forehead as you would a big, red X in a factory's conveyer line. Don't think of it as a stamp that marks you as defective and to be rejected because it's not an X that we'll put on your head. It's a cross.

It's not an X. It's a cross because God doesn't want you condemned or rejected, shamed or abused. Our God died on the cross to display His love for you and me, so give something up for Lent, only, in doing so, be not guilt-ridden but renewed, not condemned but set free.

Amen.

And the Devil Said
Deuteronomy 26: 1-11 and Luke 4: 1-13
Preached on March 10, 2019

There's something very special about being in a church like this one. Personally, there's something very special about returning to the church where I grew up. Our church has changed, of course, since I was a kid, but there are parts of this church that still smell the same.

I don't mean to say that we have a mold or mildew problem.

What I mean is that there's something about the stairwell that leads down to the room we call Track 25 where our kids have their Sunday school. That stairwell smells exactly the same way it did when I was a kid going down to have Sunday school in that same room, and every time I walk down those stairs I am overcome by the power of memory.

When some of you walk into our historic Sanctuary, I imagine that the same thing happens. Memories come rushing back. Maybe you see your mother singing in the choir or your father serving communion. You might remember your children, now grown, being baptized, or how you felt to walk down the aisle on your wedding day. What I'm talking about is a bit like time travel, but it really happens. By such flashbacks, we know that the words of Faulkner are true: the past isn't gone; it isn't even past.

Such an understanding of the past, strange as it may seem, embodies the Hebrew word for "remember." You know that when words are translated from one language to another, sometimes part of the true essence of the words gets lost. That's just the way it is with language; any language. Were we to translate a phrase like, "Well, bless your heart" into Spanish, a literal translation wouldn't do it justice.

Likewise, when Jesus was at the table with His disciples the first time, He broke the bread and poured the wine, thereby serving the first communion, He said, "Do this in remembrance of me." We have to be careful about our English translation because by saying that, He didn't mean, "When you do these 2,000 years from now, remember Me, think of Me, or don't forget my name." Instead, what He meant was, "When you do this 2,000 years or 10,000 years from now, it's a chance for you to recognize that I am present with you still."

That's a different thing.

It's a bit of a time collapse, only when God is eternal, what is time anyway? Our religion is full of these rituals that connect the great, historic, deeds of God with our present.

That's what's happening in our first Scripture lesson.

This is one of my favorite passages in the whole Bible: Deuteronomy 26: 1-11. Deuteronomy can be boring, but Jesus quotes this book often, so we are wise to pay attention to it. In the passage that I read, the people bring forth their offerings, their first fruits, but once they've done it, they say something. They participate in a short liturgy:

A wandering Aramean was my ancestor, they said.

He went down into Egypt and lived there as an alien,

few in number and there he became a great nation,

mighty and populous.

That was all a historically accurate statement, only then they said:

"When the Egyptians treated us harshly" (that wasn't technically true),

"And afflicted us" (the people who said it hadn't technically been afflicted),

"By imposing hard labor on us" (not technically true either because the people who said these words had never been in Egypt).

The personal pronoun "us" is, in a sense, a fabrication, for everyone who had personally been enslaved in Egypt by the time Deuteronomy was written or this liturgy would have been used was already dead. Still, they say:

When the Egyptians treated us harshly and afflicted us,

by imposing hard labor on us,

we cried to the Lord, the God of our ancestors;

the Lord heard our voice and saw our affliction,

our toil and our oppression.

While none of this is historically accurate (for remember back in Sunday school when you learned that before anyone entered the Promised Land where this liturgy was used, the generation who knew slavery in Egypt had to die), what Deuteronomy calls each consecutive generation to do is to make their history present again. Deuteronomy calls each generation to make the suffering of their ancestors real once more. This liturgy calls each generation, ours included, to make the mighty power of God who liberates people, not a memory, but a present reality possible now as it was then.

177

If any of that sounds strange, know that this isn't a strange, new idea.

That's what happens in here all the time.

We don't remember Jesus as historical fact. Instead, we evoke His memory and are reminded that not only did He live among us, he still does. We don't just think about the mighty deeds of God, studying them like we do ancient history. When we remember, the memory becomes a current reality.

Lent is the same.

We give something up, chocolate maybe, but Lent's not a diet. It's more than that. When we observe a Lenten discipline, we join Jesus on His journey through the desert, or we remember that He joins us on ours.

This is important.

It's important to know that Jesus is with us, for Satan is not confined to ancient history either. He also whispers in our ears today. "Command this stone to become bread," the devil said to Jesus, only he didn't just say that to Jesus, he says that to us.

"Eat, drink, and be merry," he urged. I ask you, could there be a more persistent temptation in our 21st Century than this? Constantly, we, too, are told to drink because "It's five o'clock somewhere," or to eat because "You're not you when you're hungry." We are so constantly bombarded by the voice of temptation urging us to satisfy our cravings, as though satisfying physical desire could bring true satisfaction.

It cannot.

Scripture and the hymns tell us that again and again. There's a hymn that I love, but it's probably one that no one but me likes to sing. It's called "God Marked a Line and Told the Sea." It's so bad that they left it out of our new hymnals, which says something because they put a lot of hymns that only a preacher could love in there. In this hymn, the 5th stanza goes like this:

> We are not free when we're confined,
>
> to every whish that sweeps the mind,
>
> But free when freely we accept,
>
> the sacred bounds that must be kept.

You hear that? I won't sing it, and I won't ask you to, but I want you to know it because these words are true. The devil's knocking on your door, day in and day out, saying: "Command this stone to become a loaf of bread."

"Come on," he says, "just use that credit card. You can pay for it later."

"Have a bite. It's delicious. Maybe it's bad for you but live a little."

Now I'm not trying to advocate for suffering through Lent or denying yourself for the sake of denying. My grandmother was on a diet pretty much for her entire life. Tab was all she'd drink, and I always wanted her to eat, drink, and be merry a little bit more than she did. On the other hand, the point I'm trying to make is that attempting to satisfy the desires of the flesh is like working to fill up a bottomless pit. Constantly searching for physical pleasure is a slavery all its own.

At some point, we all have to say, "Enough."

I have enough.

I've eaten enough.

My one spouse, she's enough.

Yet, on TV and your computer is the constant temptation to be unsatisfied with what you have. That's why we must call on Jesus.

We must see Him present with us, providing us encouragement as we face the same temptation that He did. We need Him, for the devil has more to say.

The devil also led Him up and showed Him in an instant all the kingdoms of the world, and the devil said to Him, "To you I will give their glory and all this authority. If you will worship me, it will all be yours."

Do you know anyone who would take him up on this offer?

Do you know anyone who already has?

The human desire for power is so great that constantly in the headlines is the story of some tyrant who oversteps decency, manipulates the democratic process, or abandons his moral character.

For what? It is to put himself in the place of God.

This is a temptation that too many face and too many fall prey to, so in Venezuela, there are two presidents, in North Korea there's a dictator with a nuclear arsenal, and here, there is a news story every day about an attorney, a campaign manager, or somebody who took the devil up on his offer. In a quest to gain power at any cost, even for the price of his own soul, too many fall prey to the devil.

What are we to say about these things?

What are we to do?

When we hear the tempter's whisper, we must call on the King of Kings and Lord of Lords, who refused to step beyond the limit of His power.

Even He bowed before somebody.

Even He was always mindful that God was in control.

Therefore, we must join Him in worship of the God who rules heaven and the earth, constantly mindful that He doesn't need our help or advice, and that when we take on too much power or authority, it rots our souls.

The devil still speaks.

He's speaking now and too many are listening, but he has more to say. Then, Satan said, "If you are the Son of God, throw yourself down from here."

How strong is the desire for self-preservation in the human heart?

It is so strong that we will compromise the truth to go on living, will turn our backs on those whom we love to save our own skin, and won't change our ways even if our ways are holding us back from joy. "Save yourself," the devil says, but we must listen instead to the One who says, "For those who want to save their life will lose it, and those who lose their life for my sake will save it." Lent is a gift we've been given. We've been given it because we are all the time living these unexamined lives. We even defend our unexamined lives, mindful only of what we stand to lose, blind to what we stand to gain if we would leave our broken ways behind.

Let us be bold not to save ourselves.

Let us die to the ways of sin, leaving behind our broken ways, that we might rise with Christ.

Let us ignore the persistent lies of Satan, to follow the One who still walks beside us and still leads to Eternal Life.

Amen.

The Love We Resist
Genesis 15: 1-15 and Luke 13: 31-35
Preached on March 17, 2019

On April 28th, more than nine years ago, my life changed forever when I held our oldest daughter, Lily, for the first time. I looked at her, so perfectly tiny and helpless, and suddenly came to the realization that I could become one of those people who puts his kid on a leash.

You know who I'm talking about?

Now the people who put their dogs in strollers? I still don't get that, but I had also judged those parents who put their kids on leashes until I held that baby girl and understood.

Becoming a parent changes you. It just does.

There's a new TV show called *Workin' Moms* about mothers who also work full-time. The main characters are always conflicted about whether they should be staying home with their children instead of going back to work. This is a show that's very easy for many modern parents to relate to, but my favorite scene is when a mother is jogging through the woods with her infant son in a stroller.

You can imagine. It's as though she's running on one of the Kennesaw Mountain Trails, and she comes face to face with what many of us who run on those trails fear most, if irrationally. She's running through the woods and comes upon the Kodiak bear, who'd recently escaped from the zoo.

She was running, thinking about work, she had her headphones in her ears, so she didn't notice the bear until she was right up on it. The bear had been eating garbage, and he reared up on his back legs and roared at this mother, who took her stand between her baby and the bear to roar even louder right back.

The bear knew not to mess with this lady and turned around.

It was incredible, but such is love.

That's what love looks like. Parents want to protect their children. If they made Babybjörn baby carriers big enough to hold a 7- and a 9-year-old, I'd have our girls strapped to my chest right now.

Once they have cell phones, I'll have those things tapped in a second.

They had better lock their diaries. I'm not kidding.

I've heard, though, that that's not what a parent is supposed to do. You have to give a child a little bit of space and freedom, but still in this father's heart is the desire to protect his children from the world. I want to protect them from what's out there, especially the parts that they are determined not to talk about with me.

Jesus said it like this: "Jerusalem, Jerusalem, how I long to gather you under my wings like a mother hen, but you were not willing."

Unlike Abraham in our first Scripture lesson, who feels darkness descend at the thought of his descendants suffering, Jesus knows that He could help His people through all their hardship, "but they were not willing," He said.

This morning Jesus is talking about that very real feeling of watching the ones whom we love resist accepting the help that they need.

He's talking about resisting the urge to scoop a child up, even if she's twenty, to protect her from the whole wide world.

He's holding back, knowing that there is no need for a child to keep secrets or face demons alone, if only he would ask for help.

"Jerusalem, Jerusalem, how I long to gather you under my wings like a mother hen, but you were not willing."

And why not?

You wouldn't ask that if you could remember what it was like to be a teenager.

Sometimes parents are the last to know.

On April 20, 1999, Sue Klebold's son Dylan and his friend Eric killed thirteen and wounded more than twenty, before taking their own lives in a murder-suicide. Dylan's mother, Sue, gave a speech a couple years ago, trying to explain what it feels like to have raised a child who would do such a thing. She stood up there to testify to the reality of feeling like the paramount example of failed parenting, to constantly apologize for the pain that her son caused, and to still love him despite what he did.

She said that so often people will ask her, "How could you not have known?" and every time, it feels like a punch to the gut because it was only after her son's death that she learned about his pain, hatred, and depression.

She knew neither that he had been buying guns nor that he had been bullied.

He had never told her about his hurt over not feeling accepted, nor his determination to have vengeance on those who had the acceptance that he wanted.

She had to learn about her son as the nation was learning about him, for there were all these secrets that he kept from her.

In the dark days that followed her son's death, she reached the conclusion that "if love were enough to stop someone who is suicidal [from hurting themselves or other people], suicides would hardly happen."[13] For love is there, but when someone is unwilling to talk or ask for help, love is not always enough.

Having heard what Jesus says in the Gospel of Luke, I say that finding what or who is to blame for the rash of pointless violence that continues in our nation and our world is difficult. Obviously, the violence is inexcusable, but what the church must also be prepared to fight are the secrets and the shame.

The Lord calls us out of our hidden lives, to stand before Him in truth and to take shelter under His wings, while the message we learned this week that some parents send to their children is that who they truly are must be covered up by fake college applications and photoshopped athletic histories.

The Roman Catholic Church is in trouble today, too, not just for the atrocities committed against children, but that the atrocities were covered up and the victims told to be quiet. Can you imagine?

Can you imagine encouraging silence, when we are already so good at hiding who we really are?

I heard a friend say, "I have come to the conclusion that buying craft supplies and actually using them are two separate hobbies." That's the case with a lot of us. We hide our reality behind our aspirations, and we just put a fresh coat of paint on our pain.

We cover up our broken hearts with our church clothes because even we Christians must be reminded that we are safe in His arms and protected under His wings, no matter what we've done or where we've been.

It's hard to accept, but we must accept it, and we must be bold to trust His love enough to reveal our brokenness, or we'll never heal.

I remember so well a couple sent to see a marriage counselor against their will. "We don't need marriage counseling," the husband said in the first

---

[13] https://www.youtube.com/watch?v=BXlnrFpCu0c&app=desktop

session, and so the counselor responded, "then you may as well go because if you aren't willing then I can't help you."

"Jerusalem, Jerusalem, how I long to gather you under my wings like a mother hen, but you were not willing!"

I wonder if that sounds like your mother.

In some ways it sounds like mine, very much like mine. I remembered this past week how years ago she wanted to protect me from cigarettes. Not only was she on my case, I am confident that she enlisted the help of my doctor, who told me during an appointment when I was thirteen or fourteen years old that my asthma was so bad that if I ever so much as tried a puff of a cigarette, I might just die, right on the spot.

Regardless of whether or not that was true, I don't know because I'm still too scared to try. That's not entirely true, but she was successful overall. I never really smoked, just chewed tobacco. The moment of parenting that I'll always remember best, though, was when I failed Spanish. It's true. I did. That's what happens if you never study or pay attention in class.

My parents would ask me how Spanish was going. I'd tell them it was going fine. Then, the report card came home, and the cat was out of the bag.

It was a real live F.

I would have hidden it under the bed if I could have. I would have gladly accepted my parents' offers to fake my transcripts had they offered. Unfortunately, they saw it and weren't about to cover it up, so I started packing my bags for military school.

That's not what happened.

They were angry, but once the dust cleared, my mother went to a drawer in the china cabinet, and she brought out one of her old report cards. "Read it," she said. Her grades were lower than I expected, plus there was a note from the teacher. I don't remember it exactly, but it said something like, "Cathy never stops talking. She is a nuisance in class, and it's no wonder her grades need such improvement." I couldn't believe it.

I looked at my mother, who, after reading this note and seeing those grades, looked a little bit different. It's like I'd never noticed before that she was a real person.

I think about this experience now and realize how important it was for me to know that she needs a Savior, too.

A friend back in Tennessee once brought home a report card with three F's and a D in History. His father shook it in his face and said, "What do you have to say for yourself?"

My friend responded, "Looks like I need to stop spending all my time focused on History."

Or maybe we all need to focus a little more on history.

Maybe we all need to do a better job of remembering that we were all once wretched, once lost, once blind.

That we were all once young, angry, and foolish.

For it is not by pretending that we were ever perfect that we will encourage other to make their way under the wings of His mercy.

We can only show them the way by turning toward Him ourselves.

Repent and be forgiven.

Leave behind what weighs you down and confines you to the shadow.

Speak and be heard.

Listen and be saved.

Be gathered under the mighty wings of mercy, for His is a wondrous love that none of us deserves but that everyone needs.

Amen.

Listen, So That You May Live
Isaiah 55: 1-9 and Luke 13: 1-9
Preached on March 24, 2019

My family has now been glad to call Marietta home for about a year and a half. It will be two years in July, which isn't that long, so people are still kind to ask us how we're settling in and what we think about the place. Of course, I grew up here, but it's still new, so Dr. Sam Matthews, newly retired pastor of First United Methodist Church, asked me about it over lunch last Monday.

"What is it like? How is your family settling in?" he asked.

I told him how fortunate I felt to be living in a place and serving a church like this one, and he responded, "you'll be asked to preach the funerals of a lot of people who made it that way."

He's right about that.

I've already preached the funerals of some people who have made this place great, whose legacy benefits me and my family.

Already, I've preached the funerals of some who made this community and this church what it is. When that's the case, the funerals become a chance for us to celebrate the life of saints who ran their races well. Even in the midst of grief, we take time to thank God for the lives of those who have gone on. We don't think so much about why they died or take their deaths as some kind of warning; instead, we focus on how they lived.

That's not how people always deal with death, though.

Someone dies, and the first question some people ask is: "Was he sick?"

"Was it cancer?"

"Did she smoke?"

This may be a natural way to be. Someone dies, and we want to know why. Human beings can't help but ask the question, "Why?" especially when trying to understand the great tragedies of life. That being the case, you can understand why in our second Scripture lesson, it sounds like it was just accepted knowledge that those who died when the Tower of Siloam fell had it coming. Many just assumed that the Galileans whose blood Pilate had mingled with their sacrifices must have done something to deserve it.

That's just the way we deal with death sometimes. We hear about a tragedy, and we ask, "Why?"

Before you think we're not still like that, consider all the people you know who still take the paper just for the obituaries.

People think a lot about death.

We'd talk a lot about obituaries back in Tennessee.

A woman back in Tennessee named Wanda Turner used to criticize people if their obituaries were too long. She showed me one that she was disgusted with and said, "It's an obituary, not a resume! Do these people think God's reading these things to decide who gets into heaven?"

We all knew not to die and let our obituary be too long or Wanda Turner would talk bad about us.

That woman was incredible.

I could tell Wanda Turner stories all day.

She was in her nineties, still coming to church every Sunday, and one morning she was standing by the coffee pot outside the Sanctuary before the service started.

"Miss Wanda, how are you?" I asked.

She said, "Pastor, I'm doing pretty well. At my age, there's not much sin that even tempts me, much less that I could follow through on."

Wanda Turner was something else, but she gets us to an important point.

Like death, sin can become an obsession, especially other people's sin. We want to make sense out of death, and so we blame the victims, but Jesus won't stand for that:

"At that very time there were some present who told him about the Galileans whose blood Pilate had mingled with their sacrifices. [But] He asked them, 'Do you think that because these Galileans suffered in this way, they were worse sinners than all other Galileans?'"

Jesus responds with this question because those present who told Him about the dead Galileans were thinking that their deaths must be a punishment for their sin. Because they died, they must have done something worse than what everyone else was doing. This is a human tendency. Sometimes we revel in the sin of the deceased to assure ourselves that we won't be next, though death is largely out of our control.

We don't like that, so we come up with little algorithms:

187

I don't smoke, so I won't get cancer.

I don't eat red meat, so I won't have a heart attack.

I won't have my kids vaccinated, and they won't get autism.

The ones who died must have done something to deserve it.

Yet, sometimes bad things just happen.

Now, no one wants to hear that. We like to hear about what we can control, so this week *The New York Times* reported that doctors are wondering whether or not we should be eating eggs. I wouldn't worry too much about it, though. We won't be throwing out our eggs. Tomorrow, it will just be something different, but some pay attention to these things because we all want to avoid death and suffering. We try to avoid sin, cigarettes, cholesterol, and a bunch of other stuff, only avoiding death and really living aren't the same thing.

To help us really live, Jesus tells a parable:

> A man had a fig tree planted in his vineyard; and he came looking for fruit on it and found none. So he said to the gardener, 'See here! For three years I have come looking for fruit on this fig tree, and still I find none. Cut it down! Why should it be wasting soil?' [But the gardener] replied, 'Sir, let it alone for one more year.'

What's the point of the parable?

Well, we are the fig tree, the gardener is Jesus, and if your name wasn't in the obituaries this morning, then he's bought you a little more time. What are you going to do with it?

That's a good question, isn't it?

It's the right one to ask because we can't fear death wondering if we might be next. No. We must wake up each morning knowing we might be, for the only thing that separates us who are alive and them, who have passed on, is that for some reason the Good Lord saw fit to give us a little bit more time. What will we do with it?

Jane Sullivan told me that she heard about a 104-year-old woman whose friends asked her what she wanted to be sure and do before she died. The woman said, "I've never been arrested, and I think I'd like that."

Isn't that incredible?

Along those same lines, I saw a C.S. Lewis quote: "You can't go back and change the beginning, but you can start where you are and change the ending."

There's more to living than not dying.

There's more to today than the fact that you and I woke up on this side of the grave. Today, we have a chance to change how we've been living that we might live more abundantly.

Back in 2016, I had the honor of officiating at the funeral of a 102-year-old woman. She didn't want me to preach. I was the same age as her great-grandchildren, so she never really saw me as her pastor. Even though I went to visit her often, she always just kind of saw me as a kid. That was OK. The man who preached was a long-time friend of hers. They met when she was eighty, so that means they had more than twenty years to solidify their relationship.

She gave this man instructions for what to say at her funeral, and so she told him not to make his part in the funeral a eulogy about the deceased. "Don't talk about me," she told him, "because if they don't know me by now then they've missed their chance. Talk instead about Jesus because they haven't missed their chance to get to know him."

If we are all fig trees, fruitless fig trees, we have been spared by the Gardener who can change us. He sees in us the potential to bear fruit, and desires to fertilize and work our soil so that we might do just that.

Yet, this charge to bear fruit is also a gift.

Today, we can't go back and change the beginning of our stories, but we can start where we are and change the endings.

I want to say that this is a good message for our church, right now and in this moment.

You might know, possibly because I've talked about it a lot, that three years ago our church found herself in the midst of a big conflict. The stories in the news about the United Methodist Church recently may be giving you flashbacks. As a result of decisions made to keep our Presbyterian doors open wide to the children of God who love someone of the same gender, there were many who left this church to start another one.

The paper got ahold of our dirty laundry, so right there in the *Marietta Daily Journal* were stories about us, full of discord and conflict.

That's true. That's what happened, and we can't go back and change it.

Yet, let me tell you something more important. This morning, that same paper announced which church was voted as The Best Place to Worship in Cobb County, and we are it.

They told us last Thursday, and all weekend I've been wishing I could tell Harris Hines about it.

All weekend I've been wishing I could call up Bob Stephens and so many others to let them know how far we've come, but while they helped us get here, they aren't here to see it.

We are though.

We are.

We can't change the past, but we can change the ending.

We can live today, right now, with a new focus and a new future.

We can focus on the power of the Good News and the love of God rather than debate who is in and who is out.

We can lift our voices in praise to the God of all creation rather the wring our hands, worried, anxious, and afraid.

Today, "Let us lay aside every weight and the sin that clings so closely and let us run with perseverance the race that is set before us, looking to Jesus the pioneer and perfecter of our faith."

Today, let us do so, for we have fruit to bear.

Amen.

Everything Old Has Passed Away
2 Corinthians 5: 16-21 and Luke 15: 1-3 and 11b-32
Preached on March 31, 2019

We call this room a Sanctuary. That's a good word. It's a word that disassociates this room from places like a courthouse or an exam room. Do you know what I mean?

The word "sanctuary" connotates safety. This is meant to be a place of refuge and forgiveness, which is something that we all need because in so many other places, we're being poked and prodded, feeling examined or exposed.

I remember how much I feared the summertime, not because I feared getting out of school. No. What I feared was going to the pool and taking my shirt off in public. The swimming pool can be a scary place that way. Putting yourself out there without the protection of being fully clothed isn't easy to do, and so the doctor's office is worse.

You have to get on a scale.

I don't like that. Then you have to answer a bunch of questions. A doctor once told me that whatever I told him, he multiplied by three.

"How often do you eat fast food?" he'd ask. I'd tell him about twice a week, which he'd multiply by three to get six, which was closer to the truth.

The doctor's office is a place of healing, but it can feel like a place of shame, and sometimes it starts before you even get into the exam room.

I once was in the waiting room reading a preacher book, a Bible commentary. The guy next to me noticed, which I assumed was bad because he just looked like one of those guys I didn't want to engage in a religious conversation.

He started telling me about how he reads the Bible every day.

Hearing him say that made me a little nervous, so just as I was preparing to tell him, "Yes, I have been saved," he said, "I read the Bible every day because it tells me what God is like and how I should be."

Now there's something valuable that I might have missed.

Many of us read the Bible. We all do, but what are we looking for?

Getting to our second Scripture lesson for this morning from the Gospel of Luke, according to the great reformer, Martin Luther, we have here "the

Gospel in miniature." The Parable of the Prodigal Son reduces the Gospel to its most essential message, for it tells us succinctly:

1. What God is like.
2. How we should be.

First, what is God like?

You've heard it before, that God is "Our Father, Who Art in Heaven." Father can be a perfectly appropriate metaphor for God, so long as we pick the right kind of father.

It's been said that among major league baseball players, when asked, "What part of playing baseball as a kid did you dread the most," a majority answered, "the ride home with my dad."

The other day, I saw a great sign put up at a little league field. It was a set of rules for parents:

1. Remember that they are just kids.
2. And that the coaches are volunteers.
3. Recognize that this is meant to be fun.
4. Leave the umpires alone and remember that your kids can hear what you say to them.
5. And win or lose, buy your child some ice cream.

I like those rules because I remember standing in left field out at Oregon Park, and some dad yelled to his son, "hit it to the kid in left field; it looks like he's asleep." If you're wondering how that made me feel, know that this happened at least thirty years ago, but I still remember exactly what this dad said.

The idea of a sanctuary is nice then because so many places are not like what this place is meant to be. The idea of having a Father in heaven? Well, whether you think that sounds great or terrifying depends on what kind of father we are talking about.

My dad was most always kind, which I now know is truly a gift because there are all kinds of different dads.

I've heard of a father who disowned one of his daughters.

Another who returned the letters sent by his son with no response, other than sending back the son's letters with the grammar corrected.

If this is a place focused on a Father in heaven, is it any wonder that some people see this room, not as a Sanctuary where they are safe and protected, but as an exam room where they are judged and condemned?

Last Tuesday, we were planning for this worship service, debating whether or not it's best to sit or stand during the Prayer of Confession.

If you wonder what your church staff does during the week, well, there you have it.

We decided that sitting during the Prayer of Confession was the best because to sit with your head bowed is a more penitential position than standing, only then we wondered when and how to invite you to stand again. Rev. Joe Brice suggested that after confessing our sins, he might just say, "Would the defendant please rise."

He won't ever do that, but this idea gets us to the heart of the matter.

If we hear this story of the Prodigal Son:

- With the guilty young man who asked for his inheritance early,
- Who was basically saying, "Dad, I wish you were dead, so I could have what you're leaving me in the will."
- Then took the money and squandered it all on loose living,
- Then so lost track of himself and the standards by which he was raised that he found himself looking longingly at the sloop the pigs were eating,
- And then in desperation went back to his father in the hopes of being brought on as one of the hired hands,
- What do we expect after confessing our sins and hearing the words: would the defendant please rise?

Condemnation?

Some received that from their fathers.

Shame?

In some families, shame was never in short supply.

What were punishments like in your house? After wrecking the car at sixteen, did they ever let you forget it? Did you ever feel like there was reconciliation again?

If your earthly father has inspired in you a distrust or fear of God, then hear what God is like, for "while he was still far off, his father saw him and was filled with compassion; he ran and put his arms around him and kissed him."

That's what God is like. Don't let anyone tell you otherwise. That's what God is like.

Then how should we be?

That's in this story, too.

"Now his elder son was in the field; and when he came and approached the house, he heard music and dancing. He called one of the slaves and asked what was going on." When he found out that his prodigal brother had returned, rather than welcome him like the father, this older son did what so often we do; he became angry and refused to go to the party.

> His father came out and began to plead with him. But he answered his father, "Listen! For all these years I have been working like a slave for you, and I have never disobeyed your command; yet you have never given me even a young goat so that I might celebrate with my friends. But when this son of yours came back, who has devoured your property with prostitutes, you killed the fatted calf for him!"

If we go to the Bible to learn what God is like and how we should be, in this older brother, we hear a warning about how we too often are.

We don't always open the doors of this church wide enough.

Too often we accept God's grace, while failing to pass it on.

We take pride in our moral fiber, while failing to recognize that the ones we've left out, fenced in, turned our back on, lashed out at, or sent an angry email to are our brothers or sisters.

This is a parable of Jesus that not only tells us what God is like, but how we should be, and how we should be is not like the older brother, for the older brother is more focused on what his brother is getting than what he has received according to the father's mercy.

Sometimes the grass appears so green on the other side that we fail to see what's underneath our own feet.

Sometimes we focus so on our neighbors' sin that we fail to see how we need forgiveness.

Sometimes we are so angry that our brother has crossed a finish line that we fail to see how we've won the race.

Within us all is a prodigal son who needs forgiveness, and an older brother who forgets about grace.

The Cherokee said that within us all are two wolves:

"One is evil. He is envy, greed, arrogance, self-pity, guilt, resentment, inferiority, and false pride. But the other is good. He is love, hope, humility, kindness, and compassion."

194

As they fight within us all, the question is, which one will win?

The old Cherokee teachers said, "The one we feed."

That poor older brother.

He was busy refusing the good feast of the father to feed on his own resentment and refusing drinking from the cup of salvation that he might drink his fill of inferiority and false pride.

He's not so unlike us, for the Father would welcome many into this house that we would look down our noses at.

The Father would welcome with open arms many whom we still resent, holding close the memory of how they squandered their inheritance and left us to hold things together.

What kind of God do we honor with such behavior?

Not the God of Scripture.

Not the God of Grace and Redemption.

No. When we act so entitled, we are blind to the truth of the Gospel, for in God's Kingdom, spring has come again, so we must not allow winter to linger on in our hearts.

"From now on, regard no one from a human point of view; [for] anyone who is in Christ is a new creation; everything old has passed away; see, everything has become new!"

Amen.

Do You Perceive It?
Isaiah 43: 16-21 and John 12: 1-8

Preached on April 7, 2019

Have you ever tried to be in two places at one time? I say, "tried to be in two places at one time" because no one really can. It seems the best we can do is be present in one, and when we try to be in two, we generally end up being in neither.

Trying to be in two places at one time makes for good comedy, however.

I remember watching *Saved by the Bell* after school. This was a teen-drama that came on TV every afternoon during the week, and the most popular boy on the show, Zach Morris, once asked two different girls out on a date for the same night and at the same restaurant. It didn't end well, and neither did it end well in the movie *Mrs. Doubtfire*, when a character played by Robin Williams is trying to meet with a business associate on one side of the restaurant as himself, while trying to enjoy dinner with his children, his ex-wife, and her new husband on the other side of the restaurant,   where he is trying to keep up the act of being an aging, female, British nanny.

Thinking of situations like these and many others, the challenges of being in two places at once become obvious. We still try because sometimes life seems to demand it of us.

In our second Scripture lesson from the Gospel of John, imagine being Martha. While you may want to just enjoy dinner with your guests, sitting down to relax with them at the table doesn't seem possible. If anyone is going to eat, then somebody has to go back and forth between the table and the kitchen.

Someone has to cook.

Did Mary think of that?

Maybe Martha wanted to sit at Jesus' feet to fully hear and comprehend what He had to say, too, or maybe she would have enjoyed sitting next to her brother Lazarus, freshly raised from the dead. Someone had to be in the kitchen, and so Martha was trying to be in two places at one time. You know what this is like.

Maybe after dinner your spouse and kids went outside to play basketball in the driveway. You wanted to play, too, but someone has to wash the dishes. Maybe your preschooler came home from gymnastics ready to offer you a full demonstration of what she's learned. You're trying to watch, but as she displays cartwheel after cartwheel, she could see that your attention was compromised because there's laundry to fold, bills to pay, and emails to send.

I've heard mothers respond to their children's cries for attention by asking, "Is anyone bleeding?" That makes it easy to decide what to pay attention to first. The rest of the time, it's really hard to decide where to be fully present, so, at dinner in Bethany, we have Martha going in between the kitchen and the table, just like every parent I know.

Why?

Because that's life.

I imagine that your perception of which demand gets priority changes should you become a grandparent because those who are lucky enough to become grandparents have had a lifetime to learn that the laundry will always be there, but the grandchildren will grow up. Since we can't really be in two places at once, we have to decide which really is the better part. Interestingly, Mary already knows.

She is fully present, focused solely on Jesus, while, like Martha, we have to think about it.

We think about the plates pilling up in the sink.

We fold laundry and cut the grass.

What will the neighbors think if we don't?

People say that we should dance like no one is looking. Have you ever done that? Neither have I. Instead, I worry about decency and decorum like all the dinner guests in that house. Jesus came to Bethany, the home of Lazarus, and there they gave a dinner for Him. If I were among those invited, I'd try to play by the rules of the house just as they did. If Martha set the table with more than two forks at my place, I might not know which one to use first, so I'd sit back to watch what everyone else does.

That's what guests should do.

One summer during college, I was sent by our denomination down to Argentina to be a missionary intern. There, if you order ice cream, they put a little spoon in your cone. I didn't know what it was for, but I'm glad I watched everyone else, because in South America one of the most vulgar things you can do is lick an ice cream cone out in public. It's just not done. Of course, it's hard to enjoy an ice cream cone if you're so conscious of social decorum. However, you have to think about these things when you're invited over to someone's house for dinner.

197

You get too immersed in enjoying something, and you might make a scene.

That's why Mary is the only one anointing Jesus' feet.

The other guests are sitting back, trying to do things decently and in order, not realizing that just as you can't be in two places at once, you also can't do two things at once. You can't be both decent and devoted, and Mary picked the better part.

She knew that we always have the chance to be respectable, while ice cream tends to melt.

She doesn't care that it's considered scandalous for a woman to let down her hair in front of a man.

She doesn't care that some will say that she's making them embarrassed, that she's being a poor host, or that the perfume she poured on her Savior's feet could have been sold to the poor.

Judas is right about that, of course.

Nard is a perfume made from a plant that grows in the Himalayas. Because of its distant origins, even a little of this oil would have been expensive. A small vile might have cost a week's wages. We know from Judas' observation that Mary poured three hundred denarii's worth, a full year's salary for a low wage worker in that region. Some say that the perfume would be worth as much as ten-thousand dollars today.

Ten-thousand dollars poured out on His feet.

Can you imagine?

Do you know what MUST Ministries can do with $10,000? Do you know what her children or her sister's children might have done should she have invested $10,000? We're told that responsible people have to think through their decisions.

We have to be mindful of the future.

Not only do we challenge ourselves to be in two places at once or to think about being both decent and devoted, our lives also call us to try and be in the present while mindful of the future. Not Mary, for Mary is so completely present with Jesus.

She acts, knowing that the poor will always be with her, but Jesus only had a little more time. It's true. At this point in the course of His life, His days were numbered. Our second Scripture lesson began, "Six days before Passover Jesus came to Bethany."

That's six days before the Last Supper.

Six days before He was betrayed.

Six days before He was arrested, tried, and sentenced to death.

That means it was about a week before he was crucified. That's why she gave Him everything that she had: all her attention, all that she could give. She was before the Lord undistracted, completely devoted, and fully present. She poured out all of who she was to this Man who meant everything. Her act of devotion was so beautiful, so pure, and so costly that I imagine, not only did the smell of this perfume fill the room, but were we to stand at the foot of His cross several days after this dinner, we might still have smelled the love she poured out coming off His feet as He breathed His last on the cross.

Maybe He smelled it.

As He was dying, perhaps He smelled the perfume coming off His feet and remembered that as the world turned its back, Mary still loved Him. As for the rest of us, well, even when we are having dinner with just one person, still we are distracted. Therefore, we must be warned not to reach the end our days like Emily in the Thornton Wilder play *Our Town,* lamenting how,

"It goes so fast. We don't have time to look at one another.

I didn't realize. All that was going on in life and we never noticed."

The Prophet Isaiah calls us to be more like Mary, asking, "Do you not perceive it?" I don't, for sometimes I'm busy in the kitchen, as though anyone ever lay on his death bed embarrassed over the dishes left unwashed in the sink. Other times, I'm too worried about what everyone thinks, even though I know that when our girls go off to college, I'll have forgotten what I missed their soccer games for, but they'll remember whether or not I was there. Then sometimes, all I can think about is what tomorrow will hold, so I must remember to pay attention to the One who holds tomorrow.

Today, let us all try and take a lesson from Mary.

Soon, He will make his way to the cross, and just as she poured out everything that she had as a sign of her love, so He will pour out everything He has for us. Today, perceive the wondrous love of His body broken for our sake; His blood shed for the forgiveness of our sins.

Amen.

As He Came Near
Psalm 118: 1-2, 19-29 and Luke 19: 28-44

Preached on April 14, 2019

This second Scripture lesson from the Gospel of Luke is so familiar and is read so often that it's possible to miss how strange it is. It is strange. It starts out strange, when you think about it. Consider how the owner felt when she woke up and went looking for the colt she'd been saving up to buy, or consider this plan Jesus comes up with;

You can tell He's not used to stealing colts.

"Go into the village ahead of you, and as you enter it you will find tied there a colt that has never been ridden. Untie it and bring it here. [And] if anyone asks you, 'Why are you untying it?' just say this, 'The Lord needs it.'"

This plan is strange, and it requires a lot of His disciples.

Think about it.

I didn't have a bike lock last Thursday. Our daughter Cece needed to borrow mine, and as I set my bike, unlocked, in the nice bike rack right outside our church, I wondered how I would feel if some guys walked off with my bike. Would I feel any better if they told me, "The Lord needs it"? "Well, I need to get home. What about that?"

How would you feel if you were the owner of that colt, or how would we feel if we were the disciples asked to go and take it?

I suppose the point is that we would feel the same as we should feel every day, for every day Jesus requires us to step beyond what we are comfortable with. Every day, He calls us to follow Him as He leads us beyond what we are used to and toward the Kingdom of God.

"Take up your cross, the Savior said" is how the hymn goes.

> If you would my disciple be;
>
> Take up your cross with willing heart,
>
> and humbly follow after me.
>
> Let not its weight fill your weak spirit with alarm;
>
> Christ's strength shall bear your spirit up
>
> and brace your heart and nerve your arm.

That's a good hymn to sing, though it's a hard hymn to live.

Some might like the song, "Jesus Take the Wheel," but most of the time we're His worst backseat drivers. That's why I admire those two disciples made horse thieves; they heard Him speak, and they obeyed.

I don't always do that, so I can relate to the Pharisees in the crowd.

There they were. As He rode along, people kept spreading their cloaks on the road.

> As He was approaching the path down from the Mount of Olives, the whole multitude of the disciples began to praise God joyfully with a loud voice for all the deeds of power that they had seen, [but] some of the Pharisees in the crowd said to him, "Teacher, order your disciples to stop."

I told you before; this is familiar passage of Scripture.

You've heard it so many times that the weird parts seem normal. Consider for a moment how strange this is, for as Jesus rides His borrowed colt, the Pharisees were in there with the rest of the crowd.

It's easy to miss that detail because the Pharisees are often painted with such a broad brush that we'd never imagine them there, happy about Jesus riding into Jerusalem.

From Sunday school lessons, it's easy to see them as one-dimensional, as those upright and haughty religious authorities who opposed Jesus.

We sometimes think of them as self-righteous, and so heavenly-minded as to have been no earthly good.

We have to be careful about such assumptions, for the Gospel writer tells us that they were not sitting off to the side of the road glaring at the disciples, but that they were "in the crowd," part of the parade, maybe just as happy about Jesus entering the city of Jerusalem as every other disciple of Jesus Christ. Yet, they were still Pharisees, and the thing that separates a Pharisee from a disciple is often a thin line.

They might have been happy about Him entering the city, but they probably wouldn't have borrowed a colt for Him.

They didn't want to cause too much of a fuss.

That doesn't make them bad.

That doesn't make them evil.

It just makes them cautious. Right?

You can understand. Nicodemus was such a Pharisee. He, too, was a member of this religious group that enjoyed authority among the people and toleration by the Romans. Nicodemus was even a member of that high court of religious authority called the Sanhedrin. He was admired by the devoted, and being a man rooted in the ancient Scripture, saw in Jesus the embodiment of his same ideals. He wanted to know this Man, and so he went to Him saying,

"Rabbi, we know that you are a teacher who has come from God;

for no one can do these signs that you do apart from the presence of God."

What a thing to say! However, Nicodemus was only able to say such a thing in the presence of Jesus at night.

He went to go see the Savior when no one else was looking.

He would only step into His presence when it wouldn't cost him the admiration of his peers and the approval of the powers that be, so it makes sense that those Pharisees were in the crowd because this is Jesus we're talking about. Yet, He didn't ask a couple Pharisees to go borrow a colt for Him.

He didn't call on Nicodemus to help Him out.

No.

The difference between a Pharisee and a disciple is that disciples live the Gospel out in the light of day.

Disciples are still Christians even when the Gospel makes them a little uncomfortable.

Disciples still follow even when it costs them.

That's a level of devotion that's not for everybody because it gets dangerous.

Did you notice what the people were singing?

"Blessed is the king who comes in the name of the Lord!

Blessed is the king."

These are treasonous words because if Jesus is the king, it means that Caesar's not.

Caesar doesn't want to hear that.

The Pharisees know this about Caesar, and so they chose to keep quiet themselves and to try and keep the crowds quiet. For disciples, that's not always an option.

Last week, we heard again about Mary, and when it came time for her to choose between appearing like a respectable, decent, and orderly hostess or stepping out and taking a risk as a devoted disciple, she poured $10,000 worth of perfume out on His feet and wiped them with her hair. That was a bold thing to do.

You can imagine how the Pharisees reacted.

They were there, of course, because Pharisees want to be at the party where Jesus is a guest, but when they leave the table, they still want to live in the same world they've always lived in. Pharisees like Jesus. They just don't want Him changing too much.

Pharisees don't want to get their hands dirty.

They try to follow Jesus while keeping the peace.

They ask, "Can't we just keep quiet and still believe?"

They say, "I'd love to follow Jesus, so long as it doesn't cost me anything," but on Palm Sunday, the Pharisees find out that following Jesus requires them to take a risk.

That's just what happens when He comes near.

On Palm Sunday "as he came near," it so quickly became clear who His real disciples were. It's one of those moments, like on a threshing floor when the grain stays but the chaff is swept away with the wind, so today, when He comes near once again, like every Pharisee or disciple in that crowd, we, too, must be ready to make a choice.

Will we allow Him to purify us?

Are we ready to take such a risk?

For nothing will be gained unless we are willing to make some changes.

There will always be evil systems that benefit from our silence.

There will always be corrupt forces that urge us to keep quiet.

There will always be parts of our own souls that resist the kind of purification that Christ brings as He draws near; therefore, we must decide if we are willing to let our light shine for all to see. That's a hard thing to do; yet, that's what's required of us when He comes near.

I've recently benefitted from a book about the ministry of Dr. Frank Harrington. Sheila Tyler let me borrow her copy. In this biography of that great preacher who served the Lord so well at Peachtree Presbyterian Church, is the story of a relative. During the dark days of segregation, he heard a crowd of African American men and women march through the street singing. Dr. Harrington remembers how this relative of his, loving and faithful in so many ways, just wanted the crowd to quiet down. Yet, what were they singing?

"We shall overcome.

We shall overcome."

We always have a choice to make:

Will we sing with the parade, or will we swallow our desire for justice down once more to keep the peace?

Will we say something to the friend who always drinks too much, or will we watch as her children lay a blanket on her sleeping body?

The Pharisees among us and within us will say, "Just keep quiet. Let her sleep," but will change come from our silence?

When will we speak?

When will we sing?

When will we let the rolling waters flow, rather than try to hold back the flood?

Each moment we spend hiding the problem rather than inviting Him to help us is a moment wasted.

Each second we spend tolerating brokenness is a moment spent carrying a heavy burden that He would free us from.

Each day we spend trying to hold up the corruption of Rome is a day we could have spent building a better future.

Each lie we live is time wasted when we could have been rejoicing in the truth.

These Pharisees who want everyone quiet are just hoping to keep the peace. Consider, then, the Prophets who said, "We say peace, peace, when there is no peace."

If you want peace, then as He comes near, sing.

As He comes near, dance.

As He comes near, let him change you and rejoice as He changes the world.

Amen.

Malchus' Ear
Scripture Lesson: John 18: 1-11
Preached on April 19, 2019

Most days when it's nice out, and some days when it's not nice, I ride my bike here to the church. That's a benefit of living close by that I'm grateful for. Last Monday morning, as I was riding here, I got to the bridge just behind the church. It's the bridge that takes Kennesaw over the 120 Loop, which is probably the part of the ride that scares me the most. The road narrows there, and people speed up to get over the railroad tracks, so during this part of my ride, I always illegally ride on the sidewalk.

Well, last Monday, there were two people walking on the sidewalk.

One was Ginny Brogan, a member here, who tolerated me as I squeezed past her.

The other was a man I didn't know, and as I passed by him on my bike, he said, just loud enough for me to hear, "You know it's illegal to ride a bike on the sidewalk."

I didn't know this man, and his words struck me, so I thought about stopping to apologize or explain myself. Then, though, the thought occurred to me, "what if he asks who I am and where I'm going?"

How is it going to look to this man I've never met before, or how is it going to reflect on this church, if I so blatantly disregard the standards of public safety on my way to the church?

He could say, "Well, I was thinking of going to First Presbyterian Church this Easter Sunday to visit, but now that the preacher nearly pushed me off the sidewalk and into oncoming traffic, I think I'd rather not."

This is the kind of stuff that I spend a lot of time thinking about because it's this kind of experience that makes the Gospel come alive. Consider this man and imagine yourself in our Scripture lesson.

What did Malchus think about those disciples, those first Christians, after Peter cut off his ear?

What did the slave Malchus, doing nothing more than minding his own business, obeying his master's wishes, think about the Prince of Peace when His right-hand man, Peter, comes at him with a sword?

How, then, was the Gospel proclaimed?

How was the Kingdom advanced?

Into whose hands has Christ entrusted His Church?

Peter, that's who. And me. And you.

Whom the Gospel has been entrusted to doesn't always lead to its advancement.

That's true, and you know what's worse?

I couldn't stop thinking about the guy who chastised me on the sidewalk for a full thirty minutes. He never made it into the church, which made me realize that he was probably just using our parking lot to go over to the new Marietta Square Market.

I became resentful then.

How dare he? This only goes to reinforce my point.

I ask you: who are we? To whom has Christ entrusted His church?

I can be so resentful as to brood over perceived wrongdoing for days, even when I'm in the wrong.

I can be so arrogant as to disregard public safety rules, as though I were the exception.

Who am I to carry forth His message, I ask you? Maybe after me giving you this look at my inner brokenness, you're asking the same thing.

This has always been the case, though.

The Gospel has always been entrusted to broken people.

Peter, named so because Christ called him to be the Rock that the Church would be built upon, not only sliced off this slave's ear, he also denied Christ three times.

Judas betrayed Him of course, but like our preacher last Wednesday, Rev. Brian Smith of First United Methodist Church said, "I believe we make such a fuss over His betrayal because we don't like to face the fact that we all betray Him all the time."

Who can say that she has fully loved her neighbor as herself?

Who can say that he has loved the Lord with all his heart, and soul, and mind?

It is this week that we must journey with Him to the cross, not because we are worthy, but because we are in need.

For there He was, the perfect Lamb of God, and while Peter denied Him three times, when they came to arrest Him, Jesus replied, "I am he" whom you are looking for.

While Judas sold Him for a bag of coins, Jesus told those who came to arrest Him, "If you are looking for me, let these men go" for He refused to lose a single one.

As they took Him away in chains, Peter had to do something, of course.

Peter always just does something.

He reacted.

He drew his sword, but despite Peter's refusal to accept the events that were unfolding before him, Jesus said, "Put your sword back into its sheath. Am I not to drink the cup that the Father has given me?"

He did, of course.

For you and for me, He drank the cup, took the beatings, and faced the cross.

In the Gospel of Luke, He even gave Malchus back his ear, which is easy for me to believe because He is all the time paying the price for my sins.

On this Good Friday, draw near to His cross and be a witness to the Father's love.

Draw near to His cross today and come to know the One who rights all our wrongs.

Draw near to His cross today and discover grace enough to cover all our sins.

What have these worship services been about all this Holy Week more than that we all need Him?

Regardless of where we go to church, we all count on Him, so we, the Church, cannot spend so much time cutting off ears, for once Malchus has lost his ear, he cannot hear the Gospel. Consider who needs to hear the freedom of the Gospel more than a Roman slave?

Like so many church folks, though, Peter just cut off his ear.

Rather than offer him the grace and mercy he had received from the Lord; he was like those priests who abuse their power.

He was like those Pharisees who walked the sidewalks in their robes, indifferent to the needs of the poor.

He was like this pastor, who wants the sidewalk to himself, unable to see that God's children are walking here.

Peter reacted, failing to recognize his brother.

Too often, that's exactly what the Church does.

The Greeks wish to see Jesus, but the Church only sees the specks in their eyes, failing to see the planks coming out our own.

Then, when there's no Malchus around, we turn on each other.

Peter and Paul couldn't even get along, always fighting and bickering. Peter's call was to build up the church, but he wanted to subdivide it, so the old joke goes about a man on a deserted island who builds for himself three huts: "That's my house, that's my church, and that's the church I used to go to before I got mad and left."

I'm not any different, though.

I used to look down my nose at Roman Catholics, until I married into a family of them.

I used to think of Methodists as our denomination's competition, until my sister-in-law fell in love with one.

I used to think that the world sure would be a better place if only there were more Presbyterians in it who think like me, but I've learned something. I've learned that we cannot defeat our enemy if we spend all our time fighting each other.

We are not following Him if we're arguing over who sits at His right hand.

Back in Tennessee, it was about the same. Before coming here, a year and a half ago, I served the First Presbyterian Church of Columbia, Tennessee. We were surrounded up there by the Church of Christ. There was a Church of Christ church on every corner, but Presbyterians were wary of them because the Church of Christ was sure that everyone but them was going to hell.

I got offended by that.

It hurt my feelings, and in an effort to understand, I asked the county historian about it. I wanted to learn if there was some hundred-year-old feud I didn't know about.

He told me not to worry about it.

He said, "Joe, it's not just that the Church of Christ thinks the folks at the Presbyterian Church are going to hell. The ones at Greymere Church of Christ think that the West 7th Street Church of Christ is going to hell, and they think that the Eastside Church of Christ is going to hell, and they all think the folks at Murry Hills are going to hell because they let a woman speak in the pulpit."

What happened is every time the church got in an argument; one group left to start the perfect church. Yet, while today there's one on every corner and a new one popping up every year, the Kingdom has yet to come, and Christ has yet to be glorified because we keep on dying by our own sword.

I read in the paper just yesterday an article that made me so mad. One Christian politician was again telling the world that this other Christian politician isn't even a real Christian.

Is that what this world needs?

Is that going to build up His Church?

What good is it really doing, us, all the time, tearing each other down and cutting off each other's ears?

We have to do not as the world does.

Instead, we must do in remembrance of Him.

We must listen to Him as He tells us about the new way to be.

Those of us who still have ears on our heads and half a brain between them, we must hear Him and obey.

It may be that the Church has cut off one of your ears.

If that's the case, I'm sorry.

I'm truly sorry for every cruel mark that the Church has left on this world, whether it be in judgement of one of God's children, disregard for one of His people, slander, gossip, condoning evil, or propping it up.

Like Peter, we, the Church, on this Good Friday, have some apologizing to do. We must be prepared to confess our sins, and we must be prepared for a new way of being.

Today, more than ever, we must be mindful of the truth that the world is watching what we do, and worse than that, the world is learning who our Savior is based on how we behave.

Yesterday, I rode my bike, and when I got to that bridge, I saw a mother coming toward me on the sidewalk, pushing one of those big, double strollers that takes up the whole sidewalk.

I stopped my bike and looked back for oncoming traffic before braving the road.

You know what? There was a white car behind me that had already stopped.

In that moment, I realized that the world is not so cruel a place, especially when we realize that Malchus is our brother and not our enemy.

Amen.

He Washed His Disciples Feet
John 13: 1-17 and 31b-35

Preached on April 18, 2019

At this exact time, just one week ago, I was at the Brave's game, but I wasn't just at the Brave's game. We were invited by neighbors to join them at the Delta Sky360 Club.

That place is incredible. It's one of those places where customer service is running on overdrive. There was a lady in the elevator who asked our floor so we wouldn't have to sully our fingertips pushing the elevator buttons ourselves. At the entrance to the club were two greeters. There was a waitress who got our drinks after we sat down at a table with a tablecloth; then, we ate our fill at the five different buffets available.

When we arrived at our leather stadium seats, there was even a man assigned to our section, and from time to time, he'd just offer us things like ice-cream sandwiches and fruit cups. This wasn't the time for fruit cups, so after having eaten before the game from two of the five different buffets, at about the sixth inning, I returned to the club to sample from the other three.

However, when I got there, the staff was shutting things down, so when I got back to the seat, our waiter asked me why I was empty-handed and looking so disappointed. I told him I was thinking about having a hot dog, but that the hot dog buffet line had closed. Well, he went off and found me one. He may have grilled it himself for all I know.

What a shock it is to go from being treated like a king in the Delta Sky360 Club exactly one week ago, to today hearing how the King of Kings washed His disciples' feet.

What a shock it is to go from the kind of service where my wish was their command to hearing how the Lord of Lords knelt on the floor like a servant.

What a shock it is to acknowledge the reality that I love to be the one who is fussed over and given special treatment to hear now that I am to imitate the One who said, "If I, your Lord and Teacher, have washed your feet, you also ought to wash one another's feet."

In Him is this clear picture of servanthood.

In Him is the true picture of power, leadership, lordship, and honor.

In Him is the defining picture of humility and grace, glory and majesty.

Yet, what do we see when we look out into our world or into our own hearts?

In grocery stores and restaurants, people bag our groceries and refill our glasses.

We pull up at the drive-thru at Chick-Fil-a and to our every request, some smiling person says, "It's my pleasure."

We love the spaciousness of first-class seating, so we don't have to sit too close to strangers.

We pay for pedicures so someone else can deal with our feet; yet, the One who created the heavens and the earth takes ours in His hands to wash them Himself.

In this one act comes the magnitude of our Gospel calling.

It is a shocking thing that Christ has done, for it is a drastic change of life that He calls us to.

Just imagine how it would look if Ted Turner were down there at the Delta Club washing the wait staff's feet.

Just imagine what it would have been like if I brought our waiter a hot dog instead of waiting for him to bring me one, or enough about feet. Just imagine what it would be like if, in calling your doctor's office, you actually got her on the phone.

Can you imagine?

Maybe you can. I hope you can. I know there are some wonderful doctors who treat every one of their patients as though he were Christ Himself, but sometimes the distance between people can be so far.

There are some who consider themselves too great to associate with the masses, while others begin to believe that their lot in life is to make a living off whatever crumbs fall to the floor.

We live in a culture of hierarchy while tonight we hear about the God who draws near. The God who draws so near as to step down from heaven to take on human flesh, so near as to kneel at His disciples' feet.

Tonight, He invites us to gather around a table that is unlike any other.

It was a meal rooted in the history of God's continual sacrifice on behalf of His people. A moment in time when He redeemed slaves from Egypt and called them His children. The Jewish people kept this tradition and passed it down, for it is so easy to forget how precious we are in His sight.

This table, not unlike the one He invited his disciples to that Passover Sadder so long ago, is still a table that requires no reservation, for He treats us like royalty.

No bill will come, for the cost of the meal has already been paid.

Our Host, our Savior, makes of us just this one request:

"Very truly, I tell you, servants are not greater than their master, nor are messengers greater than the one who sent them. If you know these things, you are blessed if you do them."

So many of you have already done it.

I've seen it.

A Baptist named Diane Brown Renfrow posted on Facebook: "Patti Kendrick and I are doing lunch every day at First Presbyterian Marietta. Two misfits welcomed here. Holy Week Services Downtown, Monday through Friday. Lunch afterwards in the Great Hall. The Presbyterians specialize in hospitality."

What she was talking about is how each day this week, guests have come to worship in this Sanctuary. Preachers from neighboring churches have preached. Following the service, they've made their way to our Great Hall, where they have been treated, not like guests, but like friends.

Each day, more than thirty volunteers prepared and served soup and sandwiches, cookies and coffee for some who have only ever been in our church for funerals, and for others who left this church to join another.

Every one of them was treated with honor.

Each one of them was given grace.

This is what the Lord requires of those who come to this table. He invites us all, and none of us deserves it for He is higher than high, bigger than big, the very essence of what is holy and good.

He calls on us to come and eat, though we betray Him, deny Him, and are slow to follow where He leads. Despite our unworthiness, He still calls us to come and eat, and only requires that we invite others who deserve to come no more than we do.

"I give you a new commandment, He said, that you love one another. Just as I have loved you, you also should love one another. By this everyone will know that you are my disciples, if you have love for one another."

This was His last request before He went on not only to wash His disciples' feet, but to give His life for those who did not even recognize Him.

Let us live honoring His last request.

Amen.

He Is Risen
Isaiah 65: 17-25 and John 20: 1-18

Preached on April 21, 2019

It is an uncommon gift to be here this Easter morning. It is a gift just to gather here for worship in this place because simply having a church to worship in is a miracle that we must not take for granted.

This week in the headlines made it clear.

The Cathedral of Notre Dame was burning on Monday. From that moment on and throughout the week, this tragedy had so many searching for words. I read one journalist who wrote,

> The image of Notre Dame burning took my breath away. And yes, I was speechless. A series of thoughts raced through my mind, some fairly apocalyptic. It wasn't just Notre Dame – "Our Lady" – that was being destroyed. To my mind, I was witnessing the immolation of Western Civilization. The words that kept repeating themselves as I tried to make sense of what I was seeing were simpler: This is so wrong.

It is wrong. It just is.

Just days before Easter, the Cathedral that took 200 years to build stood as something constant, something that could be counted on, was going up in smoke. This same journalist wrote, "Ah, yes, wars and revolutions come and go, but Notre Dame stands." That's how it's been in Paris for 674 years, up until this week, when the city learned that even Notre Dame can be gone in an instant.

In Louisiana, I imagine there are at least three churches feeling very much the same thing. Three churches there were intentionally burned in racist violence between March 26th and April 2nd. What these congregations lost in the fire is the same as what we would have lost. Their church buildings held generations of worshipers, hosted thousands of baptisms, weddings, and funerals. Those sanctuaries were places of safety, reminding worshipers of God's presence among them despite wars, divorces, disappointments, and deaths.

For many, the church building that they lost was their constant, their grounding, their foundation, and despite the changing tides of popular culture and the ebbs and flows of human life, that constant of theirs was gone all at once.

It's wrong.

It's just wrong not to have a church on Easter.

Our church mourns with our sister Presbyterian church in Wetumpka, Alabama, who lost their historic sanctuary to a tornado last January. This month's Sunday school offerings will be sent to them, to help them rebuild. This is what the church should do.

Like those French billionaires and others who have pledged fortunes to help rebuild the cathedral, we must help as we can, for everyone needs a place to worship God. However, we must not fool ourselves. Rebuilding isn't going to fix everything because the comfort and healing that the broken-hearted seek doesn't come from a building.

The Source of the grace and forgiveness that we all need is not stone but flesh and blood.

This room may point us towards God and make us aware of His presence, but while this is God's house, this is not the only place God lives.

Still, so often we mistake the container for the contents.

We look at the edifice forgetting that what lies inside her walls will stand for all eternity.

We go to the tomb, and ask, where is He?

That's what Mary did.

She went to that place, expecting to see a stone sealing the tomb of her Savior. Her meager hope was to visit the place where His remains had been laid to rest. It's as though she went to visit the grave to lay some flowers upon it, only to see that someone had run her car into His headstone, dug up His casket, and tossed it to the side.

Witnessing such desecration, she's not just disappointed.

She's not just concerned.

She's not just brokenhearted.

She must have been more than all that.

I imagine that she was that fierce blend of anger and sadness that those who knew her recognized and were wise to get out of her way. From the tomb, I can see her storming off to notify the disciples. Two of them rushed back to the tomb with her, but after seeing the tomb empty, the disciples just returned to their homes.

That they just returned to their homes makes sense in a way.

Our daughter Lily and I went to the library last Friday. It was closed, so we went back home. Likewise, I often go by the bank too late and find the door locked. When I do, I don't wait around expecting it to open. I go back home.

Then, this week, I went to Kroger looking for Root Beer Peeps (Yes, they make those now.). I thought they were sold out because they weren't with the regular peeps. I almost went back home empty-handed, but it turned out Kroger had them. I was just looking for them in the wrong place.

Mary was looking for Him in the tomb when a voice broke the silence, asking,

"Woman, why are you weeping?

Whom are you looking for?"

Supposing Him to be the gardener, she said to Him, "Sir, if you have carried him away, tell me where you have laid him, and I will take him away."

Did you hear that?

"Supposing him to be the gardener."

She was right there outside the tomb, tears clouding her vision. She was so consumed by despair, anger, and helplessness that she didn't recognize Him. She was so sure that if He were anywhere, it would be in that tomb. If He wasn't in there, He couldn't possibly be walking around. She was so sure it wasn't Jesus talking to her that she thought the man standing before her was the gardener because her imagination did not prepare her to see Him standing there alive and well.

Remember, also, that this is Mary we're talking about.

If Mary was temporarily blind to the presence of Christ, it should be no surprise that hope is hard for us because all the time we're looking for Him in the wrong places, too hopeless to see all around us the proof that He can never die.

Like the Psalmist, we lift up our eyes to the hills, though our hope doesn't come from the hills. It comes from the Lord.

We bow down on our knees in the Sanctuary, though churches are but one place where He may be found.

It's like how we long to be held in the arms of our mothers or fathers, but their love for us is not waiting in the graveyard, it is living in our hearts.

This is how the evil one takes advantage of us.

He uses our tunnel vision against us.

We are always looking for God in the same old places, so bad luck tries to destroy our faith by setting the Cathedral on fire.

Despair stalks the graveyard and draws our focus towards the tombstone with its two dates trying to tell us that life can begin and end.

Two men flew airplanes into the Twin Towers thinking this would defeat the soul of our nation, but if freedom and democracy live in a building and not in our hearts, we are hopeless already, for Christ is not in the tomb, but that hardly means He's dead.

Yesterday, the New York Times reported:

"For centuries, the Notre-Dame Cathedral has enshrined an evolving notion of what it means to be French."

This cathedral may enshrine what it means to be French, but I say, what it means to be Christian is to stand back and watch Him rise from the ashes.

Our identity is not tied to a building.

Our faith does not depend on what can be built of stone.

Our hope cannot be toppled or crushed by trials and disappointments, tragedies or strife, temporary suffering or seemingly endless frustration because every day, the sun rises, and there, we see Him.

In every infant born, He smiles upon us.

Each time we dare sing Halleluiahs in the face of death, we celebrate the God who has won the victory.

No matter how much evil lurks on this earth, from the back alleyways of our city to the halls of congress, we cannot be discouraged, for Christ has risen.

That truth has to change the way we live because saying that we believe it and letting that truth rule our lives can be two different things.

Sara and I ran a six-mile race out in Covington just yesterday. I want you to know that I ran faster than I ever have before. I finished in the top ten of my age group. There were only eight men in my age group, but that's hardly the point. At about mile five I was feeling tired, and there were two signs at the five-mile marker: one that said, "Runners, this way," and the other that said, "Hospital, this way."

It's so easy just to stop running, especially when we can't see that He's with us. Yet, it is in the moments of despair that we must ask ourselves: is He gone, or are we looking in the wrong place? This Easter morning, nearly 200 Christians were killed because their churches in Sri Lanka were bombed. This event is an atrocity, but if terror was their intent, then those bombers do not understand us.

Surely, they think we will see the rubble and will give up.

They believe that we will see the dust settle and will know we are defeated.

Yet, we know the power that rises up from ash heaps and dances to defy the power of death.

We will keep running, then, for we are on a journey toward the New Jerusalem, and not even death can stop the One we follow.

A New Heaven and a New Earth awaits where the former things shall not be remembered or come to mind.

No more shall there be in it an infant that lives for but a few days, or an old person who does not live out a lifetime.

Before we call, He will answer.

While we are yet speaking, He will hear.

The wolf and the lamb will feed together, and in that day that He is bringing, we will finally stop hurting and destroying each other, for we will see Christ alive in our neighbor. We will know that He lives on in the desperate immigrant, in the thirsty and the hungry, the broken and the outcast.

He is not gone.

He is not dead.

He has risen.

Amen.

Part 8: Beyond Easter

From the shepherds and wise men who celebrated His birth, to those who witnessed His resurrection, Jesus transformed the lives He touched. What becomes clear after His resurrection is that His purpose is to transform the world.

The following sermons are based on those post-Resurrection appearances when the resurrected Lord is loose on the earth, inspiring the faithful and changing everything.

Those Who Have Not Seen
John 20: 19-31
Preached on April 28, 2019

This Sunday morning, I feel the need to defend the disciple Thomas.

Have you ever felt like he needed defending?

Out of all the disciples, besides Judas, I believe Thomas is the one with the worst reputation. Sometimes, we pick on Peter, but while we pick on him, we also acknowledge how Peter redeems himself and becomes a great hero of the Church.

I don't believe Thomas is any less heroic, while all the time we criticize him. We call him "Doubting Thomas," which isn't fair. We don't call Peter "Denying Peter," do we?

I believe it's important to take some time to understand why it was that he wouldn't just trust what the disciples were telling him. If we had a little more empathy for the guy, we might learn something important from him.

In our second Scripture lesson for this morning, the disciples were telling Thomas that Christ had risen. For years, Christians have been wondering why Thomas couldn't just take their word for it. However, can you imagine how their story must have sounded to him? Considering their behavior, could Thomas really just accept the testimony of the same guys who had pledged to follow Jesus till the end, then deserted Him?

Could he possibly trust Peter who had denied the Savior three times?

Looking at this situation rationally, in cross examination, any attorney or judge among us would find plenty of reason to dismiss the testimony of this group of witnesses because they had all, in their own ways, failed to prove themselves as trustworthy and honorable.

Worse than that, they were all afraid.

People will say almost anything when they're afraid.

That might have been what Thomas was thinking.

Surely, he was disappointed in them for being so cowardly, for Thomas consistently proved himself to be the most lionhearted among them. A significant detail in this account we've just read from the Gospel of John is there in the first verse:

223

"When it was evening on that day, the first day of the week, and the doors of the house where the disciples had met were locked for fear of the Jews, Jesus came and stood among them."

This group of people were so scared that they'd huddled up in this one house, locked the door, and weren't going anywhere, but where is Thomas?

When Jesus came and stood among them, Thomas wasn't there.

Thomas is the only one who wasn't hiding behind the locked doors.

Did you notice that?

It's important to think through this detail, that he's the only one courageous enough to leave this locked room. This kind of courage is consistent with the other episodes in John's Gospel where Thomas is mentioned.

While we've been told our whole lives not to be like Thomas, in the eleventh chapter, Mary and Martha had just sent word that their brother Lazarus was dying. The other disciples are scared to go, afraid that if they go back into Judea, those who oppose Jesus will kill Him and his followers. They may have been right about that, but when Jesus insists that they go anyway, marked men or not, Thomas says, "Let us also go, that we may die with him."

Throughout the entire Gospel, Thomas is the picture of courage.

While the other disciples want to stay where it's safe, only Thomas is willing to say, "Let us also go, that we may die with him." Only Thomas is willing to leave the security of locked doors to do whatever it was that courageous people were doing in the wake of the Lord's crucifixion.

Knowing this about him, we must see his doubts as but another example of his courage.

The disciples said to him, "We have seen the Lord," but he said to them, "Unless I see the mark of the nails in his hands, and put my finger in the mark of the nails and my hand in his side, I will not believe."

History calls him Doubting Thomas because of this, only do you know what a weaker man would have done? Do you know what a coward would have done? All around us are people who are too afraid to admit what they don't know and can't understand, but Thomas was bold to say what stood in the way of his belief.

How many folks do you know who just go along with what their friends say and do for fear of rejection? Thomas was so courageous that he just put himself out there.

This is a rare quality.

So many, when faced with a choice between speaking up and keeping quiet would have blended in with those disciples despite their scruples and suspicions, but not Thomas. While sometimes it is easier to agree with popular opinion rather than struggle to find out the truth, Thomas was determined to know, even if it meant seeing the wounds and taking in the gory details of His death.

That's why I believe he has something important to teach us, for while it's easy to just take someone else's word for it, it's not always right.

Even now, there are those who would just tell us what *The Mueller Report* says.

There are those who say that by it our President is exonerated. Others tell us that by the same report, he is fit to be impeached. We all wonder to whom we should be listening, but you know what Thomas would do? He would read it himself.

Likewise, in the wake of another shooting rooted in anti-Semitism, consider how there are still so many who fear the Jews as those disciples did, blaming them for any manner of grievance. Thomas demands we question our fears and our prejudices.

"Show me the proof," he says.

Do you know how many lives would be saved if we all demanded our fears and prejudices be validated before acting on them?

In the same way, there are those who tell us what to think about illegal immigrants. Some say they're criminals, others say they're friends, but do you know what Thomas would do? He would go and get to know one.

When I worked as a lawn maintenance man, I was one of the only employees able to get a valid driver's license, but my crew of illegal immigrants wasn't made up of drug dealers, as some politicians have characterized. No. Back in Mexico, one had been a doctor, another was a dance instructor.

You see, too often, we take someone else's word for it, but Thomas refuses. He says, "Let me see Him myself. Show me His wounds."

This is crucial guidance, for in our world today, there are so many who think they know without truly understanding. Think about those who think they know everything about homosexuality, but none of them really knows a thing until his son or daughter has come into the kitchen saying, "Dad, I'm gay."

This is where we need the courage of Thomas, for it's one thing to be told what to think and to swallow it; it's another thing to touch the wounds left by a society who drowns too many in shame.

That's what Thomas did.

He touched those wounds, and for all these years, we've been telling children not to be like Thomas, but when I look out on the world to see how many people are like lemmings jumping off a ledge because of the fools they listen to, I wish our world had a few more people like Thomas in it.

He asked to touch His wounds.

We can all learn a lot if we aren't afraid to touch the wounds.

Of course, no one likes to see that kind of thing.

People often don't like to talk about the wounds.

It's not polite.

Back in high school, I went on our church's ski trip with a broken nose. The doctor had straightened it out and bandaged it, but my mom wanted me to keep it protected by wearing a catcher's mask on the ski slope.

"What will people say about me if they see me skiing with a catcher's mask on?" I asked her. Well, no one had the courage to ask me about it, so I never had to find out.

People don't often have the courage to ask about the wounds.

People don't really like to talk about them.

Columbia, Tennessee was a community with a wound that no one much liked to talk about. We lived there while I served the First Presbyterian Church for nearly seven years, and one of the things I learned not to ask about too much was the Race Riot of 1946.

From books and whispered conversations, I learned that an African American soldier returned from World War II, unprepared to submit again to segregation. When he stepped out of line, pushing a store clerk who was mean to his mother through a window, a mob assembled, and someone bought a length of rope. Hearing the rumors, his family hid him and protected him. In fact, every African American family in town, it seemed, stood armed and ready to defend him.

They had seen the last of lynching in their town and weren't about to let it happen again. However, the town was in an uproar. The National Guard was called in. This was all quite concerning, though hardly a shot was fired. Just the same, the county jail was filled up with African American men who were arrested for defending this young soldier. Then, Thurgood Marshall came to town to defend them.

This was his first major legal victory.

Today, the riot is sometimes called the Prelude to the Civil Rights Movement, but after Thurgood Marshall won the legal battle, he had to be snuck out of Columbia in the trunk of a car.

Years later, when Thurgood Marshall rose to be one of our nation's Associate Justices of the Supreme Court, a young African American man went to meet him in his chambers.

He said, "Justice Marshall. I'm from Columbia, Tennessee. I want to thank you for the good work you did back there."

The Justice was humble. He wouldn't take much credit, but then asked, "To get out of Columbia, did they have to sneak you out in the trunk of a car?"

"No, sir," he said.

"Then I guess I did do something good in Columbia," Justice Marshall responded.

That's a good story. Unfortunately, it's a story about wounds.

That's just because all the best stories involve wounds and a force that's stronger than them. What Thomas was brave enough to see is that the realities of life may even leave wounds on Christ, but God heals them, and those who have the courage to look at those wounds will know just how powerful our God is.

What Thomas discovered is that love always wins.

Death shall not have the final world.

The light always shines in the darkest of times if only we are bold enough to look for it.

Blessed are those who believe these things without having to see them, but for those of us who need proof, we need only seek the wounds to find it.

From every brokenness that He heals, we know the power of God.

Amen.

Follow Me
Psalm 30 and John 21: 1-19
Preached on May 5, 2019

The book of Exodus tells about manna in the wilderness: "a fine flaky substance, as fine as frost on the ground" that the Israelites lived on as they traveled through the wilderness, from slavery in Egypt to freedom in the Promised Land. An interesting thing about this manna is that it had an expiration date. Some of the people tried to keep some of their manna from one day into the next, but it "bred worms and became foul."

That sounds gross, but a lot of things are that way.

Mostly, they are obvious: milk, fish, house guests. However, other things go foul, too. Many things, not immediately obvious, will collect worms and become foul if they aren't used responsibly and in a timely manner: money, for one, and time, for another.

Officially, the Presbyterian Church has called today "Wills Emphasis Sunday." It seems odd to add "Wills Emphasis Sunday" to a church calendar that includes Easter and Christmas, but wills are important. Considering what greed does to human hearts and how either want or abundance can hurt families, wills are worth thinking about.

You've seen how siblings will become more like circling vultures in times of death when an inheritance is contested, so making a will must be emphasized because money will collect worms and become foul when selfishness invades our hearts.

Time is that way, too.

Last Friday, I was at the zoo chaperoning a field trip, and right next to the nice, open gorilla habitat that's there now is a statue of Willie B. As a child I remember going to visit Willie B the gorilla in his one room in the ape house. I remember how sad he looked in there, and how someone got him a TV. I remember staring at him, confined to his four walls, all alone and with nothing to do but watch TV. It was sad because watching TV all the time when you were born to live in the jungle will do something to you, just as fishing will do something to you if you were born to change the world.

After everything they'd seen and heard, they went fishing.

Now, if there is plenty of time to be a disciple, then there's no harm in spending an evening going fishing. It had been a stressful chain of events for the disciples, after all.

They saw their Lord arrested and crucified.

They were terrified of being arrested and killed themselves, so these men acted out of fear and ran or denied Him.

Then there was the funeral, which is physically and emotionally exhausting in and of itself, but after the funeral, His body disappeared from the tomb.

That wasn't expected.

The empty tomb demanded that they stretch their minds according to what they never imagined possible. Then, He appeared to them, risen from the dead, inviting them to see and touch the wounds left by a cruel society, but healed by God.

Can you imagine a more eventful few days?

Had I been in their position, after all that, I would have wanted to take a long nap, eat a big dinner, and spend the next few days at home. Maybe you would have hiked the mountain or hit the golf course. These disciples decided to go fishing.

In one sense, if they were just doing that to relax, then you can understand why. Maybe they needed a break, but there's a difference between taking a break and putting your life on hold. That's a real temptation.

There's a thing now called a gap year that's meant to be a break. After high school, some students wisely take a year to consider what they want to do with their lives. This year of thinking and exploring can lead to students going to college or their careers more mature and directed than they would be otherwise, which is good. If you go to college, it's good to go knowing what you want to do with your life and motivated to get the training to go and do it. However, some take a gap year, travel and relax, and decide that's what they'd like to do with their lives.

I remember being a senior in college thinking I'd like to make a life out of being in college.

It was great.

My friends were there.

There were parties to go to.

My parents paid for everything.

That won't work forever because education is meant to prepare us for life. If we put off living, we'll collect worms and become foul. Do you know anyone like that?

The disciples went fishing, but this was symbolic more than it was relaxing. After everything they'd been through, the Gospel of John is telling us here that they ended up where Jesus had found them in the beginning.

To Jesus, it must have seemed as though all His work and all His teaching had done nothing. It's as though the end of year Milestone results had come in, and His students had the same score they had at the beginning of the school year. They went back to fishing, and this is bad because time has an expiration date.

If we don't use the time we have to the glory of God, we will collect worms and become foul.

I didn't take a gap year in between high school and college, but after graduating college and before starting seminary, I fell back on the only work experience I had: lawn maintenance. After all that tuition my parents paid, I went back to doing the thing that I had done before college over at the Winnwood Retirement Community. The only thing different was that after college, I got a job cutting grass in Buckhead instead of Marietta.

In case my parents' concern with this career choice hadn't made the point clearly enough, I've told you before how I remember a woman pointing me out as I worked in her yard and whispering too loudly to her children: "That's why you go to college kids, so you don't have to do that."

It's not that there's anything wrong with a career in lawn maintenance, but Jesus is making the same point to Peter. While we can serve the Lord anywhere, there's a big difference between using our time and our treasure in service to God and killing time and wasting our money.

There's a difference between relaxing and avoiding.

There's a difference between sleeping in and hiding from the world.

There's a difference between looking at your phone to check the time and looking at your phone to check out from your life.

Some people fish to make a living; other people fish to take a break from what they've been doing, while these disciples were fishing to put off doing what they've been called by God to do. That's why Jesus had to show up once again.

Described in our second Scripture lesson is the third time the Resurrected Jesus revealed Himself to His disciples. He has to keep showing up to tell them what they should have known and get them to do what they should have been doing.

That's the way it is with people, though.

We have to be encouraged, then encouraged again, and sometimes something still holds us back from doing what we know we should. I'll run into people at the grocery store who will say, "Pastor, I've been meaning to get back to church."

"That's great," I'll say. "A lot has changed. How long has it been?"

"Ten years or so," they'll say, and might add, "In fact, it's been so long that now I'm afraid everyone will wonder where I've been and what I've been doing."

One of the worst things about procrastination is that if you put something off for long enough, you feel too ashamed to just go and do it.

So it was with Peter.

Jesus called to him. He was so excited but notice this detail: "When Simon Peter heard that it was the Lord, he put on some clothes, for he was naked, and jumped into the sea."

What does it mean that he put on clothes to go swimming?

Most people don't do that, but I know a woman who was taking a shower when a tornado swept through town, and her last, most desperate prayer was, "Please, Lord, don't let me die and my body be found naked."

That's how it is.

When we're innocent babies, completely comfortable in our own skin, we just wander around regardless of who sees what. Then, something changes.

Adam and Eve ate of the forbidden fruit; then, they made clothes to cover their nakedness.

A child wonders if he's too thin or too big and is afraid to take his shirt off.

We cover up ourselves with make-up or whatever, hiding ourselves even before the God who stitched us together in our mother's wombs.

Here the Gospel writer is telling us that Peter was excited to see Jesus, but in seeing Him, he felt such shame that he had to get dressed before jumping in the water. He couldn't stand before Him like a newborn, innocent baby. No, he had denied the Savior three times, then didn't know what to do with himself, so he went back to fishing.

You can imagine.

What happens next on the shore is significant. Jesus said to them, "Come and have breakfast." When they had finished breakfast, Jesus said to Simon Peter, "Simon son of John, do you love me more than these?"

He said to him, "Yes, Lord; you know that I love you."

Jesus said to him, "Feed my lambs."

A second time he said to him, "Simon son of John, do you love me?"

He said to him, "Yes, Lord; you know that I love you."

Jesus said to him, "Tend my sheep."

He said to him the third time, "Simon son of John, do you love me?"

Peter felt hurt because he said to him the third time, "Do you love me?" but maybe you know why the question, like his denial, came in threes. Maybe now you also know why Jesus had to show up to Peter again.

All the time, we put off what must be done, for shame holds us in the past while the future passes us by, so Jesus said to him, "Feed my sheep. Very truly, I tell you, when you were younger, you used to fasten your own belt and go wherever you wished. But when you grow old, you will stretch out your hands and someone else will fasten a belt around you and take you where you do not wish to go."

I didn't understand this part of the story for a long time, but now I do.

As a new Associate Pastor, I was honored to be asked by a mother to baptize her child. However, the Senior Pastor wanted to do it. Well, that might have been OK, had I told the mother before we made it to the baptismal font. When the Senior Pastor took the child from her, as the water was marking her infant's head, this mother was holding back tears and rage. The look on her face made me want to go fishing.

I told my friend George all about it the next morning over breakfast.

He looked me in the eye and said, "Well, Joe, you really messed up."

That's not exactly what he said. What he really said can't be repeated in church. Then, he said, "But it's OK because you're going to do it differently next time."

We only have so much time before we run out of it.

Because the clock is ticking, this church has to be the kind of place where people are set free from shame to live their lives because that's what Jesus does. He doesn't give Peter a guilt trip for dragging his feet.

Instead, He fed him, forgave him, and sent him out to feed God's sheep.

The question he asked Peter is the same one He asks us: will you feed His sheep?

We don't have enough time to fish any longer.

Live today for all it's worth and pass on the grace and forgiveness that you have received while you still can.

Amen.

In Over Our Heads, But Not Alone
Psalm 23 and Acts 9: 36-43

Preached on May 12, 2019

You might know the comic strip *B.C.* It runs daily in the *Marietta Daily Journal*, as well as most other papers, and is set at the dawn of time in the age of cavemen and cavewomen yet offers subtle commentary on our lives today.

Last Wednesday, that was especially true.

In the first frame of the comic, the caveman or "cave-husband" announces, "I've invented the dishwasher." Obviously, this is the first dishwasher ever invented, so in the second frame, he demonstrates how one would place a plate in the rack of his new invention, as this is something that's never been done before. But as he's bending over and placing the plate in the rack in the third frame, the cavewoman comes up behind him to say, "Good grief! You're doing that all wrong!"

Husbands, has that ever happened to you?

Every day that happens to me. The truth is, though, to do things correctly, I often do need supervision. That's true of many of us. On this Mother's Day, we have to give thanks to God for those women who keep us out of trouble. Most men need their mothers, spouses, sisters, and daughters for exactly this reason. If it weren't for them, many of us would be wearing only the t-shirts on top in our drawers and the same ties we bought fifteen years ago.

However, I should be careful about generalizing.

Not all men are this way.

Take Thomas for example.

A few weeks ago, I preached a sermon on the disciple Thomas who doubts the other disciples when they tell him the Lord has risen from the dead. I tried to make the case that when Thomas doubts them, in asking for proof, he's actually being courageous. That would be consistent with his character illustrated elsewhere in the Gospels.

In the Gospel of John, Jesus said:

> Do not let your hearts be troubled.
>
> Believe in God, believe also in me.
>
> In my Father's house there are many dwelling places.

If it were not so, would I have told you that I go to prepare a place for you?

And if I go and prepare a place for you, I will come again and will take you to myself, so that where I am there you may be also.

And you know the way to the place where I am going.

You've heard these verses. They're read at most funerals. In response, you can imagine all the disciples saying, "Sure, we know the way." However, Thomas said to him, "Lord, we do not know where you are going. How can we know the way?" because he was the only man courageous enough to ask for directions.

What he didn't know, he asked about.

That was Thomas.

What about Peter?

Peter is the one in the spotlight this week. He's been called on to raise a beloved woman from dead. That sounds easy enough, right?

The thing about Peter is that Jesus always believed in Peter more than Peter believed in himself. Do you remember when Jesus was walking out on the water, and He called Peter to walk out with Him? In the fourteenth chapter of Matthew's Gospel, Jesus was walking on the sea.

Peter saw Him with the other disciples and said, "Lord, if it is you, command me to come to you on the water."

Jesus said, "Come."

Peter got out of the boat they were in and started walking on the water, but then, he noticed a strong wind, became frightened, and started to sink.

What did Jesus do?

Peter cried out in his distress, and Jesus saved him. That's what Jesus does when He's around, but what happens when Jesus isn't there to bail him out?

That's a question many mothers ask of their children:

"What are you going to do when I'm not here to remind you to do your homework, pack your lunch, do your laundry, pay your bills, and make sure you pay attention to road signs?"

On Wednesday, page two of the *Marietta Daily Journal* was an article entitled: "Bridge beam struck, take 19." If you need a good reason to subscribe to the *Marietta Daily Journal*, coverage of trucks ignoring the height restrictions on the historic Concord Road Covered Bridge alone makes our local paper invaluable. The truck that did it last week was hauling a trailer, and I can imagine that the driver's wife or mother wasn't with him in the truck because if she had been, she would have been doing the same thing the cavewoman was doing in the *B.C.* comic: "Good grief, you're doing this all wrong! It says it right there on the sign. The trailer is too tall, honey."

You can imagine what it would be like if Peter were driving that truck. Without Jesus helping him through life, he gets in all kinds of trouble. He wants to walk out on the water with the Lord. Jesus tells him, "Don't be afraid. Have faith."

Peter can't do it.

He starts sinking.

What will happen to Peter without Jesus around?

Today is Mother's Day. This is a day to acknowledge that, just like Peter, without certain people, we, too, would be a mess.

I used to send our girls to preschool un-ponytailed.

I'd have to say to their teacher, handing her a rubber band and brush, "Would you please help me with this? I just can't do it."

We pack to go on a trip. Sara asks our girls and me whether or not we packed enough underwear. This is how it is. On Mother's Day, we have to give thanks for the people who were there helping us figure out how to make it in this world, and we do have to figure it out because at some point, we have to do it without Mama there to help us.

For Peter, it wasn't Mama. It was Jesus, but it's the same thing.

He had seen Jesus do what the widows were asking Peter to do, only it's one thing to ride in the back seat of a car, and it's another thing to drive. When Peter found himself in an upper room with Tabitha laying in state, clean and completely dead, you can imagine why he asked everyone to leave the room where she lay. It's so he could panic.

"Please come to us without delay," was the message these widows sent to Peter.

"I thought they just wanted me to preach," I can imagine Peter saying, only there's more to being a disciple than preaching. Being a disciple also demands a lot of doing, so Peter went, and I've been asked to do enough that was out of my comfort zone and beyond my abilities to have some idea of what it must have felt like for him to be there in that room with Tabitha, a crowd of her friends full of unrealistic expectations right on the other side of the door.

There are so many moments in life that demand too much from us.

The worst is when I realize so clearly that there's no one else to help.

It has to be me.

Mama wasn't there to do it for him.

Jesus wasn't around to do it, either.

It had to be Peter.

Do you know what that feels like?

I can just imagine what images thinking this way might bring up to your consciousness.

In this room today are sons who became fathers.

There are daughters who became mothers.

Some are here who then became mothers to their own mothers.

Right here in this Sanctuary are those who long ago went to doctors when they were sick, then became doctors themselves, only now, in retirement, they have to get used to being the patients again.

I'm up here preaching this morning, but who's in the choir? The man I grew up listening to is there. Here I am, and if you think it doesn't terrify me every time, you'd be wrong because it does. However, walking out in faith into unchartered territory is what life demands. Jesus calls us to walk out on the water and into the room where the dead woman lies, for if we only do what we're comfortable doing, we never find out what He'll do through us if we just trust Him.

If we never have to walk through the valley of the shadow of death, we never learn that just when we think we're all alone, we're not.

"Though I walk through the darkest valley, I fear no evil;"

Why?

"For you are with me."

That's how it was with Peter.

He "put all of them outside, and then he knelt down and prayed." What did he pray, you might wonder? I don't know what he prayed, but had it been me, my prayer would have been something like, "Lord, I don't know how I got into this, but You're going to have to get me out, so work through me, please!"

It must have been like the prayer uttered by all those who have to say goodbye but don't believe they have the strength to do it;

the kind of prayer voiced by those who need a miracle to make it in a world without their mother by their sides.

It must have been like the prayer moaned by the desperate and overwhelmed who know what it feels like to drown, in or away from the water.

Peter must have prayed the same prayer that we all pray when we suddenly realize that "if it is to be, it is up to me." That's a Harvey Mackay quote. He is a seven-time *New York Times* best-selling author, who wrote, among other books, one called *Beware of the Naked Man Who Offers You His Shirt*.

Jean Ray quoted him to me, and it struck me because I have an idea of what it must have felt like to be in that room; to know that it fell to you to speak, but to realize as you utter the words that you're not alone at all because this is exactly what you'd been prepared for.

After praying, he turned to the body and said, "Tabitha, get up."

It's a powerful moment, but it's in moments like this that we so truly know that we're hardly alone and that we are capable of far more than we ever dreamed.

However, our fear would keep us from even trying.

Too often, we're so consumed with fear, we just sink down into the water. Fear that we're not enough and never will be ensures that we never live up to what we're capable of.

Last Thursday in the paper was a quote from Laurence J. Peter, a Canadian-born educator who said, "Television has changed the American child from an irresistible force into an immovable object."

I got a lot of material out of the *MDJ* this week, didn't I?

Regardless, Mr. Peter is right.

Those who only watch TV fall asleep to what they're capable of, while those kids who walk into our Club 3:30 program hear something else. Their graduation was last Wednesday night, and the speech that struck me the most was from one of the graduates of the program, now a college graduate, and former recipient of the Peggy Bullard Scholarship.

Daniel Leon got up there and said, "I want to thank all of you who helped me with my homework, but especially Libba Schell, who would say to me week after week, "One day, you're going to be my doctor or my lawyer." What a gift that was to him, as now he goes out into the world knowing he has the potential to do far more than he'd ever imagined.

Like him and like Peter, we have to walk out onto the water, knowing that life may be overwhelming, but we're never alone.

Even when it fell to Peter to say the words, still Christ was with him. For when we walk through the valley of the shadow of death, He is with us, and even when we walk out these doors to do who knows what and to go who knows where, we may be in over our heads, but we are never alone.

Amen.

And She Prevailed Upon Us
John 14: 23-29 and Acts 16: 9-15

Preached on May 26, 2019

This second Scripture lesson that I've just read contains one of my favorite phrases used in the whole Bible: "And she prevailed upon us." It's not a verse that anyone should commit to memory because it contains some life-changing theological truth. This phrase in Acts 16:15 isn't like John 3:16, "For God so loved the world that he gave his only Son, so that everyone who believes in him may not perish but may have eternal life."

Memorize that one because it will change your life, but remember Acts 16: 15, "And she prevailed upon us." because in five words, the author of the book of Acts describes my whole childhood. Maybe it describes my whole life, and to know the story of the Christian Church is to understand that there are many heroes like Paul, whose names we know, who had to be pushed to realize their full potential by certain women whose names we might have forgotten.

In reality, the book of Acts is the story of the likes of Peter and Paul, who would have been nothing were it not for the likes of Lydia.

That's something like my story.

I was raised in a family of strong women.

My father's mother raised him and his two sisters in a loving household, despite her husband's alcoholism. My mother's mother, Mrs. Peggy Bivens, was such a force that I never once challenged her, questioned her, or tested her.

I remember one morning at her house when we were kids sitting at her kitchen table. Because we were coming to visit, she bought some muffins from Sam's, especially for my sister.

This purchase was special because it was out of character.

She stocked her pantry inspired by weight loss crazes of the 1980's. She mostly lived on Tab cola and Special K cereal, so I remember her putting one of these calorie-laden Sam's muffins in front of my sister and saying, "Elizabeth, I bought these special for you."

In that moment, my sister did something I thought was unadvisable.

She said, "But Nanny (that's what we called her), I don't like those anymore."

After she said that, I remember my grandmother trying to convince my sister that, in fact, yes, she did still like those muffins. My sister refused to submit to our grandmother's determination to influence what she liked and didn't like, which is the kind of thing that happens when there are two strong women in a family, neither willing to be prevailed upon.

What my sister did is not what I would have done.

Had it been me, it wouldn't have mattered if they were peanut butter muffins and I had a peanut allergy. I'd rather face anaphylactic shock than to defy the iron will of my grandmother.

A couple times I remember trying to tell her that I wasn't hungry.

Did you ever try that? Have your grandchildren ever tried that? Telling your grandmother that you aren't hungry when she thinks you look too skinny is an exercise in futility. All this is just to say that I can imagine what it was like for Paul meeting Lydia.

"And she prevailed upon us" is how our second Scripture lesson ended, and I know what that means.

Now, being prevailed upon can be either good or bad. If you always allow yourself to be prevailed upon, you'll lose yourself. Peer pressure can be like that, and peer pressure can be just plain evil, but in this instance, had Paul stood his ground, his bullheaded insistence might have stifled the spread of the Gospel. Thanks be to God that "she prevailed" upon him because when she did, she expanded the spread of the Gospel beyond what any of the disciples might have imagined.

Those disciples were prone to being narrow-minded, despite the Savior's best intentions. Without Jesus around to correct them, surely, He was nervous about whom He was leaving His Church to. In our first Scripture lesson, Jesus had to warn the disciples, "Do not let your hearts be troubled, and do not let them be afraid."

He told them that He would be ascending into heaven, leaving the work of spreading the Gospel to the ends of the earth to them, but for them to do it, He must have known that they were going to need a little help because that's how we are.

The choir sang, "every time I feel the spirit," which makes me tap my foot a little bit. Already, that's pushing me beyond my Presbyterian comfort zone.

However, if we are to feel the Spirit, we have to be ready to sway to the music.

We must be swept up in a greater vision, beyond what we could have imagined.

241

If we never allow ourselves to be prevailed upon by God's vision for our lives, we'll never live into our full potential, which is bigger than whatever we had been planning for ourselves.

I received an inspirational email last week. I'm on the High Point University mailing list because this woman I was having breakfast with at a conference prevailed upon me. Signing up for the email was easier than fighting her on it, and just this week, the inspiring email said: "If you don't imagine, nothing ever happens at all."

That's a quote from someone named John Green.

I don't know who that is, but he's right. However, I'd add to it because what God does in our lives would defy our imagination, which is unfortunate for us because what's beyond our imagination scares us.

I'll give you a personal example.

About two years ago, a man named Jim Goodlet called me. At the time, I was happily serving a church in Columbia, Tennessee. Jim left me a message telling me that he was chairing a Pastor Nominating Committee to find a new pastor to serve the church I grew up in.

Now why did I imagine he was calling me?

I imagined he was calling me so I could give him the names of some people who might actually be qualified for the position. Never did I imagine that he would want to talk with me. Then, a couple weeks later, after a few phone interviews, Jim Goodlet tried to get me to come down here to interview in person.

Now that made it a little too real.

I got scared then.

Why would I do that, I wondered?

Why would I even think about going down to Marietta, Georgia when I was perfectly happy in Columbia, Tennessee?

I told Jim that on the phone one day about two years ago, but guess what happened?

He prevailed upon me, and it's one of the best things that has ever happened in my life.

How often is that the case? So often the best things in life, the greatest gifts we ever receive, are just like that.

We get called out of our comfort zones.

C.S. Lewis said it's like a child making mud pies in the alleyway receiving an invitation to the seashore. What will she do? Will she go? Will she stay? Will she choose what is unknown and far beyond her reality, or will she stick to the small joy of what she has. Will she allow God's vision for her life to prevail upon her?

Years ago, our church faced the same choice with this Sanctuary. This Sanctuary was built to seat 400 worshipers. That's a lot of people, especially when you consider that this Sanctuary that was built to seat 400 was built by a congregation of 96 members in 1853.

What were they thinking?

There may have had some slow-growth, fiscally-responsible members of the congregation who suggested that they pace themselves, but someone like Lydia prevailed upon them, and here we are today.

You see, this is the way it goes.

We have one idea in our heads. We settle into certain expectations get used to certain things, but every once in a while, someone like Lydia calls us to do something bigger.

It happened in the neighborhood around Kennesaw Avenue last Thursday.

Last Thursday, if you drove on Maple Avenue or some of the other streets around the Westside School, you might have noticed that so many of the mailboxes were decorated. Signs were up congratulating someone named Floyd. I didn't know who that was, so I asked Chris Harrison, our neighbor, and he told me that their mailman, Floyd, was retiring after thirty-five years of delivering the mail. His wife, Katherine, said, "I've lived in a house on Floyd's route for so long that I've had a relationship with Floyd the mailman longer than with my husband, Chris."

This kind of thing doesn't happen all the time.

It doesn't happen all the time that a mail carrier works for thirty-five years and retires.

It doesn't happen all the time that a neighborhood even stops to notice something like that, but someone like Lydia prevailed upon all of them.

In that neighborhood, her name isn't Lydia. One's name is Sarah Bullington; another's name is Becky Poole, and I can imagine how those initial conversations went:

"We should do something for Floyd," one said to her husband.

"Sure, we should," he responded, and then went back to watching the Braves on TV. However, these women weren't going to let this occasion pass without notice, so they prevailed upon their husbands and their neighbors. They had a party in the street, raised enough money to send Floyd to Hawaii, and the whole story ended up on CNN. That's what happens when we listen to the likes of Lydia, while all too often we resist these kinds of voices.

By doing so, we stifle the Spirit.

We settle for mud pies when God invites us to the beach.

Lydia invites us to change the world, but we busy ourselves rearranging the furniture on the deck of the *Titanic*.

She reminds us that God speaks of justice on earth and righteousness in government, but what do we settled for? On the eve of Memorial Day, I realize how important the voice of Lydia is, for as the war drums beat again, we must listen to the voices of those mothers and fathers whose children will never come home to learn again the price of war.

Lydia would remind us, if we are faithful enough to listen, that while we have grown used to wartime, God would lead us in the ways of peace.

Too often, we don't imagine enough.

We don't allow God's vision for the future to prevail upon us.

To use Rev. Cassie Wait's image from last Sunday, "We don't pull up enough seats to the table, limiting God's grace." Yet, what would have happened had Paul ignored Lydia's voice?

He started out this passage in Asia Minor, what is now Turkey. You can read in Scripture about the great signs and wonders performed through Paul and others during his ministry there, but today, the skyline of every city in Asia Minor is dotted with minarets. A journalist trying to follow the footsteps of Paul in Turkey arrived for mass at the Church of Saint Paul in 1998 and joined a congregation of five other Christians. Look at Macedonia, on the other hand; on the cover of your bulletin is a picture of the ceiling of what is called the Church of Saint Lydia in Macedonia, which we now call Greece.

Thanks be to God she prevailed upon him, and may God, through the likes of such a woman, prevail upon you.

Amen.

Why Do You Stand Looking?
Ephesians 1: 15-23 and Acts 1: 1-11

Preached on June 2, 2019

My family and I spent the last week in Santa Fe, New Mexico. We traveled there with Sara's family. All of us were in one, big house, which was an adventure in and of itself. There was also the challenge that fell mostly to Sara of managing all the wants and needs of this group of people who all wanted to do different things while also wanting to stick together.

One day during the trip, we drove out to a pilgrimage site. That trip made its way to the agenda because, while both their daughters married protestant ministers, Sara's mother and father are Roman Catholic. Since we were staying so close to El Santuario de Chimayo, a shrine and pilgrimage site that attracts about 300,000 people each year, they both wanted to go and check it out, having heard that it is like the Lourdes of the Southwest. I was excited to go, too, as Presbyterians don't often get to go to these kinds of places.

All over the site were pictures of people who had been healed. There were crutches left by those who didn't need them any longer. It's a place with a supposed miraculous soil that comes from a holy well, where a man named Don Bernardo Abeyta found a crucifix in 1810 while doing penance. According to this legend, Christ met him out there in the New Mexico desert. This is a story that many people believe, but Presbyterians tend to be skeptical of this kind of thing. However, thinking of Acts, it should come as no surprise that the Lord would be present in New Mexico, for just as Don Bernardo found a crucifix there in 1810 while doing penance, last week, we celebrated the Apostle Paul who went all the way to Macedonia and joined God who was already at work there.

Likewise, in Acts, Peter went to visit a Roman Centurion named Cornelius, only to find that God had prepared even the heart of one who served the Empire to hear him preach the Gospel. It's miraculous, and I've had the same experience in my life of being surprised by the presence of God in faraway places.

As a high school student, I thought that we were sent by this church to bring the light of Christ to Mexico. We went there to build houses, just as a group from our church is doing now, only every time we went, we discovered that God had beat us there. We have to remember that because, as the disciples saw Jesus ascend into heaven, they were slow to see Him present in the world. Watching Him, they were stuck for a moment, still staring up at the sky.

245

Of course they were, for too often we become obsessed with where we saw God at work last, rather than focus our attention on where God is at work now.

I believe the life of faith is something like learning to ride a bike. In one moment, just as the disciples had Jesus there, so you knew that your father was holding the seat. Then, as you and the bike moved forward, even though he promised not to, a good father always lets go. Remember that for a few moments everything was fine. You were riding a bike, and it was as miraculous as Peter walking on the water. However, you then looked back to where your father once was, namely, holding the seat. Not seeing him where he was supposed to be, but far behind, celebrating your independence and gesturing that you look forward and not backward, you lost balance and fell. That's because life, like riding a bike, requires that we pay more attention to where we are going than where we've been.

Christ ascended into heaven, and the disciples were transfixed, staring up at the clouds. Suddenly, two men in white robes stood by them.

They said, "Men of Galilee, why do you stand looking up toward heaven?"

It's as though they were saying: "He's not up there in the clouds anymore. You have to stop looking for Him there, or you'll fall."

While we were out west, we visited the cliff dwellings at Bandoleer National Park. This was an exciting place to go because there we saw human residences, thousands of years old. They were ancient apartment buildings made of wood and mud. It was incredible; so incredible that Lily and Cece's cousin Sam wasn't paying attention to where he was going. He was looking up, and so he slipped and fell and scraped his knee and elbow.

It happened on my watch, so I picked him up and brushed him off.

He needed a Band-Aid, which of course, I did not have. Luckily, a woman in a blue hat stopped and pulled one out of her little purse. That made him feel better. The icing on the cake was the piece of gum that she pulled out of her purse next.

When Sara caught up, this lady said to her, "He did just fine."

I said, "Thank you." because I thought she was talking about me.

She wasn't. She was talking about Sam, and now I see this experience as one of those little miracles. So far, this woman in the blue hat has worked more wonders than the dirt I got out of the well at El Santuario de Chimayo.

That's not immediately obvious, however, because so often we just brush off such acts of the Spirit as though they were happenstance.

246

Likewise, years ago, I was visiting a lonely woman in her home. She was going on and on about how no one from the church ever speaks to her. I was empathetic because it's always tragic when the church fails at being the church, but it happens, so I apologized. However, then, the phone rang. It was a member of the church calling to check on her. I could hear the conversation. "I've missed seeing you and just wanted to see how you were," says the church member on the line. Once she hung up, thanking this woman from the church, ironically, she just launched right back into it, "No one from the church even knows me!"

She failed to see Jesus right before her because she was focused somewhere else.

Too often we are this way.

Chaining our focus on where He was, we fail to see where He is.

Confining Him to our expectations, we think we know where and when He'll show up and miss Him when He is present on His own terms rather than ours.

In this way, the past becomes a prison to too many, despite the fact that God is even now opening the door to freedom and new life. Then, idolatry convinces us that we know God, whereas God has been defying our expectations since the beginning of time. So rarely do we open our eyes enough to recognize that Christ is at work, just not always where we expect Him to be.

This is an important lesson for our church today because we have not yet reached the Promised Land, though we are tempted to mistake the bygone days for it. Nor have we missed out on it, for we have yet to see the peak of what God will do among us. However, how God is moving in the present may look different from the past, and where God will lead us demands that we leave so much of our past behind. We don't really know how God will move among us next, but we must choose looking for Him at work in new and mysterious ways over nostalgia or regret.

There's danger in both.

Nostalgia doesn't seem dangerous. Neither does looking up at the clouds, but there are Christians who are so heavenly-minded that they're no earthly good. There are living people so consumed with ancient history that they risk becoming dusty relics themselves.

We sometimes honor the memory of the departed over paying attention to the newborn.

247

We can be so regretful that we abdicate the promise of the future.

We grow so used to hurt that we fail to see the miracle worker even when He stands before us. We just look up at the clouds, blind to God all around us. That's why we must hear them asking, "Men and women of Marietta, why do you stand looking up toward heaven?" This God of ours incarnate in Christ Jesus is alive and well, leading us into a new future.

I know it's coming, too, because as I was working on this sermon, we were way up in the clouds, flying back home from Santa Fe, New Mexico, and I didn't see Him there. However, I remembered where He promised He would be:

For I was hungry, and you gave me food,

I was thirsty and you gave me something to drink,

I was a stranger and you welcomed me,

I was naked and you gave me clothing,

I was sick and you took care of me,

I was in prison and you visited me.

For truly the King of Heaven said, "Just as you did it to one of the least of these who are members of my family, you did it to me."

Let us look into the future knowing that He's leading us onward and let us go out into the world today expecting for Him to meet us there.

Amen.

In Defiance of Babel
Genesis 11: 1-9 and Acts 2: 1-21

Preached on June 9, 2019

It's amazing how relevant Scripture is. The great theologian of the 20th Century, Karl Barth, would advise his students to prepare their sermons with the Bible in one hand and the newspaper in the other. He wanted them to be watching as ancient Scripture comes alive day after day.

This seemed eerily relevant advice last Monday morning as I read the *Marietta Daily Journal*. You may know that our current Habitat for Humanity house is a joint effort. Just yesterday, members of our church, coordinated by Tim Hammond and the Mission Council, were scheduled to join together with Methodists, Episcopalians, Catholics, and Unitarians, as well as members from Temple Kol Emeth Synagogue and two mosques to build a new home for a single mother named Belinda and her two children.

We're working together with all of them, but this is the funny part: considering all the different religious groups involved in the build, last Monday morning, our paper quoted the project's co-chair who said, "We call it our Tower of Babel."

Now that we've read what God did at the Tower of Babel, I'm not sure I'm glad that's how he referred to the house. However, I get his point. We live in this world where, most of the time, different people can't do anything like this. It's as though we're all speaking different languages. Oftentimes, even those who speak the same language can't understand each other.

If you need proof of the massive level of misunderstanding prevalent in our culture, of course, the obvious example is always Washington, D.C. where "the aisle" is like some deep, unbridgeable chasm. Yet, there's no need to look all the way to Washington for a failure to communicate. Spouses often can't understand each other.

Neighbors don't always know each other's names.

Then, there's always someone at the family reunion who seems to have come from a completely different planet rather than the same gene pool.

The two Scripture lessons we've just read tell two of the accounts where all that changes: first, in Genesis, when "The whole earth had one language and the same words," and then, in Acts, when the gathered believers began "to speak in other languages, as the Spirit gave them ability." Recorded then, are at least two brief instances when we all understood each other. Because such understanding is rare, it's good to pay attention to both these passages of Scripture, but we must also pay attention to how they are different. These two Scripture lessons are very different in the sense that in one instance, humankind uses their common tongue to work together to build a tower so that they might "make a name for [them]selves," while in the other, it was not humankind, but God who was glorified.

That's a significant difference in motivation.

The difference reminds me of a great quote: "It's amazing how much can be accomplished if no one cares who gets the credit." So often we care about that: trying to "make a name for ourselves," though it is a bad idea. Be it Ancient Egypt, Mussolini's Rome, or wherever else masses of soldiers goose step in identical uniforms, when self-interest, vain glory, and pride guide the project, not only a tower, but tyranny is being created.

"Let us make a name for ourselves," they said in our first Scripture lesson.

These are dangerous words.

> [So] The Lord came down to see the city and the tower, which mortals had built. And the Lord said, "Look, they are one people, and they have all one language; and this is only the beginning of what they will do; nothing that they propose to do will now be impossible for them. Come, let us go down, and confuse their language there, so that they will not understand one another's speech."

I used to think that God confused the languages of those who were building the Tower of Babel because God was threatened by what humanity was able to do. However, on the heels of the 75th Anniversary of D-Day, I know that what God was worried about was how whenever humans are able to build a tower, we nearly always also build a gas chamber.

Every time one nation sets her mind on making a name for herself, she does so with violence and inhumanity towards other nations and ethnicities.

Should someone say, "Let's prove, once and for all, that Marietta is better than everyone else," the football team will face recruitment violations, the mayor will be tempted to accept bribes, and the Chamber of Commerce will turn into a den of graft and favors. That's because when making a name for ourselves is the goal, winning becomes more important than righteousness, control more important than justice, order more important than grace, silence more important than hope, and survival more important than love.

Last Thursday night, our girls had a swim meet.

I had the honor of being a line judge.

My duty was to report which kid won each race. Did you know that on each side of the pool there have to be two line judges? One parent from each team has to be there to judge the line because even in a kid's swim-team competition, if one subdivision has the chance to "make a name for [her]self" honesty and integrity are bulldozed in the pursuit of vain glory.

On the other hand, something different happened at Pentecost.

They weren't speaking the same language, but they could all understand each other. Did you notice that?

"All of them were filled with the Holy Spirit and began to speak in other languages, as the Spirit gave them ability… And at this sound the crowd gathered and was bewildered, because each one heard them speaking in the native language of each."

Scripture doesn't say that each person in Jerusalem could suddenly understand one language. What Scripture says when describing Pentecost is that each could understand the voice of God speaking to them in his own language. One Bible Scholar named Diamonthi Niles translates this passage saying, "each one heard them speaking in her mother tongue."

I like that.

I like that because Siri can't understand my accent.

Neither can Alexa.

I once heard about an airport in Wisconsin posting a "help wanted" add for telephone operators who could speak Spanish, German, Mandarin, and Southern. I hate that we live in a world where everyone is supposed to speak like a news anchor and where "ain't"' is not a word.

On Pentecost it was different because God's love is different.

Those who seek to make a name for themselves push us towards uniformity. Commerce wants to give every kid a mass-produced Happy Meal and will judge every woman by the same standards of beauty, but God speaks to us in the voice that we don't have to think to understand.

Industrial progress makes us cogs in a wheel to build their towers, stations on an assembly line to build their fleets. Our jobs can demand that we do things the same way, again and again, all according to the manual rather than our creativity, but God sees us as individuals who are uniquely suited to serve His greater purpose.

Scripture tells us that those who are determined to make a name for themselves will violate and objectify us every time. Then, Scripture also proclaims over and over again that God speaks to us in words of love because all our God wants is that we would be saved. As Peter explained to the crowds:

In the last days it will be, God declares,

That I will pour out my Spirit upon all flesh,

And your sons and daughters shall prophesy,

And your young men shall see visions,

And your old men shall dream dreams.

Even upon my slaves, both men and women,

In those days I will pour out my Spirit;

Then everyone who calls on the name of the Lord shall be saved.

The crucial word there is at the end: "everyone."

That word "everyone" is so different from "us." "Then everyone who calls on the name of the Lord will be saved" is so different from, "Let us make a name for ourselves." For there to be an "us," there must be a "them," but are we not all children of Abraham?

Of course, "everyone" is a problematic word as well.

The idea that everyone would get a trophy or that everyone is a winner feels like a culture of pampering rather than reality. On the other hand, how wonderful the world would be if everyone was happy for whoever won the trophy; if everyone celebrated whoever was given the honor of having his name on a mighty sea vessel, tall tower, or scenic park; if everyone sought good and no one cared who got the credit, and everyone did what she believed was right without worrying so much about who benefited. When life is one, long competition between "us" and "them," sooner or later, everyone loses. On the other hand, if the Spirit moves again and we all realize once more that life is one, long blessing from God to all His children, then truly, everyone will be saved.

Early this morning, Jim MacDonald, a great leader in our church, sent me the message Tim Hammond emailed to all of yesterday's Habitat for Humanity volunteers. I didn't ask Tim if I could quote him up here because he would have said no, and this is just too important to miss:

Hello friends, sisters, and brothers, I have been thinking about this day. We had to get up too early; we had to get on a bus and ride to Mableton; we had to endure incredible rain, slosh through mud, and bump into each other trying to accomplish jobs under the confines of one roof. But I want to be clear about this day. We arose early to come together as missionaries in service to our Lord Jesus Christ. We sloshed through rain and mud with smiles. Under that roof we saw each other, not as people in our way, but as those we might serve. We did our best to give Belinda a safe place to live and take care of her family, as well as worship Christ. Friends, today we cemented our family ties.

To God be the glory.

Amen.

Part 9: A Heritage of Faith

The following sermons are based on the account of some of Israel's great prophets. They were preached during the summer, which at First Presbyterian Church means that they were preached in the historic, antebellum Sanctuary.

Just as the prophetic heritage inspires these sermons, so does the local heritage of this congregation, as I attempted to respond to all that was happening in the news the summer of 2019.

Help Along the Way
Galatians 3: 23-29 and 1 Kings 19: 1-15a

Preached on June 23, 2019

Being around kids during the summer reminds me of how obsessed with fairness they can be. Whether here at the church or out on the playground, it seems like, "It's not fair!" is all I ever hear. Again and again, it's "but she got a bigger piece," and "I had to sit in the back seat last time." Kids can be obsessed with justice, and so often they're paying more attention to what everyone else is doing than what's really going on around them.

I heard a radio show this week all about a preschool classroom where the teacher, so tired of her class tattling on each other, placed an old, red rotary phone in the back of the room, and, without plugging it in to anything, told her students that if they needed to tell on one of their friends, they could go and tell it to "the tattle phone." It was a revolutionary success in that the kids used it instead of constantly streaming to her. Someone had the bright idea to plug this phone in to a recorder so that the radio audience could hear what kids were saying, and this is some of what they said: Ramona wasn't listening to the teacher, and Eli hit Kevin. When Vera was playing family with Tommy, he kept trying to wake her up when she was pretending to be asleep. Also, Sally pushed Billy, and Thomas passed gas right in Eugene's face, and he didn't even say excuse me.

The funny thing about all this is that, as far as these kids knew, when they got upset and told on their friends into the tattle phone, there was no one on the other end listening who could do anything about it. This segment of the radio show ended with one child who went home and told his father that the tattle phone was broken. I'm sure his dad was thinking, "What do you mean it's broken. It never worked." His son said, "Dad, the tattle phone is broken. I told the phone that my friend Nicky was pinching me, but after I told the tattle phone, he still didn't stop." Now, some of us have learned this lesson already.

The world isn't fair, and sometimes you go tell the tattle phone, but no one is listening, or you go and tell your teacher, but she says something like, "Well, life's not fair." That being the case, parents have to teach their children that sometimes they must stand up for themselves. Grandfathers lecture their grandchildren about personal responsibility, for sometimes you go looking for someone to help and find out that you're that someone.

The Prophet Elijah stood up to do something about it.

257

He's a great hero in the Bible.

The backstory to today's second Scripture lesson is that there was an evil queen named Jezebel. She was married to the King of Israel, but he was kind of a joke. Because of that, there was no one else to stand up to the Queen's idolatry and oppression; therefore, Elijah stood up to her.

It was a great success, too.

There was a legendary contest between her god, Baal, and Elijah's God. Two altars were set up. The God who rained down fire and lit His respective altar won, and Elijah did it. He triumphed, only then Queen Jezebel decided not to give up and to just have Elijah killed instead.

That's where the unfairness of the situation gets to him.

The Prophet Elijah runs for his life. He went a day's journey into the wilderness because after standing up against Queen Jezebel and all her priests, still unrighteousness and idolatry ruled Israel. He sat down under a solitary broom tree and asked that he might die saying, "It is enough now, O Lord, take away my life for I am no better than my ancestors."

Then, he fell asleep. An angel of the Lord woke him and fed him that he might go forty more days, making it all the way to Horeb, the Mount of God. Then, the word of the Lord came to him saying, "What are you doing here, Elijah?"

He answered, "I have been very zealous for the Lord, the God of hosts; for the Israelites have forsaken your covenant, thrown down your altars, and killed your prophets with the sword. I alone am left, and they are seeking my life, to take it away."

None of this is very fair, and Elijah was right to tell God all about it. He was right to tattle on Jezebel and to defend his own righteousness, for among all the great villains of Scripture, she's one of the worst. Also, among all heroes of our faith, Elijah is among the most faithful. However, seeing his words in print, the part of his speech that seems funny to me now is how often he uses the pronoun "I."

"I am no better than my ancestors," he said.

"I have been very zealous for the Lord, the God of hosts."

Then, while they "have forsaken your covenant, thrown down your altars, and killed your prophets with the sword. I alone am left."

Even though there comes a time when we must stand up for ourselves and can no longer spend all our time tattling to our teachers, this kind of self-centeredness will cloud our vision of reality. Once we've learned to stand up for ourselves, we're not yet out of danger, for if we live into a lie that it's all up to us, we're exactly where the Evil One wants us because this way of thinking and being blinds us to God and holds us far from the truth of how things actually are.

Thinking again of the radio show from the preschool, the journalist who set up and listened to the tattle phone asked the preschool teacher, "About how much of their time is spent concerned with tattling?"

She said, "This isn't scientific, but I'd say most of it."

The journalist responded to this statement by saying, "It's amazing that in a world where they can't feed themselves, dress themselves, or take themselves anywhere, literally able to do nothing on their own, they become so obsessed with fairness." Maybe we laugh about that irony when thinking of little kids, but I can't help but assume that God feels the same way about us.

I can't help but imagine God feeling the same way about Elijah.

"I, I, I," Elijah said to God, but it doesn't matter whether we're down on ourselves, defending ourselves, or trying to show the world that someone else is really the problem, so long as we are the focus, we can't see God at work, feeding us, dressing us, and watching over us by night. In order to get Elijah's focus away from himself, a voice calls him out to the edge of a cliff on top of a mountain.

You can imagine what this was like, for maybe you know already that sometimes clarity comes when we stand on the peak to see the great wide world around us. That was the case with a friend of mine named Jim Hodges. Jim was a member of the first church I served, and he was diagnosed with lung cancer.

For a while, things were OK. He just had to walk around with an oxygen pump, but then he was hospitalized. I remember well the day he called to tell me that the doctor said it wouldn't be long, that he didn't have much time left. We were close, so it was hard for me to see him like that. When I got to his hospital room, his wife, Carol, excused herself, and I sat down by his bed. The first thing I asked was if he was afraid. Jim paused. Then, he said, "I'm afraid Carol doesn't really understand the maintenance schedule for the HVAC contract." After another pause, he said, "Joe, I don't know what I'm going to do when I see Him."

I wasn't sure who Him was at first, so I just listened as he continued talking.

"When I see Him, what will I do? Will I laugh? Will I cry? Will I sing? When I see Jesus, I'm not sure I'll know what to do." Now Jim was from Texas and this happened in a hospital over in Lilburn, but as far as I'm concerned, he could have been meditating on top of a mountain in Tibet for how enlightened he was. His mind wasn't on cancer because he could see so far beyond it.

There's no question in my mind that there is no more miserable person than the one who thinks only of himself. I believe that those who love their neighbors as themselves have unlocked the secret to happiness, and those who trust the Lord have a joy within them that no hardship can touch, for they see beyond temporary hardship to love and joy. That matters because we're the kind of people who will spend all our time tattling on our friends, instead of rejoicing in our blessings.

I've caught myself complaining about writing a stack of thank-you notes rather than celebrating the gifts I've received. We rage at the dying of the night, forgetting the glory of our days or the promise of our future, but when we stand at the cliff, we see beyond the temporary to glimpse the eternal.

Then, we are like David who defeated Goliath; like Paul who changed the world; like Jim, who defeated cancer, even though it took his life.

For when we focus away from ourselves, we see our Creator, Redeemer, and Sustainer, our ever-present help in times of need.

Amen.

"Wash and Be Clean"
Galatians 6: 7-16 and 2 Kings 5: 1-14

Preached on July 7, 2019

This second Scripture lesson is focused on a great and infamous man named Naaman, who was healed by the power of God, but what nearly prevented him from being healed is what I'm most interested in this morning. There are things that get in the way of healing, especially when it comes to those who care a lot about what people think of them.

You've heard of Wilt Chamberlain.

According to some he was the greatest basketball player of all time, having once scored one hundred points by himself in a single game. That's the most anyone has ever scored in a professional basketball game. It's probably the most anyone will ever score in a professional basketball game, but what's so interesting about this game that took place in Hershey, Pennsylvania in 1962, is that when he scored over a hundred points by himself in this single game, Wilt Chamberlain made nearly all of his foul shots.

Now, why did he make nearly all of his foul shots in this game when he typically made less than half of them? It's because for this season and only this season, Wilt Chamberlain shot his foul shots underhanded, using a technique I grew up calling "the granny shot."

From the foul line that night in Hersey, Pennsylvania, Chamberlain made twenty-eight out of thirty of his foul shots granny-style when he normally made twelve or thirteen out of thirty shooting them with his hands over his head. Now if Wilt Chamberlain, all seven feet, 275 pounds of Wilt Chamberlain, could dramatically increase his ability to make foul shots by using the granny shot, why would he ever shoot foul shots any other way? According to Chamberlain himself, it was because he thought shooting underhanded made him look like ridiculous. In fact, in his autobiography, Chamberlain wrote, "I felt silly, like a sissy, shooting underhanded. I know I was wrong. I know some of the best foul shooters in history shot that way... I just couldn't do it."

Generally speaking, one might say that there are two kinds of people in this world. There's the kind of person who can understand why Wilt Chamberlain went back to shooting foul shots the way that he did and the other kind of person who thinks he's crazy to have cared so much about what other people thought.

Which kind of person was Naaman?

Right there at the beginning of our second Scripture lesson, we read, "Naaman, commander of the army of the king of Aram, was a great man and in high favor with his master, because by him the Lord had given victory to Aram. The man, though a mighty warrior, suffered from leprosy." You wouldn't call a man who suffered from leprosy vain, but a man like this has to spend a fair amount of time thinking about how he is perceived. A commander or a general must spend time thinking about how he is seen in the eyes of his troops.

That was true of George Washington.

Just after the Fourth of July, it's good to be thinking of him, but let it be known that as a general, he executed his own soldiers if they deserted their posts. He did this because no one who gives orders can risk appearing weak. That's true of both generals and parents, so if I make the declaration that everyone must eat five bites of soup before she leaves the table, no one can leave until she's done it. Once the children see weakness, they'll take advantage of it.

Imagine then, how it felt to Naaman, commander of the army of Aram, when he came with his horses and chariots and halted at the entrance of the Prophet Elisha's house, and Elisha sent out a messenger. I expect that Naaman rode up with a proper procession of troops on horseback and troops in chariots. Maybe it was something like the ancient world's equivalent to the parade through Washington D.C. last Thursday with tanks on display and flyovers. However, in this case, after the pomp and circumstance, the great commander, the giver of orders, a severe man who demanded respect and couldn't stand to look silly in front of his troops, is left waiting outside the house of a prophet he's never met because Elisha won't even pay him the honor of a proper greeting.

All the way there, as they rode on their chariots, surely people were shaking in their boots. Children were climbing into their mother's arms and rushing inside, and even the King of Israel tore his clothes and cried out in a panic. However, then they stop at the house of the Prophet Elisha, the dust settles, the commander dismounts, and Elisha didn't even come out to see about the commotion. Then, Elisha sent a messenger to him, with directions so simple the foreign commander surely wondered why he had traveled so far: "Go, wash in the Jordan seven times, and your flesh shall be restored, and you shall be clean."

The commander of an army just can't be disrespected that way.

After seeing how the Prophet didn't even come out to see him, Naaman's power and authority were in question, so understandably,

> Naaman became angry and went away, saying, "I thought that for me he would surely come out, and stand and call on the name of the Lord his God, and would wave his hand over the spot, and cure the leprosy! Are not Abana and Pharpar, the rivers of Damascus, better than all the waters of Israel? Could I not wash in them, and be clean?"

I guess not because sometimes the cure requires surrender.

It could be that the cure even requires humiliation.

Sometimes, the cure requires that you and I address our vanity and stop worrying so much about what everyone else thinks so that we can finally do what must be done.

Statements like those assume that people suffer from a level of vanity. I'm not trying to call anyone in particular vain this morning. I'm trying to call everyone vain this morning, myself especially. Vanity is a problem because sometimes it's vanity that keeps basketball players from being better basketball players, commanders of armies from being cured from their leprosy, sick people from getting better, aging people from aging gracefully, and sinners from being set free. Sometimes our Achilles heel is just so preventable.

Sometimes we could all too easily do something about what ails us, but don't.

Why? Dr. Martin Luther King Jr. once declared that "our thinking is often anthropocentric rather than theocentric." He goes on to explain:

> The question which is usually asked is, "What will my neighbor think…" or "what will my friends think…" Somehow [we] forget to ask the question, "What will God think." And so [we] live in fear because [we] are bogged down on the horizontal plane with only a modicum of devotion to the vertical.

What does God require of Naaman the General, but to wash and be clean?

Then, what kept him from it?

The answer is pride, vanity, and the maintenance of his own reputation.

If the great preacher William Sloane Coffin was right in saying that "faith is not believing without proof but trusting without reservation," then it might be safe to conclude that Naaman's struggle to get into the water of the Jordan River isn't like the leap of faith where you walk on water. It's not so radical

263

or dramatic as that. It's maybe more like the struggle of every boy who's been invited onto the dance floor by a young girl but is afraid because he thinks he can't dance.

Should he bow to vanity?

Should he listen to the jeers of his friends?

Should Naaman risk forsaking the respect of his troops?

Thinking this way, it's easy to see that the maintenance of reputation can be a problem, for while we all long for approval, some long for the approval even of those who hold them back from doing what is best. In the same way, the soul of our nation is threatened by an evil that we are afraid to really talk about, for fear of how we'll be perceived.

On the border, there are children separated from their parents. A father drowned with his child on his back, but in the age of partisan politics, we must be careful about what we say about it or risk being called a liberal. A man was nearly sent to prison for giving an illegal immigrant water as he crossed the desert, but it was hard for many to pardon him for fear of appearing soft on the immigration issue.

I don't know how to tell you to think or how to tell you to vote, but as a preacher, I can say that if we don't spend less time worried about how our neighbors and our friends perceive us and more attention to how we are being judged by God, we risk winning an election while continuing to suffer with spiritual leprosy.

That's how it was with Naaman.

That's how it often is with us.

Last Monday, I read the front page of the *Marietta Daily Journal*. (You know, it's been so many weeks that I've quoted the *Marietta Daily Journal*, they ought to give me a free subscription or something.) Last Monday, on the front page, were the top causes of preventable death in Cobb County. Here in Cobb County, the top cause of preventable death is heart disease, which might be managed with medication and diet.

The second is suicide.

Suicide is preventable. However, it demands we get the help that we need, and that's where it gets tricky. Going to a counselor isn't bad at all, but parking in the lot where someone might see us, that's where the struggle is.

We must take a lesson from Naaman to see that only a fool stands in the way of his own healing out of concern for how he's being perceived.

In our first Scripture lesson, the Apostle Paul wrote with his own hand:

> May I never boast of anything except the cross of our Lord Jesus Christ, by which the world [with all its pride, expectations, rumors, vanity, and shame] has been crucified to me, and I to the world [for what they say and what they think], it's all nothing. But a new creation, that is everything.

May it be so with you.

May it be so with me.

Amen.

Amos, What Do You See?
Colossians 1: 1-14 and Amos 7: 7-17
Preached on July 14, 2019

Scripture is full of wonderful metaphors. When God speaks through Scripture, we hear the divine speak in terms that we can understand, which is gracious in and of itself. God, who could so easily speak over our heads, is unlike those who use fifty-cent words to make themselves sound intelligent, and instead, speaks to us of heavenly things using what we know about already.

You can think of Jesus saying that God's love for us, who are sinful and disobedient, is like that of a father who welcomes his prodigal son back home, or a woman who loses her fortune and then finds it again. Rather than using words like "predestination" or "limited atonement," Jesus just says: faith is like a mustard seed.

Then, Paul says that the world is like a woman in labor: we suffer because new life is coming. Likewise, in our second Scripture lesson, God, through the Prophet Amos, uses something that we know, a plumb line, to explain something that we don't know or don't fully understand, the importance of righteous judgement.

Judgement is hard to understand, mostly because we don't like it.

No one likes the sound of judgement. Certainly, I don't, but to explain God's righteous judgement using the metaphor of a plumb line makes it a little bit better because this metaphor helps us to see that life lived outside certain standards of behavior is like living in a house with a crooked wall; sooner or later, it's going to fall down, and what will hurt worse than fixing the wall is it falling down on us.

That's what a plumb line is for.

A plumb line is basically just a weight with a string tied to it.

When the weight is suspended, it can show you a straight line up and down. I know you use it as a reference, though I've never actually used one. You can tell I haven't by looking at anything that I've ever built, but I frequently used something like it in Mexico.

Our church still goes to Mexico for mission trips. When I was in high school, we drove to either Monterey or Juarez in the old bus we called Woody (may he rest in peace), and there we'd stack cinderblocks to build houses. Due to

266

our inexperience with stacking cinderblocks, brick lines were used to make sure that we stacked those blocks in straight lines to build a sturdy house for a family to live in.

A brick line is something like a plumb line. One hooks a wooden block on two corners, and the string that stretches between provides a straight horizontal line to stack the cinderblocks according to. A plumb line does the same thing; it just gives you a straight vertical line. The brick line was the most important tool of the person we called a "house builder." That person was like the guy who holds the clipboard on a road maintenance crew. I loved these trips to Mexico so much that even after I was a high school student, I kept going back as a college student and was then promoted to this role of "house builder."

This was a big title, and my primary role was checking on all the brick lines. However, I wasn't very good at it. In fact, the group of high school students stacking blocks got ahead of me. They had the whole back wall of our house stacked before I had had a chance to check their lines. This wall was bowed out so far, I didn't know what to do, so I chose to just look the other way.

My friend Dave Elliot was the other house builder, and if I took the wall down, he'd be way ahead of me. I didn't want that, so I just kept going with one unstable wall to this four-walled house.

If that sounds like a horribly immature and irresponsible decision, that's because it was.

I hope you've never done anything like that, but it's hard to know what to do sometimes when things are out of whack. It's hard to know how to fix some things. There are times in life when we live in denial of problems that we're afraid of dealing with. God doesn't like it when we do that because God cares as much about the family who's going to live in the house as he does about the group who's building it and the college kid who's overseeing it. Fortunately, God knows that sometimes we get caught up in the maintenance of our own egos and fail to face the truth of who we are and what we're doing, and so God sends righteous prophets, like Amos, to warn us of the results of our bad behavior.

Our second Scripture lesson began this way:

> The Lord was standing beside a wall built with a plumb line, with a plumb line in his hand. And the Lord said to me, "Amos, what do you see?"
>
> And I said, "A plumb line."
>
> Then the Lord said, "See, I am setting a plumb line in the midst of my people Israel; I will never again pass them by; The high places shall be

made desolate, And the sanctuaries of Israel shall be laid waste, And I will rise against the house of Jeroboam with the sword."

The walls of the house of Israel are crooked, and God is going to tear them down to build them up again. That's a terrifying idea, but what's more terrifying to God is allowing His people to live in a house with crooked walls any longer. Can you imagine what it would have been like for this family to move into the house that I was building them in Mexico? Three straight walls, one crooked. I might have said something like, "Three out of four ain't bad," to which the mother would have said, "I'm not sleeping in this house. I'm not letting our children sleep in this house." Fortunately for the family who lived in that house, and fortunately for the reputation of our church in Mexico, the guy who was supervising me came by to check the walls and made us take that wall all the way down to build it back up again. Dave Elliot's house ended up being finished way ahead of mine, but it feels better to do the job right, doesn't it?

It feels better to live a righteous life, according to God's standards of justice.

It's best to live in a society where the poor and the voiceless are provided for.

It's best to live constructing walls for the well-being of all God's children.

What the book of Amos reminds us of is that God cares about all His other children as much as He cares about us, so God sends prophets who call us to tear down the crooked walls that we build which abuse the poor and the widow. Should we fail to listen, God tears them down Himself.

That's sad in a way but necessary because sometimes we don't listen, and sometimes we don't listen because Amos isn't the only one speaking. After Amos declared that the Lord is "setting a plumb line in the midst" of Israel, Amaziah the priest said to Amos, "O seer, go, flee away…never again prophesy [here]."

Why would Amaziah say this? He says this because some people can't handle the truth and don't want anyone else to have to handle it either. Amos speaks an inconvenient truth, but the truth is inconvenient to some people. It always is! Some people benefit from crooked walls and are afraid of how it will look if one has to be torn down on their watch.

Our society is not very forgiving of people who make mistakes, so rather than apologize, we deny.

Rather than start over, we cover up.

The King of Israel is probably thinking about how he'll be portrayed by his biographers and if he's keeping up with the King of Aram. Therefore, as both

Amos the Prophet and Amaziah the Priest are attempting to influence the King of Israel, he must decide whom he'll listen to.

That's how it often is.

The King is a lot like all of us.

He's glad to sweep things under the rug, which is wrong. However, under the right kind of pressure, he'd stop. With enough grace and encouragement, he would change and would act right. Unfortunately, though, Amaziah is there silencing Amos the Prophet and justifying the King's bad behavior.

I wonder if you have a friend who's like Amaziah.

Whenever you call, she's on your side.

After talking with her, you don't feel so bad or so alone.

I have friends like that.

I have friends whom I call whenever I want to complain about anything, and no matter what it is, they're ready to commiserate and slander whoever has been trying to correct my bad behavior. Then, once I'm ready to hear the truth, I go talk to my wife, Sara.

We need people who love us enough to tell us the truth. If we're lucky, then we're lucky enough to have friends who love us and support us. I hope you have a friend who loves you so much that most of the time she just listens, but who, some of the time, loves you so much she can't help but tell you when you're being irresponsible and immature. I hope that in your life you have someone who is bold enough to tell you that your crooked walls of behavior are about to collapse on top of the people you love.

That's why I don't like it when the President talks about "fake news."

I know the press is hard on him, and I know they don't get it right all the time, but I also know that while evil can be at work in those who stand in our way, sometimes the evil we must fear the most is the one who cheers us on while we're running in the wrong direction. We can't just silence the prophets. Crooked walls have to come down, and there are times in our lives when God sends people who say hard things because He loves us enough to tell us the truth. If we just brush off the prophets, the crooked walls will stay and then fall, when we could have fixed them. God holds a plumb line so that the crooked walls of society be rebuilt before they teeter and collapse on the desperate and the disenfranchised.

God holds the plumb line up to our own behavior because God cares for those who suffer under the crooked walls that we build.

You see, God isn't the housing inspector who walks around searching for code violations just to wield power. That's not what God's righteous judgement is. Our God is about rescuing us all from darkness, even the darkness of our own making, that "justice roll down like water, and righteousness like an ever-flowing stream."

May it be so.

Amen.

A Basket of Summer Fruit
Colossians 1: 15-28 and Amos 8: 1-12

Preached on July 21, 2019

A basket of summer fruit is the focus of our second Scripture lesson from the book of Amos. On the surface, this image sounds nice. Summer fruit seems nice, but what is lurking beneath the surface?

Many things about summer are this way.

Summer is nice, but then there's the heat that comes with it.

Summer vacations are nice, but then you have to come home.

Have you ever come home from vacation and everyone who was so happy while you were at the beach is now grouchy and exhausted? You pull into the driveway, and the grass is two feet tall. Coming back from vacation can be a little sobering.

You're greeted by a pile of yellowed newspapers.

Bills are spewing out of the mailbox.

You have to pick up the dogs from the kennel, and they have fleas.

You're afraid to open the milk in the refrigerator.

The saddest part for me is going out to the garden.

We've probably spent two-hundred dollars on garden stuff, like fertilizer, plants, and seeds. We spent hours pulling weeds and terracing this hill so we can plant tomatoes and cucumbers, but when I go out there after we've been away, the cucumbers are too long, and the tomatoes have rotted on the vine. When you add up the cost and the labor, two-hundred dollars is a big price tag for two rotten tomatoes. Consider such summer fruit and know that what's done is done.

When you come back from vacation, you have to deal with whatever you forgot to do.

It's the time for reaping whatever you've sown.

You can't do it over.

What's done is done.

In our second Scripture lesson, God showed the Prophet Amos "a basket of summer fruit." This is the second of the Prophet Amos' metaphors that we're encountering this summer. It's a common enough image. Surely, you have a place in the kitchen where you keep fresh fruit, but what does this metaphor mean, and what does it have to do with our lives? It means that if the summer fruit is in a basket, then the time of planting is over: that time of new beginnings has come and gone. The time of fertilizing is over, too. The time of pruning has passed as well. All that's left is for the fruit to get picked. Even if the summer fruit is a bushel of bad apples, you can't go back and do anything to change it. Amos is saying that now is the time for the people of Israel to reap what they've sown.

As we've read the rest of the passage, we know that's not a good thing. Sometimes it's not, but that doesn't change the fact that for them, it's too late to do anything differently.

It's good to live life knowing that there is a "too late" for some things. Hopefully, living with the knowledge of "too late" in our minds forces us to do the things that must be done while we have the chance to do them.

I once heard a folktale about a wild teenager who went into a forbidden forest, too disobedient to listen to everyone who warned him not to go. He was pulling down branches of ancient trees and upsetting the woodland spirits, who then, magically turned him back into a baby. The baby was returned to his mother with the stern warning, "Raise him right this time." That's not how it works, typically.

Normally, once the summer fruit has made it to the basket, that's it.

Once the car has pulled into the driveway, back from vacation, there's no point in regretting not having asked the kid up the street to cut the grass.

All the neighbors are already talking about you, so live with it.

The kids go off to college, and then, for some things, it's just too late.

My father-in-law told me a story about an Italian mail carrier. He was lazy and would often put undelivered mail in his attic. For years, he intended to deliver it, but then one day, the ceiling collapsed and fell on him in his sleep. It was too late to do anything about the undelivered mail at that point. The fruit was in the basket.

For Israel, it was too late, too, but we can learn something from Amos because it's not too late for us. We can learn something from anyone who has reached this moment of finality because we can change what we're doing now based on what Amos wishes that Israel, especially the ruling class, had done differently.

You've heard the old anecdote that no one lays on his death bed wishing he had spent more time in the office. I imagine that's true. If you remember the movie about the Holocaust, *Schindler's List*, then you know that as Oscar Schindler leaves this huge group of Jews, 1,100 men and women whom he saved from the concentration camps, he looks at his car and the gold pin on his lapel and regrets that he never sold them. He had the chance to sell these things and could have used the money to save one more life and didn't. It's a moment where he can't do any more. The time for changing anything has passed. The opportunity to do more has come and gone, and he knows in this moment, as any decent person would and as the Talmud proclaims: to save one life is to save the whole world.

On the other hand, what had the wealthy in Israel saved?

The book of Amos describes a world where those who had power did the opposite of Schindler. They weren't selling their goods to save people, but "buying the poor for silver and the needy for a pair of sandals." The faithful ask, "What is life, but our chance to make a difference and to make this world a better place?" Yet, in Amos, we hear of those who cannot wait for the Sabbath to be over that they might reopen their stores and get back to cheating their customers, as though the point of life were making money. What is it about our society that we have created so many people who believe that those who die with the most toys win, as though what we have in our bank accounts would somehow make us into bigger and better people? We, too, must heed this warning: when we reach the end of our days, when we, like summer fruit, are picked from the vine, our regret will be not having shown more kindness and generosity while we had the chance. Ours is a world of investments, property acquisitions, mansions, and yachts.

Last September, *Business Insider* reported that the world's largest private yacht, which cost more than six-hundred million dollars to build and has held the record for being the largest for more than five years, at 590 feet long, has been dethroned by an even bigger yacht.

What would you do with a boat that big? Fish? Water ski?

The new biggest yacht in the world was built by a Norwegian billionaire who ordered the construction of this new yacht to be 597 feet long, just seven feet longer than the current record holder. Why 597 feet and not just 590 feet? So many of us think that means something. So many of us join in the great rat race to have the nicest things.

In the hope that wealth will provide happiness and fulfillment, we pursue it relentlessly. Some cut the salaries of coworkers to increase the bottom line, others wager physical health with endless hours, then compromise the well-being of their families by providing for their physical needs while disregarding their emotional needs. Yet, here's the problem: it doesn't work. Money can't buy happiness.

I'm sure you've heard that before.

It's true.

Think about it like this: do you remember what happened to Mr. Banks in *Mary Poppins?* Little Michael Banks wanted to use his tuppence to buy crumbs from the bird lady. "Feed the birds, tuppence a bag," she sang. Do you remember? Mr. Banks wanted him to invest that money, instead, and so did Mr. Daws Sr., who, played by Dick Van Dyke, sang:

If you invest your tuppence wisely in the bank

Safe and sound

Soon that tuppence safely invested in the bank

Will compound

And you'll achieve that sense of conquest

As your affluence expands

In the hands of the directors

Who invest as propriety demands

Little Michael can't decide what to do. He knows what Mr. Daws Sr. wants him to do. He also knows what his father wants him to do, only he naturally seems to know that what will bring him the most joy in this moment is feeding the birds.

Watching this movie, we also know that Michael is right, for what does Mr. Banks know about happiness? What does he know about life? He's the most foolish man, bumbling through his days, blind to everyone around him. Mary Poppins says he can't see beyond his nose. Interestingly, he only finds joy once he's been fired from the bank and spends an afternoon flying a kite with his family. We choose the pursuit of wealth, but, like King Midas, whose touch turns everything to gold, like Ebenezer Scrooge, who sleeps alone in a drafty old house, like those siblings that you know, who tore each other apart at the reading of the will, we have yet to learn that kindness, generosity, and love bring us what an excess of money never will.

The tragedy of our second Scripture lesson isn't just that the poor went hungry and the impoverished never pulled themselves out because of an economic system that privileged the rich, it's that those who were rich died with regrets. They died having chosen money over people, wealth over love, and greed over generosity.

When people who make such choices have time to reflect on the way they've lived and the choices that they've made, I've never heard of one who said, "I sure am glad I'm dying with a lot of money in my bank accounts." No. Like fruit picked from the vine, when we go to meet our Maker, it will be those who gave of themselves who leave this earth having known joy, and who go knowing that their joy will not end.

Today is my birthday.

Birthdays are always sobering.

It's a moment to realize that whatever I intended to do over the last year will not be done. Another year of my life is gone. Of course, I may have many more. Harry Vaughn also had a birthday this week. He turned ninety, and now he is on his way to one hundred. When will we be picked from the vine, harvested at the end of our days? We don't know, and we can't tell, but this passage from Amos warns us again to remember that it is coming. Like a thief in the night, it comes, and when it does there is no do-over, no second chance. There will be no five-minute warning that we might quickly give away all that we've saved or make right what we've done wrong.

There is no reset button on life.

Yet, consider this: why not change now?

Why postpone the joy that comes from living out our greatest purpose?

We were created by the God who showed us how to live. He, who poured Himself out in life, invites us to follow His example, that our joy would be complete.

Amen.

CPSIA information can be obtained
at www.ICGtesting.com
Printed in the USA
LVHW031104141219
640498LV00042B/2373/P